The First Book

Kennywood: Roller Coaster Capital of the World

Kennywood revisited

In 1981, when I was writing *Kennywood: Roller Coaster Capital of the World*, I had no idea that fifteen years later I would be doing another book on the same subject. At first, I thought about merely updating my first book but finally concluded the best approach was to write a completely new book. *More Kennywood Memories* is the result. I wrote this 224-page book to add more facts about the park's early years as well as to bring the subject up to date.

More Kennywood Memories is really a companion book to *Kennywood: Roller Coaster Capital of the World*. The new book does not replace the first book because not one of the images or illustrations used in the first book appears in the second. Doing an all new second book gave me a chance to use many photographs that I could not fit into the first book, as well as a chance to add hundreds of new ones, many in color, from 1982 through 1997. Also a planned appendix at the end of the first book was deleted for space considerations. This appendix has been expanded and updated and appears in the second book.

Kennywood: Roller Coaster Capital of the World remains in print and is available from Amusement Park Journal, P.O. Box 478, Jefferson, OH 44047 and bookstores in the area for $24.95.

Other Books by Charles J. Jacques, Jr.:

Kennywood: Roller Coaster Capital of the World (1982)

Goodbye, West View Park, Goodbye (1985)

Hersheypark: The Sweetness of Success (1997)

Kennywood has become a local icon along with Heinz 57, Iron City Beer, and the Steelers. The historic amusement facility is part of the fabric of Pittsburgh and the surrounding area, and if anything would happen to it, the park would be sorely missed. Kennywood is strong and prosperous and is a welcome exception in a business where the rule has been parks failing rather than succeeding. Kennywood is a survivor, almost an anachronism, a successful urban amusement park in the 1990's.

(Photograph from Charles J. Jacques, Jr. Collection)

BY CHARLES J. JACQUES, JR.

More Kennywood Memories

DESIGNED BY
Karen Morrison

EDITED BY
Rick Shale

P.O. Box 478
Jefferson, OH 44047-0478
(440) 576-6531
fax: (440) 576-5850

Copyright © 1998 Charles J. Jacques, Jr.

All rights reserved. No part of this book may be used or reproduced in any manner whatsoever without written permission except in the case of brief quotations embodied in critical articles and reviews. Printed in the United States of America. For information write to Amusement Park Journal, P.O. Box 478, Jefferson, OH 44047.

HARDCOVER
ISBN #0-9614392-3-8

PAPERBACK
ISBN #0-9614392-4-6

Library of Congress Catalog Card Number 98-70119

"More Kennywood Memories"

Table of Contents

Preface......vii

Chapter 1	1898 - 1939	The Early Years......2
Chapter 2	1940 - 1979	The Park Faces New Challenges......22
Chapter 3	1980 - 1982	The Laser Loop......42
Chapter 4	1983 - 1984	Idlewild and More......54
Chapter 5	1985 - 1986	The Raging Rapids......72
Chapter 6	1987	Historic Kennywood......84
Chapter 7	1988	Kennywood Memories......96
Chapter 8	1989 - 1990	Sandcastle......112
Chapter 9	1991 - 1994	The Steel Phantom......130
Chapter 10	1995	Lost Kennywood......148
Chapter 11	1996 - 1997	Noah's Ark and the Pitt Fall......166

Appendix......187
Acknowledgements......213
Index......215

Dedication

This book is dedicated with love to my three children, Lynn Jacques, C.J. Jacques, and Cory Siri.

Preface

When Charles Jacques, Jr. first brought up the idea of a book on Kennywood, my response was something like this: "Well, don't expect us to subsidize a vanity publication. We won't." That did not discourage him at all. Jacques made clear the only help he wanted was access to our files and photos. To my surprise my low profile boss, Carl Henninger, told him, "No problem. Look at anything you want except our balance sheets."

We really did not expect much to come of it. You have to realize that at Kennywood nothing gets thrown away. There were rooms of correspondence and invoices dating back to 1906 when the present owners took over the park. Jacques, we figured, would probably give up.

But he was determined and made visit after visit to the park to go through the archives, copying what he thought might be helpful. Then he began asking questions to fill in the blanks. The result was not only an interesting book - *Kennywood: Roller Coaster Capital of the World* - but what ultimately turned out to be a profitable one. His book has sold over 23,000 copies.

One unfortunate thing about a book like Jacques' *Kennywood*, or in this case now two books, is that they cannot show the contribution over the years that each of our employees (today we call them team members) has made in helping make this park great. Harry Henninger, Jr. and I are almost embarrassed that we are mentioned so often in the book, but this is because Jacques uses so many quotes from newspaper and magazine articles. The writers of those articles are always looking for someone to attribute a statement to and Harry Henninger and I have often been the ones.

Jacques' book and Rick Sebak's WQED award-winning documentary, *Kennywood Memories*, have given the people of the tri-state area a deeper understanding of Kennywood, its history, and its impact on the culture of the community. *More Kennywood Memories* tells the park's story in even greater detail.

Jacques' earlier book was undoubtedly the first unsubsidized one ever written about an operating amusement park. He has done several other books on the amusement park industry since that first Kennywood effort. And now he is back with *More Kennywood Memories*. We think readers will be delighted with this new book that chronicles Kennywood's dynamic changes and expansion in the eighties and nineties and records the park's history from its origins to the present.

Carl O. Hughes 12/22/97
Chairman of the Board

Kenny's Grove in 1898 was used for picnics and family reunions.
(CHARLES J. JACQUES, JR. COLLECTION)

CHAPTER 1

1898-1939
The Early Years

"Kennywood is bound to become famous from the very start"

For 100 years, Kennywood Park has meant fun to the residents of western Pennsylvania and surrounding states. The big amusement park, located near Pittsburgh, Pennsylvania, has both a serious, historical side, being designated a National Historic Landmark, and a thrilling, exciting side, as the "Roller Coaster Capital of the World." A trip to Kennywood is truly something special. The park combines the past and the present (and some might say the future) in one diverse experience. Kennywood, with its trees, gardens, and historical buildings, is calming and reassuring while at the same time, with its roller coasters and water rides, exciting and stimulating. Kennywood is unlike any other amusement park in the world.

Development of the park started in 1898 when the Monongahela Street Railway Company, which ran from Pittsburgh through the mill towns of the Monongahela River Valley, leased a tract of ground from Anthony Kenny. A wooded section of the property, called Kenny's Grove, had been used by people of the valley since the time of the Civil War for picnics and family reunions. The farm was located on a bluff high above the Monongahela River on the trolley company's right-of-way between Homestead and Duquesne. Rather than purchasing it outright, the street railway company leased the land perhaps feeling that an amusement park might be just a passing fad. The grove was located high above steel mills, railroads, and towns which dotted the river valley. The company wanted to build a trolley park to help boost its ridership in the evenings and on weekends. The name Kennywood was chosen by Andrew Mellon who later served as secretary of the treasury, and whose family held stock in the railway. Mellon himself seemed to enjoy Kennywood, and there are stories of him putting on his gray flannels and donning a straw hat during the summer to go out to the park.

Construction began immediately on a Dance Pavilion, Casino (restaurant), and building to house a merry-go-round. During the summer and fall of 1898, the trolley company encouraged its passengers to visit the site to see the park being developed. The park bought a three-row Merry-Go-Round from Gustav A. Dentzel of Philadelphia. Trees were planted, and a small artificial lake (only three feet deep) was dug. The open-air Dance Pavilion was done in a Queen

The rustic bridge at Kennywood Park circa 1900.
(CHARLES J. JACQUES, JR. COLLECTION)

Boating on the Lagoon around a small island. In the background is the Casino (restaurant).
(LIBRARY OF CONGRESS)

Kennywood offered a sylvan setting for people who lived in the mill towns that dotted the Monongahela River Valley.
(CHARLES J. JACQUES, JR. COLLECTION)

Anne style. Its 120-foot by 70-foot floor was said to have a mirror-like surface and was surrounded by a promenade 15 feet wide that encircled the entire building and was separated from the dance floor by a small railing. Two of the three original buildings, the Casino and the Merry-Go-Round Pavilion, which was converted to a refreshment stand in the 1920's, are still in use today.

An article titled "Beautiful Kennywood" appearing in the *Pittsburg Press* on May 7, 1899, reported that "over 500 mechanics, landscape gardeners, and laborers have been at work for weeks at the new Kennywood park." The article claimed "the park would open within the next ten days," but the park was not opened until Decoration Day, May 30, 1899. The *Pittsburgh Index*, a weekly newspaper, reported the event with these prophetic words, "Kennywood is bound to become famous from the very start." (From 1890 to 1910, the United States Post Office spelled the City of Pittsburg without an "h." Some Pittsburg businesses dropped the "h" and some did not. Others, like The Pittsburgh Railway Company, appear at times with an "h" and other times without one during those years.)

Kennywood was located about 12 miles from the City of Pittsburg in the

The Old Mill was located in the wooded section of the park.
(CHARLES J. JACQUES, JR. COLLECTION)

Circa 1902.

heart of the Monongahela River Valley and directly across the river from the huge Edgar Thomson Works of the Carnegie Steel Company. It was a period when trolley lines radiated from Pittsburg and extended to the edges of the urban areas. By transferring, people could easily get to the park by street car. For many years, the trolley company would not permit the park to open a railroad station, although the Pennsylvania Railroad ran along the Monongahela River at the foot of the bluff. Picnickers who came on the Lake Erie Railroad had to get off at the Rankin Station and were required to take a street car to the park. Those traveling on the Pennsylvania Railroad stopped at Braddock Station, Braddock, Pennsylvania, where they boarded a street car to the park. The railroads provided special reduced round-trip rates, which enabled people from as far away as New Castle, Erie, Washington (Pennsylvania), Youngstown, Cleveland, Canton, Columbus, and Wheeling, to come to the park. At the turn of the century, many of the roads in the area were not paved. A road, which generally followed the old Braddock Road, served the park, but it could not be called first rate and before automobiles became popular, it was a relatively insignificant way of getting to the park.

Drinking from the spring that George Washington was said to have used during the French and Indian War. It was located on the present site of the Jack Rabbit.
(CHARLES J. JACQUES, JR. COLLECTION)

In 1906, the park's first Merry-Go-Round Pavilion housed a Carousel built by Gustav A. Dentzel.
(RICHARD L. BOWKER COLLECTION)

"Stunts on the Funny Stairway" and "You quake with mirth on the 'Earthquake Floor'" from the brochure "Kennywood the Beautiful" circa 1903.
(CHARLES J. JACQUES, JR. COLLECTION)

The Wonderland Building was open-air. It also contained the entrance to the Scenic Railway.
(LIBRARY OF CONGRESS)

A pond, refreshment stand, and the Casino in 1906. Franklin Wentzel's ice cream sign hangs on the Casino.
(LIBRARY OF CONGRESS)

The Monongahela Street Railway Company merged with the Pittsburgh Street Railway Company (PRC) in 1900, and Kennywood joined Calhoun, Oakwood, and Southern Parks that were already owned by the PRC. The *Duquesne Observer* said "Kennywood was the prettiest spot in Allegheny County, which is available at the phenomenal cost of one fare [5 cents]." The development of Kennywood was definitely served by the merger and creation of a much larger single fare area. Kennywood for years was known as the "Coolest Place in Summer." The *Pittsburgh Leader* observed, "The altitude of Kennywood Park assures a breeze all of the time. There is plenty of shade; comfortable seats..."

More attractions were soon added. In 1901, the park built The Old Mill, which was advertised as "a six minute ride on water that was cool and comfortable." The ride had scenes that were illuminated by electric lights, and music was also provided. Fred Ingersoll, president of the Amusement Construction Co., a Pittsburg concern, installed a Laughing Gallery that was said to have been imported directly from the Paris Exposition. The attraction had glass mirrors arranged to give the most amusing and grotesque distortions. Each mirror was

An open-air trolley carried an ad for Kennywood's new Racer.
(Carnegie Library of Pittsburgh)

4 feet by 7 feet, and the Laughing Gallery was advertised as "Mirrors That Really Make You Laugh."

The Pittsburgh Street Railway Company wanted to get out of the trolley park business, so in 1902 it subleased the park, first to a Boston company and the following year to a group from Aspinwall, Pennsylvania. The Aspinwall lessee, the Pittsburg Steeplechase and Amusement Company, was headed by O. D. Thompson. Thompson's company reportedly spent $141,500 on the park including bringing in a steeplechase ride that lasted only two seasons. The new owners did erect a substantial building in a world's fair style of architecture that occupied part of the former Baseball Grounds. This domed structure was remodeled many times over the years, and it served as everything from a scenic railway loading station and vaudeville theater to a fun house and finally home for a skooter ride.

The park's first roller coaster

Also in 1902, Kennywood got its first roller coaster, a Three-Way, Figure-Eight Toboggan, which was built by Frederick Ingersoll. The coaster was 85 feet wide and 225 feet long with an incline 70 feet long. The Figure Eight was less than

Boating on the Lagoon at Kennywood.
(Charles J. Jacques, Jr. Collection)

Two boys enjoy the horse and buggy on the Pony Track at Kennywood.
(Charles J. Jacques, Jr. Collection)

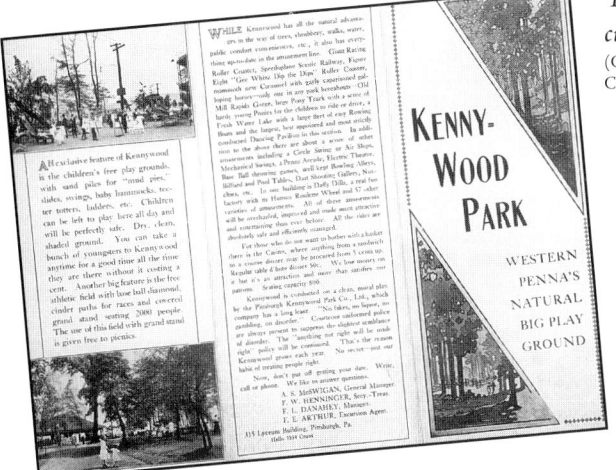

Brochure circa 1912.
(CHARLES J. JACQUES, JR. COLLECTION)

Pony Track, Casino, Circle Swing, and racing coaster from the Speed-O-Plane.
(CHARLES J. JACQUES, JR. COLLECTION)

40 feet high. The coaster did not have a train of cars connected together, but ten little cars that could hold two passengers each. The cars ran on a hard maple track.

In the early years of the century, church groups tried to get the street railway companies to close their parks on Sundays. The Pittsburgh Railway Company answered the complaints by introducing outdoor religious services at Kennywood and its other parks. The parks invited guest choirs and ministers and hired a concert band to play such numbers as "Onward Christian Soldiers" and "Nearer, My God, to Thee." This strategy helped defuse the effort to close the parks on Sunday. But attempts to enforce the Pennsylvania Blue Laws, which restricted business on Sundays, continued into the 1950's, however. In 1904 Carrie Nation, the axe-wielding prohibitionist, appeared at Kennywood, which served no alcohol on its premises.

A number of new attractions were added in the Steeplechase Building in 1904. A new vaudeville theater was constructed, and new scenery was purchased. The stage measured 40 feet by 60 feet, and the seating could accommodate 600 spectators.

An illusion (a motion picture) which "makes one imagine he is riding over Niagara Falls in the car" was added in 1905. Another new attraction was roller skating on the dance floor of the Steeplechase Building. In 1905, Kennywood advertised its Circle Swing and Scenic Railway along with 101 other attractions. One of Kennywood's most unusual promotions, a snowball fight, was held that year. More than a ton of confetti and cotton was used as snow; the stunt was apparently never repeated, however.

After subleasing the park for four years, the Pittsburgh Railway Company was forced to resume direct control in 1906 when the Pittsburg Steeplechase and Amusement Company folded. The park came under the management of the railway company's young, energetic director, Andrew S. McSwigan. McSwigan not only ran all of the company's parks, but also the Duquesne Gardens, an ice skating rink in the winter. McSwigan immediately had every building in the park painted the same color giving the park a uniform appearance. The grounds were leveled, graded, sodded, and remarked while all the paths were covered with Ligonier white stone. The "House of Trouble" and "Down-and-Out" were made free of charge. The

The cast lines up in front of a train that was used in the park's spectacular live drama "The Great Western Train Hold-Up."
(Charles J. Jacques, Jr. Collection)

Aerial view of the Speed-O-Plane, Athletic Field, and Hilarity Hall circa 1915.
(Charles J. Jacques, Jr. Collection)

admission to Wonderland, which was located in the old Steeplechase Building, was reduced to five cents. Among the new amusements McSwigan added were an Irish Village and the Grotto of Visions. The number of electric lights was doubled. The Old Mill was renamed the Fairyland Floats, and the Figure Eight's name was changed to Whirly-Whirl.

McSwigan, who had been a newspaper reporter before coming to work for the trolley company, knew how to promote the park through newspapers. The *Pittsburg Leader* reported on May 27, 1906, "beautiful Kennywood park has taken a new lease on life. Record-breaking crowds had attended the Sunday concerts so far, while the formal opening on Friday brought out an immense throng. The illumination of the park at night is a beautiful sight, it being on a greater scale than ever." Nirella's Fourteenth Regiment Band played every afternoon and evening that week while another band played at the roller skating rink.

Kennywood's other attractions in 1906 included the Dance Pavilion, rental boats, Electric Theater, Merry-Go-Round, miniature railroad, roller skating, and Scenic Railway. In addition to the regular rides and attractions, a combination Wild West Show and live drama called the "Great Western Train Hold-Up" was performed in the park the whole season. The Pittsburgh Railway lost more than $17,000 on the venture, which grossed only $11,000 but cost more than $28,000 to produce. Needless to say, it was not renewed for the following season although smaller wild west shows were presented off and on over the years.

In 1906, attractions owned by concessionaires, who paid a percentage to the park on a lease, included a fortune

Cowboys unloading the horses from a work trolley in 1906.
(Richard L. Bowker Collection)

Native Americans in a stagecoach in back of the Wonderland Building.
(Charles J. Jacques, Jr. Collection)

teller, name plate machine, chameleon, overland wagon, Laughing Gallery, weighing machines, Circle Swing, Ferris Wheel, Irish Village, the House of Mystery, photo gallery, Pony Track, swings, and shooting gallery. According to Kennywood's financial ledgers, only $50 was paid for injuries and damages during the whole 1906 season.

McSwigan and Henninger take charge

Andrew S. McSwigan with his partners Frederick W. Henninger and A. F. Megahan formed a partnership known as Pittsburg Kennywood Park Company, Limited and leased Kennywood from the Pittsburgh Railway Company in December 1906. McSwigan, Megahan, and Henninger had years of amusement park experience. McSwigan, as already noted, was general manager of all of the trolley parks owned by the Pittsburgh Railway Company. Henninger owned and operated a number of figure eight coasters including one in Exposition Park (Conneaut Lake) and another in Chester Park in Cincinnati. Henninger had helped establish West View Park and then left after only one season. Henninger did not want to be T. M. Harton's junior

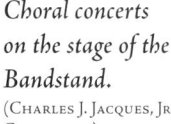

Children on the Steeplechase.
(Charles J. Jacques, Jr. Collection)

Choral concerts on the stage of the Bandstand.
(Charles J. Jacques, Jr. Collection)

Kennywood's trolley station and waiting room.
(CHARLES J. JACQUES, JR. COLLECTION)

Aerial view of Kennywood's Carousel Pavilion and Casino.
(CHARLES J. JACQUES, JR. COLLECTION)

partner and he brought Megahan, who was manager of West View Park, with him. Megahan, who had previously managed Kennywood and was considered one of the best picnic men in the business, became park manager. The three men quickly established group picnics as the foundation for renewing Kennywood's business. In 1908, Megahan withdrew from the company and sold his shares to the other two partners.

Members of the McSwigan and Henninger family would continue to operate Kennywood for the next 90 years. McSwigan became the spokesperson in dealing with the press and the public while Henninger ran the financial end of the company. They were innovators and leaders in the amusement park industry, and Kennywood's success was a direct result of their ownership and control. Kennywood had only 82 employees when McSwigan and Henninger took over. There were only two small picnic shelters, and wrought iron hand pumps were still used in the groves. Most people got to the park by street car, while a few came by foot, bicycle, horse and buggy, or automobile.

McSwigan and Henninger realized booking picnics was the most important thing they could do to make Kennywood succeed. They had a remarkable ability to solicit picnics from a wide range of groups. Schools picnics were always important, but the park also booked annual outings for communities, nationality groups, large and small corporations, labor unions, fraternal organizations, church groups, and family reunions, which helped the park to survive even in the lean years.

In the first decade of the century, Kennywood was engaged in a fierce battle for survival with a dozen other trolley parks and amusement resorts in western Pennsylvania. In 1907, the *Pittsburg Leader* carried ads for the following amusement parks: Calhoun, Coney Island (Neville Island), Dream City (Wilkinsburg), Luna Park (Oakland), Oakwood, Southern, and West View. In addition, excursions were offered by different railroads to parks like Idora (Youngstown, Ohio), Woodland

Foot race on the Athletic Field.
(CHARLES J. JACQUES, JR. COLLECTION)

The Lagoon and Dance Pavilion.
(CHARLES J. JACQUES, JR. COLLECTION)

Kennywood's first racing coaster was designed by John A. Miller.
(RICHARD L. BOWKER COLLECTION)

The Wonderland Building with the Circle Swing in the foreground.
(RICHARD L. BOWKER COLLECTION)

A crowded Woman's Cottage circa 1915.
(CHARLES J. JACQUES, JR. COLLECTION)

Beach (Ashtabula, Ohio), Cascade (New Castle), Idlewild, Aliquippa, Conneaut Lake, and Celoron on Lake Chautauqua, New York. Only Kennywood and Idlewild have survived.

Working for Kennywood, where 16-hour days were common, was grueling. Management employees were expected to work from when the park opened until it closed all summer long. To make things a little easier, McSwigan and Henninger set up the "Hungry Club" to serve at least one good meal a day to employees and for many years, the meal was served in the old Service Building. In the late-1930's, the Hungry Club's diners were moved into a dining room in the new office.

In 1910 and 1911, McSwigan and Henninger had two large roller coasters built: the first was a racing coaster The Racer, with two tracks on which two trains raced against each other. The Racer was also called Aerial Racer Joy Ride, Aerial Racer, Mountain Joy Ride, or Aerial Joy Ride. This coaster was built along the edge of the bluff overlooking the Monongahela River. The second coaster, the Speed-O-Plane, was built the following year and was an out-and-back coaster erected along the Baseball Grounds. It replaced the old Scenic Railway. The coasters were very popular and made

Landscaped floral calendar.
(CHARLES J. JACQUES, JR. COLLECTION)

Kennywood the dominant coaster park in the Pittsburgh region. They became the park's biggest attractions both literally and figuratively.

For the 1910 season, Kennywood presented vaudeville, "American Hippodrome," 15 acts for 10 cents, 5,000 seats, and "Every Act a head liner." The following year, the park suffered a fire on August 12, 1911, when the Penny Arcade, shooting gallery, and theater were destroyed. The fire also damaged the Panama Canal (Old Mill) and the Figure Eight Coaster.

In 1913, Kennywood leased, with the right to purchase for $7,500, a new "jumping horse carousel" from the T. M. Harton Company. The Carousel was to be the one built and owned by Harton at the Pittsburgh Exposition, which was located in Pittsburgh at the point, or one similar to it. As part of the agreement, Harton had to enlarge the Carousel Pavilion. He did this by removing the inside posts of the building from their original position and moving them back three feet. Harton agreed to take the park's old Dentzel Carousel in trade giving Kennywood a $2,000 credit.

In 1917, Kennywood painted all of its buildings yellow and brown. McSwigan and Henninger rebuilt The Old Mill and called it Fairyland Floats. They also

Refreshment stand with The Racer in the background.
(CHARLES J. JACQUES, JR. COLLECTION)

A wooden, arched bridge with electric lights was built in the early 1920's.
(CHARLES J. JACQUES, JR. COLLECTION)

A huge painted rabbit adorned Kennywood's first modern coaster, the Jack Rabbit.
(CHARLES J. JACQUES, JR. COLLECTION)

The park's first racing coaster was removed in 1926.
(CHARLES J. JACQUES, JR. COLLECTION)

purchased a new $10,000 shooting gallery, which was placed on the midway near The Whip and Circle Swing. During World War I, large patriotic celebrations were held featuring such bands as the Vastine Westinghouse Electric Band and the Pittsburgh Municipal Band. Everything was free to soldiers in uniform. The war created prosperity, and it was a good time for Kennywood, although some things were in short supply.

The 1920's – A golden age for the park

Kennywood almost doubled in size during the 1920's. However, the decade started on a sad note when Kennywood's president Andrew S. McSwigan, who was just 57 years old, died unexpectedly. His place was taken by his son, Andrew Brady McSwigan, who continued his father's aggressive management style. Brady McSwigan would serve as president of Kennywood from 1923 until 1964. Young McSwigan was only 26 when he assumed control and did not know much about the park, but he quickly learned. Brady McSwigan, like his father, became the chief spokesperson for the park while Frederick Henninger continued to direct the park's finances as secretary-treasurer.

The park added three wooden coasters in the 1920's. First, a ravine coaster, the Jack Rabbit, was designed in 1920 by John A. Miller of Miller and Baker. It was Kennywood's first modern coaster. It featured an 85-foot drop with a double dip (two drops in rapid succession) and a long covered passage or tunnel. The 2,132-foot-long coaster cost $50,000. The *Pittsburgh Leader* reported on June 27, 1920, "Every day the gates of the new ride are stormed by hundreds of persons all eager to try the new amusement at the same time." The article went on to say that "The Rabbit is absolutely safe. Safety straps fasten the passengers in the car. Electric appliances all over the track allow the power to be diverted and the trains stopped. Persons can ride on the Rabbit with the utmost security and peace of mind. The structure is squarely and solidly built." The article said that the other coasters, the (old) racing coaster, Speed-O-Plane, and Figure Eight were all "as popular as ever," but none of them could compare to the Jack Rabbit, and all were soon dismantled and removed from the park.

Four years later John A. Miller, who was one the greatest coaster designers of all time, returned to design another coaster, the Pippin, built in a ravine at the opposite end of the park. Later the

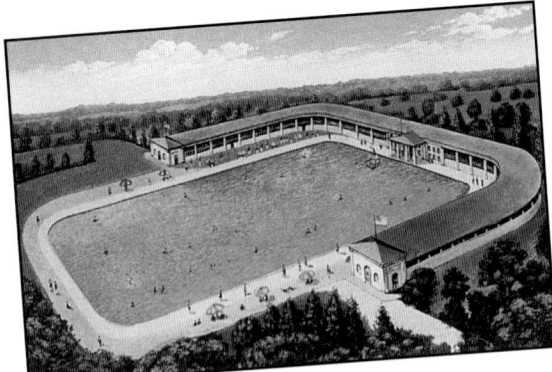

Artist's drawing of Kennywood's Swimming Pool and Bathhouse.
(Charles J. Jacques, Jr. Collection)

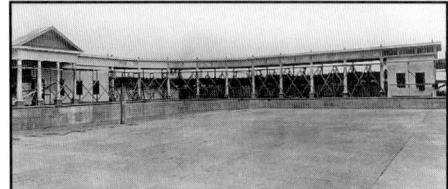

The Bathhouse and Pool under construction during the winter of 1924-25.
(Charles J. Jacques, Jr. Collection)

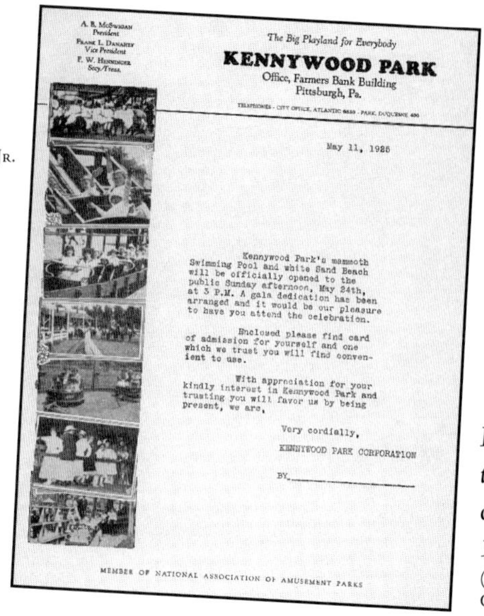

A. B. McSwigan
President
Frank L. Danahey
Vice President
F. W. Henninger
Secy./Treas.

The Big Playland for Everybody
KENNYWOOD PARK
Office, Farmers Bank Building
Pittsburgh, Pa.
TELEPHONES - CITY OFFICE, ATLANTIC [illegible] - PARK, DUQUESNE 400

May 11, 1925

Kennywood Park's mammoth Swimming Pool and white Sand Beach will be officially opened to the public Sunday afternoon, May 24th, at 3 P.M. A gala dedication has been arranged and it would be our pleasure to have you attend the celebration.

Enclosed please find card of admission for yourself and one which we trust you will find convenient to use.

With appreciation for your kindly interest in Kennywood Park and trusting you will favor us by being present, we are,

Very cordially,
KENNYWOOD PARK CORPORATION
BY_______________

MEMBER OF NATIONAL ASSOCIATION OF AMUSEMENT PARKS

Letter announcing the Swimming Pool opening on May 24, 1925.
(Charles J. Jacques, Jr. Collection)

Pippin was rebuilt and enlarged, and it became the Thunderbolt. The third coaster, built in 1927 at a cost of $75,000, was a new racing coaster, the Racer, which replaced the park's old racing coaster that had been built in 1910. This masterpiece was again designed by John A. Miller. Although the Racer appeared to have two coaster tracks, it actually had one long continuous track and the train that started on the left side of the loading station would finish on the right side and vice versa. The coaster was 72 feet high and 2,250 feet long and due to a surveying error, the coaster did not take full advantage of the ravine in which it was to drop and thus required more lumber to build.

In 1924, Brady McSwigan laid out the park's first Kiddieland with four, child-sized rides across from the Jack Rabbit. When the new Racer was built in 1927, Kennywood moved the kiddie rides to a spot the park's first racing coaster had occupied. In the late1920's, Kiddieland was further expanded until it had nine rides.

A year later (1925), the park built a huge Swimming Pool, which was designed by Lynch Brothers, New Haven, Connecticut. The Pool, which cost $150,000, was 350 feet by 180 feet and took 2,250,000 gallons of water. There was a colonial style pavilion with a 2,500-seat grandstand built over the dressing room. A 25-foot wide sand beach, which required 20 railroad carloads of white sand, surrounded the pool on three sides.

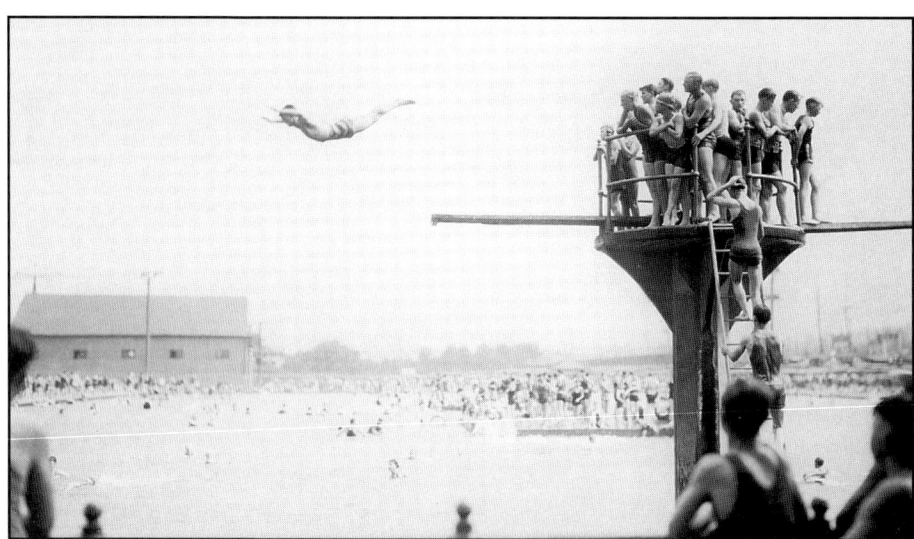

Diving Tower in the Swimming Pool.
(Kennywood Park)

Enjoying a root beer at the Tower Refreshment Stand.
(Charles J. Jacques, Jr. Collection)

By the 1920's, more people were coming to the park by automobile. Although Kennywood was located on a main trolley route, getting there by car was not as easy. In the early 1920's, directions to the park included warnings about one way streets, uneven pavement, and speed traps. To further assist motorists, Kennywood introduced in 1925 the yellow arrows with the park's name on them, which were placed strategically around the Pittsburgh district. For many years, Kennywood would leave the signs up during the winter, and it even put a few

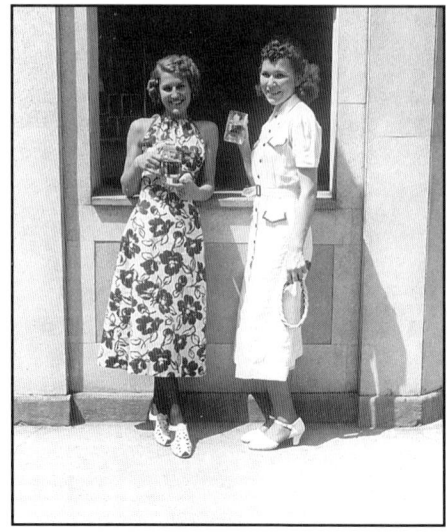

Miniature railroad was built by the Dayton Fun House and Riding Device Mfg. Co.
(KENNYWOOD PARK)

The Tumble Bug, later called the Turtle, was added in 1927.
(KENNYWOOD PARK)

Carousel horse with roached mane on the new machine built by William H. Dentzel.
(CHARLES J. JACQUES, JR. COLLECTION)

A jester head on the rounding boards was a "trademark" of a carousel built by William H. Dentzel.
(CHARLES J. JACQUES, JR. COLLECTION)

This building was constructed in 1927 to house the park's new Dentzel Carousel.
(CHARLES J. JACQUES, JR. COLLECTION)

signs up as far as 60 miles from the park.

In the 1920's, the park purchased a number of new rides including a Caterpillar, Tumble Bug, Laff-in-the-Dark, and Auto Race from Harry G. Traver of Beaver Falls, Pennsylvania. Other rides added included a Dodgem, Tilt-A-Whirl, and electric third-rail miniature railroad. In 1927, the park purchased a dazzling deluxe Park Model Ferris Wheel from the C. W. Parker Company, Leavenworth, Kansas. The wheel had ten enclosed cars that offered a view of the park and the Monongahela River Valley.

Dentzel's masterpiece

In 1927, Kennywood bought a huge, four-row carousel from William H. Dentzel Carrousells and Organs of Germantown, Pennsylvania. The park paid $25,000 for the new machine. William H. Dentzel, the owner of the business, personally supervised the installation. Less than a year after Dentzel completed the installation at Kennywood, he died. William H. Dentzel was the third generation of Dentzels to build merry-go-rounds. His grandfather, Michael Dentzel, built merry-go-rounds in Germany as early as 1839. His father, Gustav A. Dentzel, had built Kennywood's

The Dentzel Carousel was starting to show some wear in the 1930's.
(CHARLES J. JACQUES, JR. COLLECTION)

The Windmill was originally built in 1929 on an island in the Lagoon. Charlie Mach, the park's chief engineer, designed it.
(KENNYWOOD PARK)

---

first Merry-Go-Round in 1899.

Traditional laughing jester heads and angelic faces decorated the rounding boards and interior of the machine. There were 72 animals hand-carved from bass wood. The machine had 50 jumping horses in three rows and 20 stationary ones in one row along with four chariots, one lion, and one tiger, a Dentzel trademark. The park advertised the Carousel as "one of the largest and most elaborate carousels ever built." The machine was spectacular at night with 1400, 50-watt mazda lamps on it.

The park remains a bright spot during the Depression

The Depression years of the 1930's were hard on McSwigan and Henninger, but Kennywood survived with the help of ballroom dancing and school picnics. Some of the newer parks in western Pennsylvania like National in Aspinwall and Burke's Glen in Monroeville closed. Others like Conneaut Lake, Oakford, and Olympic underwent management changes or were forced into bankruptcy. Kennywood's bank closed, and one year McSwigan and Henninger had to borrow on their insurance policies to keep the park open.

Kiddie Boat Ride by Mangels circa 1927.
(KENNYWOOD PARK)

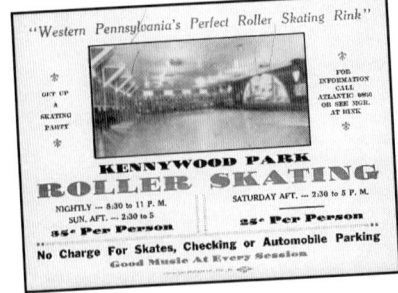

Kennywood offered roller skating in the Dance Pavilion in 1934.
(CHARLES J. JACQUES, JR. COLLECTION)

16

The Tower Refreshment Stand was built in 1929. (CHARLES J. JACQUES, JR. COLLECTION)

Kennywood's birthday cake was first made in 1931. (CHARLES J. JACQUES, JR. COLLECTION)

Many high school and amateur sporting events were held on the park's Athletic Field. (CHARLES J. JACQUES, JR. COLLECTION)

The Teddy Bear junior coaster was designed by Herbert P. Schmeck of the Philadelphia Toboggan Company and built in 1935. (CHARLES J. JACQUES, JR. COLLECTION)

In March 1930, the *Voice of Kennywood*, a monthly four-page sheet with stories and humorous sayings, edited by A. K. "Rosey" Rowswell made its debut. For the next 23 years, Rowswell would say in 100 different ways "picnics are good for Pittsburgh." The first issues stated "Golf is all right and you probably enjoy your Country Club privileges, but how about the fellows in the mill or factory who have neither the opportunity nor price of golf? An outing, with an opportunity for a bit of recreation, would bring more of a thrill to him and his family than your game of golf brings to you. It is not too late to book a picnic date for your employees at Kennywood Park."

In the early 1930's, when things were bleak, Kennywood Park was one of summertime's few bright spots. The school picnic was often the only highlight for many children who did not have enough money to go anywhere else. It was possible to go to the park and spend as little as 50 cents for a whole day's entertainment. A favorite spot was the Bug House where one could have hours of fun for the price of one 15 cent admission. It was really a big indoor playground.

A thumbnail sketch of Kennywood Park appeared in the *National Association of Amusement Parks Bulletin* in July 1932: "The

On Sundays in the late 1930's the parking lot was jammed with cars.
(CHARLES J. JACQUES, JR. COLLECTION)

13 Spook Street, Kennywood's second walk-through, was built in 1937.
(CHARLES J. JACQUES, JR. COLLECTION)

park is a real credit to our industry. Efficiently operated and conducted. Beautifully landscaped and gardened. Mouse City the hit of the season. Employees courteous, neatly uniformed and well trained. Al Wyant effectively directing operations." Over the entrance to the park's office a large sign boldly stated, "We can't please everyone - but we try."

In Kennywood's open-air Dance Pavilion appeared the most famous bands in America including Rudy Vallee, Benny Goodman, Ozzie Nelson, Harry James, Tommy and Jimmy Dorsey, and Vaughn Monroe. The big bands, along with popular local bands, attracted patrons to the park, and many of the groups appeared live on radio from Kennywood's ballroom.

In the late 1930's, Kennywood again began to flourish. McSwigan and Henninger started adding new rides, including an Eyerly Loop-O-Plane, a Spillman Ridee-O, an Auto Skooter from Lusse, Stratoship from R. E. Chambers Co., Beaver Falls, Pennsylvania, (Chambers had acquired the assets of Harry G. Traver in the early 1930's). Also added were a new fun house, 13 Spook Street, which featured a Magic Carpet, and a junior coaster, the Teddy Bear, both from the Philadelphia Toboggan Company. The park's infrastructure was upgraded with a new office building and paved sidewalks replacing the limestone walkways.

The park's huge ballroom was remodeled and redecorated for the 1936 season. The park boasted that the ballroom was more "eye-appealing" and the dance floor more "feet-compelling." The bands booked that season included Jimmy Joy, Ace Brigode, Jess Hawkins, Will Roland, Val Garvin, and Baron Elliot.

Noah's Ark signaled the end of hard times

The most famous attraction built by Kennywood during the 1930's was the Noah's Ark walk-through. With its nautical theme, high ballyhoo ship, swaying structure, and eerie fog horn, it became one of Kennywood's most identifiable symbols. Kennywood had hoped to build an ark for the 1930 season, but the depression postponed its development. The Biblical attraction set sail in 1936 (the year of the largest flood in the Pittsburgh area) with the assistance of Herbert P. Schmeck, chief engineer of the Philadelphia Toboggan Company, who helped obtain the original plans from

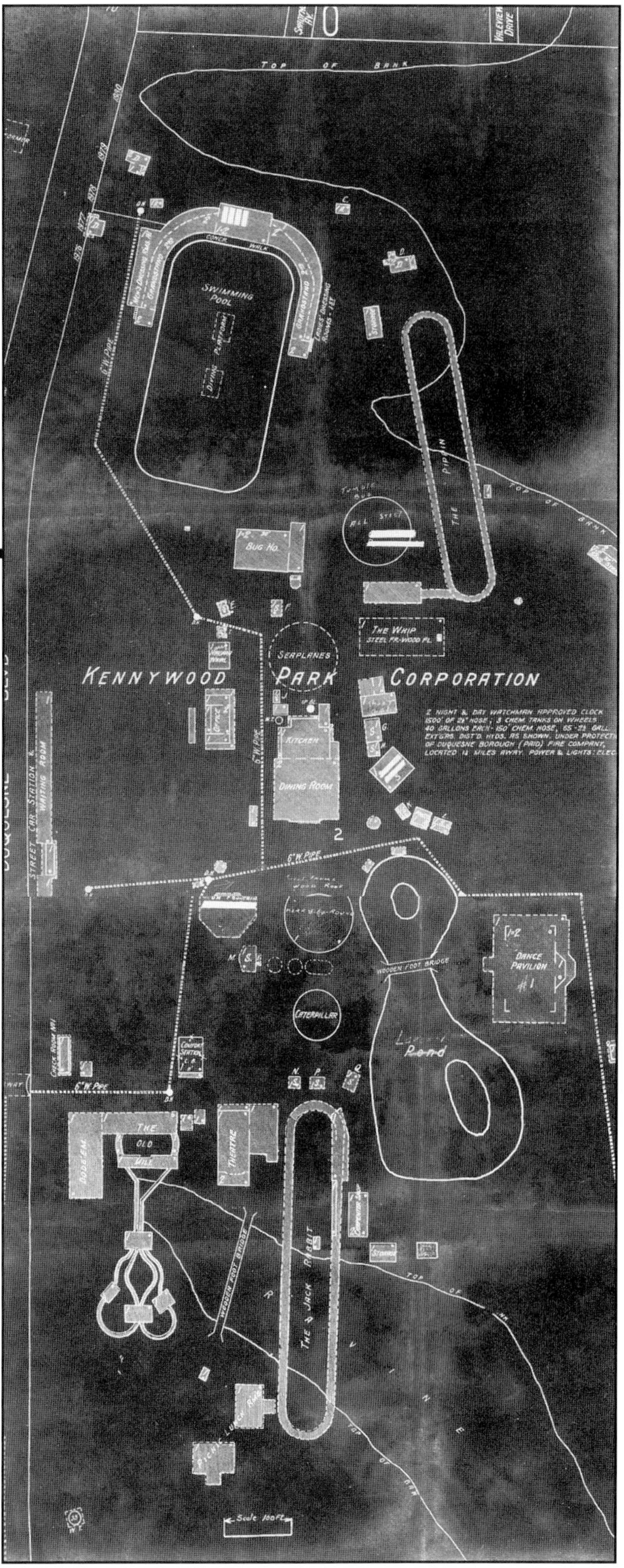

Map of the park circa 1926.

An aerial view of the park, circa 1935.

(Kennywood Park)

The Ridee-O was one of a series of major new rides purchased in the late 1930's.
(Charles J. Jacques, Jr. Collection)

a defunct company that had built the arks.

In 1936, F. W. Henninger's son, Carl, became assistant manager of the park and Erwin A. Vettel, who came from Palisades Park in New Jersey, replaced Charlie Mach as the park's chief engineer. In 1938, Brady McSwigan was elected president of the Pennsylvania Amusement Park Association, a group he had been instrumental in founding.

By 1939, Kennywood had grown from a small trolley park to the dominant amusement park in western Pennsylvania. Under the direction of the McSwigans and Henninger, Kennywood prospered and survived the worst depression America had ever seen. As the 1940's approached, Kennywood looked forward to better times.

The Swimming Pool in the 1930's.
(Charles J. Jacques, Jr. Collection)

Auto Race, later renamed the Auto Ride, was located adjacent to Kiddieland.
(Charles J. Jacques, Jr. Collection)

A publicity photo for Tommy Carlyn and his orchestra in 1939. The miniature train's engine had been modernized and was renamed the Kennywood Express.
(KENNYWOOD PARK)

Another band promotional shot from the 1930's.
(CHARLES J. JACQUES, JR. COLLECTION)

An electric fountain was added to the pool in the late 1930's.
(CHARLES J. JACQUES, JR. COLLECTION)

Three attractive women take to the swings in the free playground.
(CHARLES J. JACQUES, JR. COLLECTION)

CHAPTER 2
1940-1979
The Park Faces New Challenges

World War II and the baby boomers

In 1940, Erwin Vettel, Kennywood's head engineer, supervised the installation of The Rockets (a giant circle swing) on an island in the Lagoon. More than 110 yards of concrete and 49 tons of steel beam were used in building the ride and elevated platform. Vettel commented, "In the old days when one wanted to build a refreshment stand, all he needed was a saw horse, unplaned lumber, and the American flag. Now most building by the park required an architect, contractor, and electrical engineer. New materials like chrome and glass are now used to create streamline effects." Soon the war would interrupt all new civilian construction, and chrome and glass would not be available. Once the war began, amusement ride production stopped. All of the ride manufacturers shifted to building war-related items.

Kennywood was fortunate that shortly before America entered World War II in 1941, it was able to buy two rides: the Dipsy Doodle and Snapper, both from concessionaires who had operated them at the New York World's Fair of 1939-40. Brady McSwigan liked to rename rides. He would often change

Dipsy Doodle, a Flying Scooters ride, was added in 1941.
(CHARLES J. JACQUES, JR. COLLECTION)

The Circle Swing was moved onto an island in the Lagoon, and new modern rocket ships were purchased.
(Charles J. Jacques, Jr. Collection)

During World War II the park was able to purchase a used Ferris Wheel.
(Kennywood Park)

Auto Skooter cars were lifted off the steel floor in the off-season.
(Kennywood Park)

the generic or manufacturer's name for a ride. For example, the generic name for the Dipsy Doodle was Flying Scooters. Dipsy Doodle was suggested by Rosey Rowswell, a long-time friend of McSwigan. Rowswell, who was a radio announcer for the Pittsburgh Pirates, used the words dipsy doodle to described a Pirate pitcher's strikeout pitch. The Flying Scooters permitted its passengers to fly their own "planes" with a sail-like, canvas-covered rudder. It was a very popular ride, and it was in and out of the park several times over the next 50 years.

During the war, Kennywood suffered from severe shortages of almost everything — except people who wanted to go to the park. Sugar, tires, gasoline, ammunition for the shooting gallery, and anything made of metal were all in short supply. America adopted a strict rationing system and amusement parks were near the bottom of the priority list. It was almost impossible for Kennywood to buy anything new. The park had to struggle just to keep its rides operating due to a shortage of replacement parts. During the war, Kennywood was able to buy only one ride, a used Ferris Wheel built in 1936. The park repainted the wheel in patriotic stars and stripes.

Kennywood had trouble finding and

The Laff-in-the-Dark ride and Old Mill were located just inside the gate circa 1940.
(Charles J. Jacques, Jr. Collection)

Exiting the Laff-in-the-Dark, the couple (or at least the man) looks slightly bewildered.
(Kennywood Park)

keeping employees during the war. Often a new employee would work for a few days or a few weeks and then be drafted or leave to work in defense industries. Carl E. Henninger was named general manager of Kennywood in 1940 but soon thereafter left for Alaska to serve in the Navy where he would rise to the rank of U.S. Naval Reserve Commander. Retired employees were encouraged to return and work at the park. The park advertised in the *Pittsburgh Post-Gazette* in 1943, "Wanted 10 men for attendants on amusement rides in Kennywood Park. Good steady job out in the fresh air and sunshine." Many women were used in positions that previously had been staffed exclusively by men.

Some amusement parks that were located in rural areas like Idlewild in Ligonier and Knobels Grove near Shamokin were forced to close during the war because of travel restrictions. The rationing of tires and gasoline hurt amusement parks the most. There also was a shortage of trains during the war, and the railroads stopped offering excursions. Hershey Park, located near Harrisburg, was forced to drastically curtail its hours and close its ballroom during the war.

While some parks experienced severe

Following the war, the park developed a new Mall and built the Little Dipper coaster.
(Kennywood Park)

In 1946 the Racer received a more modern front.
(Kennywood Park)

The Looper, Pony Track, and Bubble Bounce were located adjacent to the Racer.
(CHARLES J. JACQUES, JR. COLLECTION)

The Looper permitted its passengers, by use of a foot pedal, to turn their car upside down while traveling in a circle.
(KENNYWOOD PARK)

operating problems during the war, Kennywood, because of its urban location, actually made more money than it had since the 1920's. While travel was restricted, Kennywood's location, only a few miles from Pittsburgh and its suburbs, was a definite advantage. The park was only a 25 minute trolley ride from Pittsburgh (trolleys remained a major means of transportation during the war). Gasoline rationing had a minimal effect on Kennywood because the park was only a short drive from most of the major towns in western Pennsylvania. During the war, Kennywood advertised itself as "The Place For Your Stay-At-Home Vacation." People finally had money to spend after the Great Depression of the 1930's, and they were looking for some place to spend it. After long hours in the factories, people headed to Kennywood in the evenings and weekends for dancing and amusement. War industries insured full employment and huge payrolls. With the steel mills and factories up and down the Monongahela River working near capacity the park got more than its share of smoke and soot, but McSwigan and Henninger did not mind.

Kennywood's Dance Pavilion played many regional dance bands during the early 1940's including Brad Hunt and his

The old open-front cars were still used on the Pippin until the 1960's.
(CHARLES J. JACQUES, JR. COLLECTION)

KENNYWOOD
Last Time Saturday
PEACHES
SKY REVUE
6 Girl Aerialists
Doing Daring Sky-High
Routines

Saturday, Monday & All Week
DANCE TO BOB STRONG
and his Famous Orchestra
—No Public Dancing this Friday—

Starting Sunday
THREE FRANKS
Gyrating Aerial Thrills
GASCA TRIO
Mexico's Agile Acrobats

Sunday Concert Shows
BOB STRONG, his Band
and Entertainers

BATHING, AMUSEMENTS DAILY

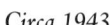

Circa 1943.

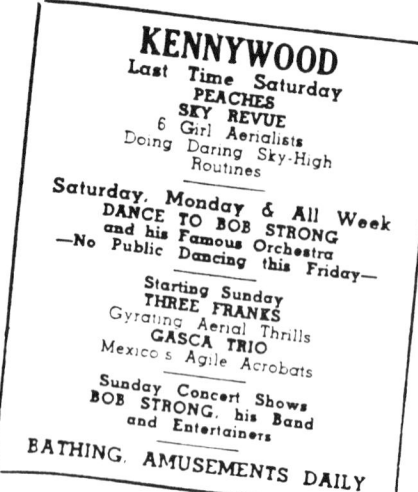

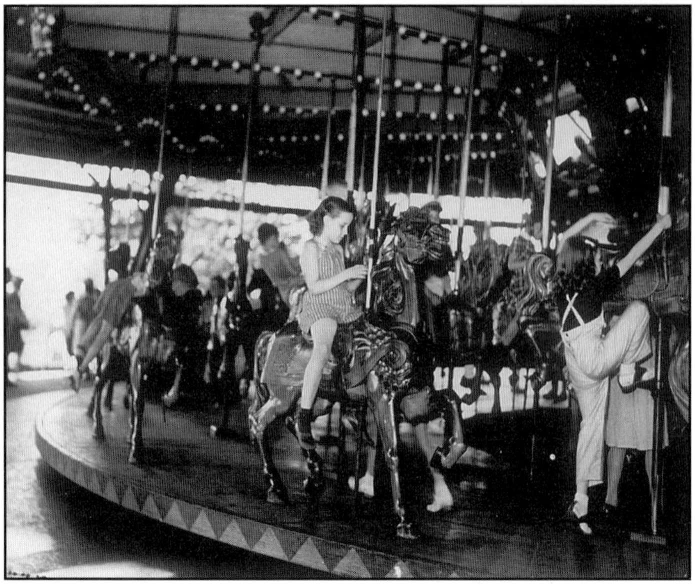

The Dentzel Carousel in the 1940's.
(Charles J. Jacques, Jr. Collection)

Orchestra, Lee Barret Orchestra, Tommy Carlyn and his Pittsburgh Orchestra, Ace Brigode and his Virginians, and Bernie Armstrong and his KDKA Orchestra. The park used fewer national bands because of the travel restrictions. In the Music Plaza (bandstand), bands like Frank Cervone's played patriotic programs on Sundays and holidays.

Thousands of service men and women in uniform were given free ride tickets by the park, and more than two million free books of tickets were given to service personnel. Men and women in uniform also received reduced admission to the Dance Pavilion and Pool. Kennywood sent a small pictorial letter called *Chatty* to former employees who were in the services. During the war, service personnel enjoyed the letter with stories and pictures of the park and lists of bands scheduled to play.

Hot dogs and cotton candy were not always available, but french fries and popcorn helped fill the void. Old rides were repaired and rebuilt. If metal parts could not be secured, the park made its own. Plaster statues replaced brass prizes at the game stands. The shooting gallery's guns were replaced by compressed air guns with pellets. The park did add a few new stunts in its fun houses and dark ride.

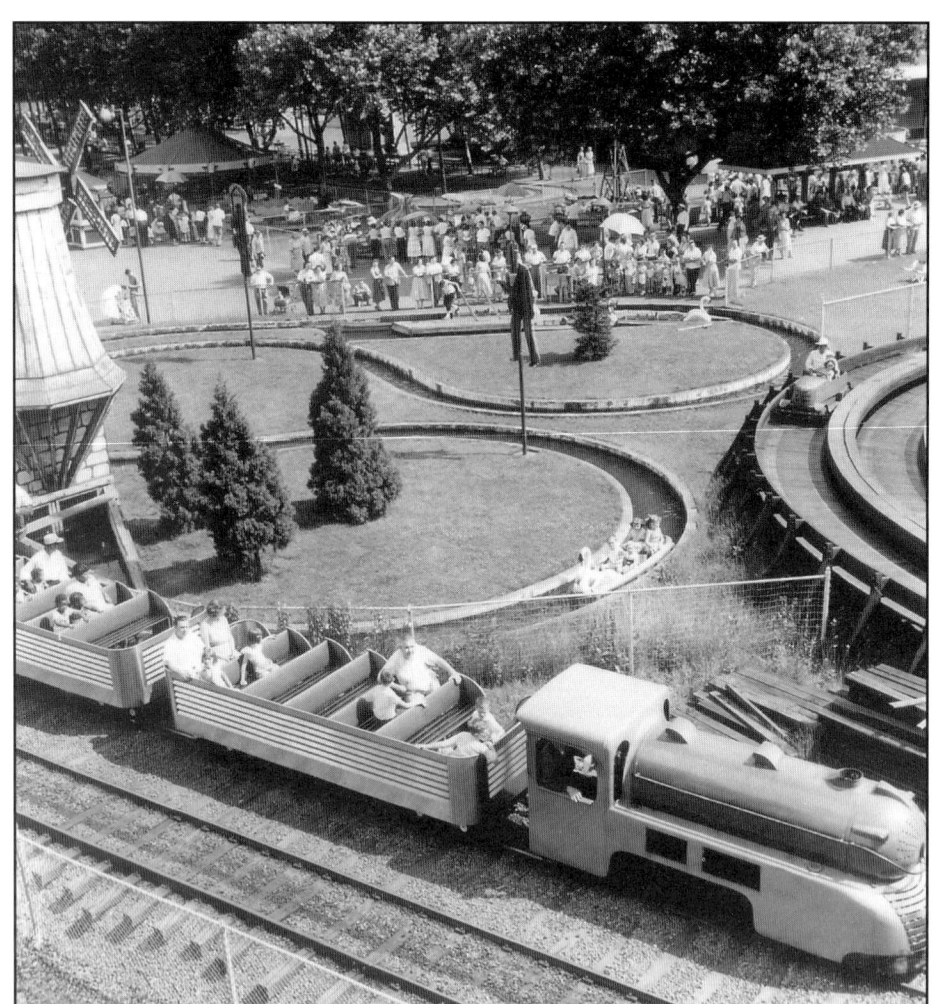

Kiddieland, Auto Race, and Little Choo Choo greeted baby boomers following World War II.
(Charles J. Jacques, Jr. Collection)

Kennywood restaurant menu in 1946. (KENNYWOOD PARK)

At the beginning of the war the fun house, 13 Spook Street, was renamed the Daffy Klub. It was a move away from terror and death, which people faced in real life, to the zany-comical.

In 1945, the park purchased three locomotives from Lillian Cagney for its miniature railroad whose engines had run at the New York World's Fair of 1939-40. The train's route, which was nearly one-half mile long, followed the edge of the bluff overlooking the Monongahela River and then made a loop running along the picnic groves and in back of Kiddieland.

In 1945, a juvenile book *Little Choo-Choo*, written by Helen Sterling and beautifully illustrated by Denison Budd, was published. At the end of the book the Little Choo-Choo goes off on a rampage all by itself and ends its exploits by "riding the steepest roller coaster in the world out at Kennywood Park in Pittsburgh." Kennywood renamed its miniature train ride Little Choo Choo in honor of the book.

Toward the end of World War II, Kennywood carried an article in the *Voice of Kennywood* encouraging returning servicemen to seek a job at the park. "Entertainment of pleasure-seekers at Kennywood Park is just the right adjustment for returning to civilian life," the article said. Carl O. Hughes, who had worked at Kennywood, followed the advice of the *Voice of Kennywood* and wrote to Brady McSwigan from the Philippines, "If you see me coming through your doorway on the 14th floor of the Farmers Bank Building [where Kennywood's main offices were located] sometime in early March, don't be surprised." Kennywood hired him as a part time publicity director in 1947. Hughes also resumed working as a sportswriter at the *Pittsburgh Press*. He became a full-time employee at Kennywood in 1956 when he was appointed assistant manager.

Following the war in 1946, Brady McSwigan was named president of the National Association of Amusement Parks, Pools and Beaches. In 1947, Kennywood celebrated its golden anniversary, 50 years of continuous operation. McSwigan wrote, "It's brought us pleasure, too, all these many years, making folks laugh and having golden days of fun at 'The Nation's Greatest Picnic Park.'" In honor of its golden anniversary, the park offered a six-night Fireworks Watercade on the Lagoon, produced by Thearle-Duffield that was attended by about 35,000. McSwigan said of the fireworks, "the pyrotechnics zoomed and boomed around at such intensity as to have our hearts right up where the tonsils should

Carl Hughes, in the Philippines in early 1947, would soon return to Kennywood. (CHARLES J. JACQUES, JR. COLLECTION)

be, so fearful are we of fire."

Kennywood had one of the largest Kiddielands in the country. In 1947, the rides in Kiddieland included a miniature Whip, carousel, Kiddie Auto Ride, Roto Whip, Tickler (miniature Virginia Reel), Ferris Wheel, Brownie Coaster, boat ride, Comet Ride, Pony Ride, a miniature Seaplane Swing, Fire Engine Ride, and a little Old Mill, which had been designed by Herb Schmeck of the Philadelphia Toboggan Company. Just outside Kiddieland were the Auto Race and the park's miniature railroad. In 1948, a junior roller coaster, The Little Dipper, was added just beyond the miniature railroad. Kiddieland rides cost five cents with a six-ticket strip for 25 cents. The Auto Race and miniature railroad were ten cents each. Kiddieland required a large staff of more than 30 because each child was placed on the ride and strapped into the seat by an employee.

Kennywood's school picnic season ran from May 15 to July 1 except Sundays. Schools were provided free street car or bus transportation, and each student attending the outing was give a strip of four, five cent FREE amusement tickets. In addition, each pupil was permitted to purchase up to one dollar fifty cents in special amusement tickets at three and one-third cents each. These tickets, which cost five cents at the park, had to be purchased at the school prior to the school's picnic. To get around the limits and to get more free tickets, students would have classmates who were not going to the picnic buy extra Kennywood tickets for them.

Some of the popular adult rides of the late 1940's and early 1950's included

Kiddieland's entrance was rebuilt in 1947.
(CHARLES J. JACQUES, JR. COLLECTION)

The Soda Fountain Stand was located in the park's original Merry-Go-Round Pavilion.
(KENNYWOOD PARK)

The Racer at night in the late 1940's.
(CHARLES J. JACQUES, JR. COLLECTION)

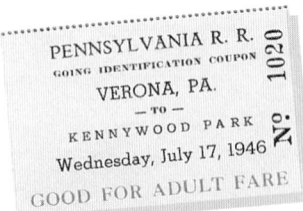

(KENNYWOOD PARK)

28

the Hurricane and Looper, both manufactured by the Allan Herschell Company. The Rotor, which was Kennywood's first ride imported from Europe, came to the park in the mid-1950's. Other rides were an Octopus and a Wild Mouse. Flying Cages was a self-powered ride, with riders trying to swing the cages over the top.

Kennywood continued to offer free entertainment on the Island Stage and at the Music Plaza (bandstand). Each afternoon at 4:30 p.m. and each evening at 9:30 p.m. the park presented two free acts, usually an aerial thriller and a ground or low act. A five piece "circus band" supplied the music. On Sundays and holidays, free concerts were presented at 3 p.m. and 8 p.m. at the Music Plaza, which could accommodate approximately 5,400 people. In the 1950's, the program consisted of dance band music and two vaudeville acts. There was no dancing in the Dance Pavilion on Sundays. The Music Plaza concerts lasted about 30 minutes, and the free acts on the Island Stage ran between 20 and 25 minutes.

Frederick W. Henninger died on September 18, 1950, after serving as secretary and treasurer of Kennywood for 44 years. Henninger was always interested in providing clean, wholesome outdoor recreation. After the war, Carl E. Henninger returned to the park and became vice president and general manager. Two other brothers also joined the management team; Robert F. Henninger became a vice president and refreshment manager, and Harry W. Henninger, Sr. succeeded his father as secretary-treasurer of the park.

In the 1950's, the Wild Mouse was known for its fast drops and quick curves.
(KENNYWOOD PARK)

Aerial view of the park in 1953.
(CHARLES J. JACQUES, JR. COLLECTION)

Robert F. Henninger
(KENNYWOOD PARK)

Harry W. Henninger, Sr.
(KENNYWOOD PARK)

**1957
FALL FANTASY
FEATURING
"MARDI GRAS
ON PARADE"
AND
FESTIVAL OF MUSIC
—
KENNYWOOD
PARK
AUGUST 18 thru 25**

Fall Fantasy Parade "Circus on Parade" in 1953.
(CHARLES J. JACQUES, JR. COLLECTION)

Kennywood learns to love a parade

Kennywood's love affair with parades started in 1950 when the park staged its first Fall Fantasy Parade to fill in one of the slowest periods of the summer season, the weeks before Labor Day. The park often had closed the week before Labor Day because of the low attendance. The first Fall Fantasy promotion was called "Alice in Wonderland Parade Spectacular" and lasted five nights. The park actually had trouble getting high school bands to march in the first parade. The name "Tournament of Music" was used for many years to describe the band part of the parade. Alice, riding in a float of her own, was selected from entries on the "Starlets on Parade" program on KDKA radio. The first Fall Fantasy Parade started promptly at 8:30 p.m. on August 29, 1950.

The idea of a parade with floats and bands was borrowed from Riverview Park in Chicago as Brady McSwigan and Carl E. Henninger had gone to Riverview the previous season (1949) to see its parade. Kennywood's first parade was designed by Modern Art Studios, Inc. of Chicago. Following the first Fall Fantasy, McSwigan reported back to Riverview Park:

A push-float in the Fall Fantasy and Tournament of Music Parade.
(CHARLES J. JACQUES, JR. COLLECTION)

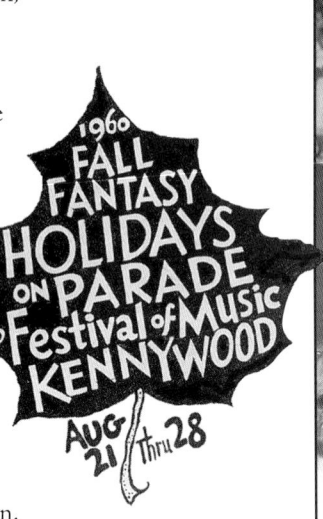

1960 FALL FANTASY HOLIDAYS ON PARADE AND Festival of Music KENNYWOOD AUG 21 thru 28

Another new ride added by the park in the 1950's was an eight-armed Octopus.
(KENNYWOOD PARK)

The Auto Race was renamed the Auto Ride and a clock was added in the 1950's.
(CHARLES J. JACQUES, JR. COLLECTION)

Hungerford cartoon circa 1956.
(CHARLES J. JACQUES, JR. COLLECTION)

Auto Ride and Kiddieland in the 1950's.
(CHARLES J. JACQUES, JR. COLLECTION)

Noah's Ark was the park's signature ride in the 1950's. To the right was Bozo, the mechanical man.
(CHARLES J. JACQUES, JR. COLLECTION)

We did not get rich on the parade. In fact broke just about even. In the face of doubtful weather all week (although we did not miss a parade) we are encouraged and want to try another one. We had some favorable comments that were quite heartening showing people appreciated our efforts.

Kennywood did hold another Fall Fantasy and then another and another until it became an important end-of-summer tradition that people in the area did not want to miss. Soon there was a waiting list of school bands that wanted to play in the parade. Bill Schmidt, the owner of Riverview Park, had only two "rules" for its parade; the parade had to have elephants and had to wind up with Santa Claus. Kennywood had a Santa Claus in a different float each year, but decided against the elephants.

Over the years, the park experienced amazing good luck with the weather during its Fall Fantasies. During the first seven years, the parade was rained out only once, in 1951. Every year the parade was given a new name. In 1952, it was "Kandy Kapers On Parade" with costumed park employees as the Peppermint Girls, the Lollypop Ladies, and Candy Canes. Some other parades in the 1950's

The Rotor, which was the park's first ride manufactured in Europe, was introduced in 1955. It was almost as much fun to watch as to ride.
(KENNYWOOD PARK)

included "Circus On Parade," "Frontier Days on Parade," and "Mardi Gras on Parade." McSwigan told Bill Schmidt the themes were often selected to be as general as possible, "There is less continuity, if any at all," he noted, "yet who cares for continuity when it comes to a parade?"

In the 1950's, Kennywood continued to call itself, with much justification, "The Nation's Greatest Picnic Park." One of the largest events was the Westinghouse picnic. According to a brochure that was specially prepared for the 1952 picnic, "There was something doing all day long from a Diaper Derby to a dinner for one thousand retired employees." The entertainment program included selections by the Westinghouse Band, the Scotch Band, and the Westinghouse Male Quartet. In the afternoon, there were athletic events in which more than 1,000 employees participated.

In 1953, Kennywood closed the ballroom and the Swimming Pool. Through the years, these facilities had been segregated and to avoid the tensions of integration, Kennywood decided to close them. They were no longer the attraction they had once been. The Dance Pavilion was converted into a walk-through (fun house) and later a dark ride, and would remain that until the structure

Welding the chain on the Pippin in 1957.
(KENNYWOOD PARK)

Dual Ferris Wheels were purchased in 1959.
(CHARLES J. JACQUES, JR. COLLECTION)

32

Although Skooter cars were supposed to go in one direction, some riders disregarded the rule.
(KENNYWOOD PARK)

With its two coaster trains, the Racer could carry more persons per hour than any other ride in the park.
(CHARLES J. JACQUES, JR. COLLECTION)

EZC (Easy Credit) Ranch Gals performing at the Music Plaza.
(CHARLES J. JACQUES, JR. COLLECTION)

Kennywood's diving platform in the 1950's. A few women were wearing two-piece suits.
(CHARLES J. JACQUES, JR. COLLECTION)

Mother Goose Tiny Tot Comfort Station was located in Kiddieland.
(CHARLES J. JACQUES, JR. COLLECTION)

33

UNEMPLOYED
FORD CITY COMMUNITY PICNIC
Present this card on Saturday, July 15, 1967 at Pavillion No. 1 between the hours of 11:30 a.m. and 1:30 p.m. in order to get your tickets for the Ford City Community Picnic.
PICNIC COMMITTEE

Kiddie Mill Ride was one of the more popular rides in Kiddieland.
(CHARLES J. JACQUES, JR. COLLECTION)

The letters on the Daffy Klub rotated back and forth to attract customers.
(CHARLES J. JACQUES, JR. COLLECTION)

The park entered the space age with miniature Flying Saucers.
(KENNYWOOD PARK)

The Jack Rabbit received new streamlined cars manufactured by the Philadelphia Toboggan Company in the 1950's.
(CHARLES J. JACQUES, JR. COLLECTION)

The Tower Refreshment Stand was decorated in a space age fashion.
(CHARLES J. JACQUES, JR. COLLECTION)

The Bubble Bounce received a new look and was moved near the park entrance.
(CHARLES J. JACQUES, JR. COLLECTION)

burned to the ground in 1975. The Swimming Pool reopened in 1956 fully integrated. When the Pool was reopened, it was given the name Sunlight.

For a few seasons in the late 1950's and early 1960's Kennywood operated two Ferris Wheels side by side. The wheels were purchased from Eli Bridge Company of Jacksonville, Illinois. The wheels were low capacity rides, but with two operating, especially on big picnic days, the park was able to handle the crowds.

On opening day 1961, Brady McSwigan's worst fears about fire were realized when Kennywood's Music Plaza burned to the ground. With the wooden buildings and coasters, the park was vulnerable. Firefighters saved the Pippin roller coaster. The original bandstand was replaced with a new one of a more modern design called Starvue Plaza.

In 1964, Brady McSwigan died after a long illness, and Carl E. Henninger replaced him as president of the park. Under McSwigan's direction, the park had undergone its period of greatest expansion in the 1920's and survived America's worst Depression in the 1930's. McSwigan was an innovator and showman who helped make Kennywood a truly great park.

Although Kennywood was really a series of corporations (one for each of the

On opening night, April 23, 1961, the park's bandstand, the Music Plaza, burned to the ground.
(KENNYWOOD PARK)

Andrew B. "Brady" McSwigan
(KENNYWOOD PARK)

major coasters, one for the park and one for the refreshment company), it had always been run like a partnership. Nothing major was done in the park without the assent of both "managing partners." This started with Andrew S. McSwigan and Frederick W. Henninger and was continued under Brady McSwigan and Frederick Henninger and, after Frederick Henninger's death, with Brady McSwigan and Carl E. Henninger. At Brady McSwigan's death there was not a "natural" heir from the McSwigan family, so Carl E. Henninger took his brother, Harry W. Henninger, Sr. and Carl O. Hughes in as his junior partners. Robert F. Henninger continued as president of the refreshment company.

Kennywood learns to adapt to changes in society

Although park revenues and attendance were still high in the 1960's, Kennywood was threatened by major changes in society. Up until the 1950's, most people would dress up to go to an amusement park and they would usually come as part of a family unit or with a school or group picnic. But starting in the 1960's and carrying into the 1970's, more people, especially teenagers, came to the park

35

Kennywood featured a photo cutout of President Kennedy and bride in the early 1960's.
(KENNYWOOD PARK)

Flying Scooters returned in 1960's and was renamed the Flyer.
(KENNYWOOD PARK)

Noah's Ark was rebuilt in 1969, and the whale's entrance was added.
(KENNYWOOD PARK)

Flying Cages, called Allez Oop by the park, was a ride in which people tried by moving side to side to get their cage to go "over the top."
(KENNYWOOD PARK)

alone or in groups and had to be controlled by the park, not parents or others. Laws were also changing and it became harder to ban people from the park without cause. Many large traditional parks like Euclid Beach in Cleveland, Palisades Park in New Jersey, and Riverview in Chicago were simply overwhelmed by these changes and closed. Kennywood stayed on top of the changes and developed new policies and procedures needed to cope with a changing society.

A second major change that Kennywood had to face was the development of super theme parks. Walt Disney started it all in 1955 with the opening of Disneyland in Anaheim, California and it was followed by other parks. Cedar Point,

The Dance Pavilion was closed and became a walk-through, the Enchanted Castle.
(KENNYWOOD PARK)

The Racer steel tracks shine in the sun.
(Photograph by Charles J. Jacques, Jr.)

although an old resort park, was being developed into a major theme park, and Coney Island, Cincinnati, became Kings Island in 1972. At first, Kennywood's management did not know how to compete with these parks or what course they should follow. It became obvious the comfortable rut the park had been in since the end World War II would no longer do. West View Park, Kennywood's major local competitor, did not change and closed in 1977. Kennywood could no longer add a new flat ride every few years and depend upon circus acts and television personalities to draw crowds.

Led by Carl E. Henninger, Kennywood's president, the park determined it had to spend more money on new rides and in rebuilding the park. In 1971, after years of unsuccessfully trying, Kennywood was finally able to purchase the ground the park was built on from the Anthony Kenny heirs. Now Kennywood could build permanent rides and make improvements without fear of having to move someday. Harry W. Henninger, Sr., the secretary-treasurer of Kennywood Park Corporation, was instrumental in arranging the purchase from the Kennys.

Even before the land was purchased, the Henningers and other park officers built the Turnpike auto ride at a cost of more than $100,000. Up until that time, the park had added many new rides, but almost all of them were portable flat rides that could be removed if the company lost its lease. All of the park's major permanent rides (the Jack Rabbit, Racer, Pippin, and Noah's Ark) and buildings (Casino, Old Mill, Merry-Go-Round Pavilion, park office) had been built prior to World War II. The Turnpike required a major, fixed installation that could not be removed and sold.

The Turnpike was a huge success, and it was quickly followed by an even more ambitious undertaking, a new roller coaster - the Thunderbolt. For a number of years, some members of management had wanted to build a new roller coaster,

Flying Coaster was named the Kangaroo when Kennywood adopted the Kangaroo as one of its symbols.
(Kennywood Park)

The Turnpike required a major fixed installation.
(Kennywood Park)

37

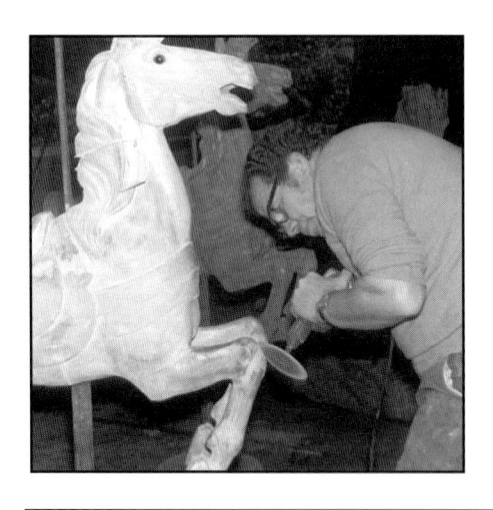

In 1976 the park's carousel was restored.
(KENNYWOOD PARK)

(Left to Right) Ken Garrett, Bill Henninger, and Harry Henninger, Jr. learning the ropes.
(PHOTOGRAPH BY CHARLES J. JACQUES, JR.)

and finally in 1966, Carl E. Henninger gave the go ahead to Andy Vettel, Kennywood's chief engineer and resident roller coaster expert, to design and build a new coaster to replace the Pippin. Using part of the old Pippin track that dipped into the ravine, Vettel designed a great new coaster. The Thunderbolt was more than 95 feet high, 2,887 feet long with sections extending down into a ravine. The coaster was known for its 90-foot drop at the end of the ride. The Thunderbolt got a giant boost, when Robert Cartmell, writing in the *New York Times* in 1976, said, "If there is an 'ultimate coaster' today, I think it is the Thunderbolt at Kennywood...king of the coasters."

In the 1970's, the park continued to expand and modernize. The area around the Lagoon was landscaped and beautified. In 1976, a new, larger Island Stage was built. The new stage was put in the same location as the old one. Major new rides were added including the Enterprise, Monster, Super Roundup, and Cuddle Up. The Carousel was completely refurbished for America's Bicentennial. Even The Old Mill and Noah's Ark were updated.

The Log Jammer flume ride, which was the park's first ride that cost more than one million dollars, opened in 1975.

Aerial view of the park in 1972.
(KENNYWOOD PARK)

During the winter of 1967-68, the Pippin roller coaster was partially demolished, and the Thunderbolt was built.
(KENNYWOOD PARK)

Circa 1968.
(CHARLES J. JACQUES, JR. COLLECTION)

Two new rides added by the park in the 1960's were the Calypso and Satellite.
(KENNYWOOD PARK)

Using new hydro-technology, the new log flume was able to pump thousands of gallons of water per minute through a trough propelling fiberglass boats. Patrons in casual clothes were willing to get wet. Although the Log Jammer was not a particularly wet ride, there was always a chance of getting sprayed during the ride or when a rider would dip his hand into the trough and splash another rider.

A new management team

Robert F. Henninger, who had served as vice president of the park and head of the Kennywood Refreshment Company, died in 1972. He had taken over the refreshment company in 1946 when it consisted of the Casino Restaurant and a handful of food stands and had helped build it into a high-volume, modern refreshment business. Robert Henninger encouraged the park to keep the Casino and remodel it. Robert Henninger was replaced by his son, F. W. "Bill" Henninger, who was working for the refreshment company.

In 1973 Carl E. Henninger was not well, so he moved up to become chairman of the board of Kennywood Park Corporation. His brother, Harry W. Henninger,

The park's Ferris Wheel was moved to a site behind the office in the late 1970's.
(PHOTOGRAPH BY CHARLES J. JACQUES, JR.)

39

The Old Mill was renamed Hardheaded Harold's Horrendously Humorous Haunted Hideaway.
(KENNYWOOD PARK)

Father Noah looking out for the slightest hint of rain.
(PHOTOGRAPH BY CHARLES J. JACQUES, JR.)

Sr., who had been secretary-treasurer of the company for many years, reluctantly agreed to become president. Harry W. Henninger, Sr. played an important role in the park's decision to build the Log Jammer. When Harry Henninger died suddenly in 1975, Carl E. Henninger named Carl O. Hughes president. Hughes was the first person who was not a McSwigan or Henninger to serve as president of the park. Carl Henninger needed someone with Hughes' experience and management ability. Harry W. Henninger, Jr., Harry Henninger, Sr.'s son, was named general manager. Carl E. Henninger, Carl O. Hughes, Harry W. Henninger, Jr. and F. W. "Bill" Henninger made up the new management team to

Painting the whale's eye.
(KENNYWOOD PARK)

The Skooter building was demolished in September 1979 to make room for the Laser Loop.
(KENNYWOOD PARK)

Snoopy was added to Noah's Ark in 1969.
(PHOTOGRAPH BY CHARLES J. JACQUES, JR.)

40

Walkway along the Lagoon.
(KENNYWOOD PARK)

The Pop Over or Sky Diver was purchased from Chance Manufacturing.
(KENNYWOOD PARK)

carry Kennywood into the 1980's.

Harry Henninger, Jr. and Bill Henninger were still in their twenties when they were named to the new management team. Although they were both Henningers, they had to prove themselves to their uncle, Carl E. Henninger, and if either of them had failed, they might not have remained with the company. In appointing Harry and Bill Henninger, perhaps Carl Henninger remembered he had been in his twenties when Brady McSwigan and his father named him general manager. Although the younger Henningers were given major responsibilities, Carl E. Henninger, who had recovered from his illness, continued to direct and supervise.

Kennywood had taken some steps to remain competitive, but much more had to be done. Spending $1,000,000 for a ride in the 1970's had seemed so precarious, but in the 1980's the park would spend many millions buying new rides, improving the park, buying a park, and building a water park. What seemed so risky in 1975 with the Log Jammer became common place in the 1980's and 1990's. The increased spending would bring increases in attendance and revenues beyond what anyone thought possible in the late 1970's.

Chapter 3
1980-1982
The Laser Loop

Looping into the eighties

Kennywood literally looped into the 1980's when it built the Laser Loop, a steel looping coaster. For most of its history, the front of the park near the main highway (Kennywood Boulevard) had not been developed. Kennywood's three wooden coasters were ravine coasters (coasters that used the valleys in the park) located at the back of the park, but starting with the Turnpike, which was built in 1966, Kennywood began making its rides more visible to people outside the park. For many years, the most conspicuous attraction to motorists as they approached the park was Noah's Ark and in many ways this made it the park's signature ride.

The Laser Loop changed the skyline of the park. Not only was the new coaster visible from Kennywood Boulevard, but it could be seen for miles around. It was the first coaster since the Speed-O-Plane that people could see while passing by the park. The new coaster was only the beginning of Kennywood making its coasters and rides more visible to those outside the park's boundaries. It was also a sign that Kennywood, though a mid-size park, was ready to compete with the major parks in the East.

A crane lifts sections of the 139-foot end into place.
(PHOTOGRAPH BY CHARLES J. JACQUES, JR.)

The Laser Loop's new cars in the unfinished station.
(PHOTOGRAPH BY CHARLES J. JACQUES, JR.)

The Laser Loop coming out of its loop. (At left)
(KENNYWOOD PARK)

Loading station and Laser Loop under construction.
(PHOTOGRAPH BY CHARLES J. JACQUES, JR.)

Two giant cranes lifted the top of the 72-foot high loop into place.
(PHOTOGRAPH BY CHARLES J. JACQUES, JR.)

Kennywood's management realized in the late 1970's that the park needed a high-tech coaster if it wanted to continue to call itself the "Roller Coaster Capital of the World." Steel coasters had been around for about 20 years, but with the development of loops and corkscrews in the mid-1970's, they had finally come into their own as an important ride in almost all modern amusement parks. The Log Jammer had been so successful and had drawn so many people that it was easier for the board of directors to spend more than a million dollars on a new steel coaster, but the question remained - what kind should it be? The new management team hoped the new coaster would be as successful as the Jammer.

Harry W. Henninger, Jr., vice president and general manager of the park, was given the job of selecting the new coaster. He was drawn to the shuttle loop because it was so compact and provided a lot of bang for the park's bucks. The Laser Loop was a high-tech, state-of-the-art ride. Rather than using a chain lift and gravity, the Laser Loop used a spinning flywheel and clutch system. Kennywood soon found out that high-tech meant more maintenance and possible breakdowns. The park repeatedly had troubles with the flywheel, clutch, pads, and pressure plates. As a season wore on, it took longer for the Laser Loop to "launch" its coaster train. In August, employees on the Laser Loop would hold their breath as the clutch whined trying to engage the flywheel. A clutch repair or replacement would shut the ride down for days, possibly a week, and in the early 1980's when the park had only five major rides (Laser Loop, Thunderbolt, Racer, Jack Rabbit, and Log Jammer), closing just one ride would seriously hurt ride capacity. (The Log Jammer had experienced very little downtime even in its first season, and the park's three wooden coasters were really low-tech rides that

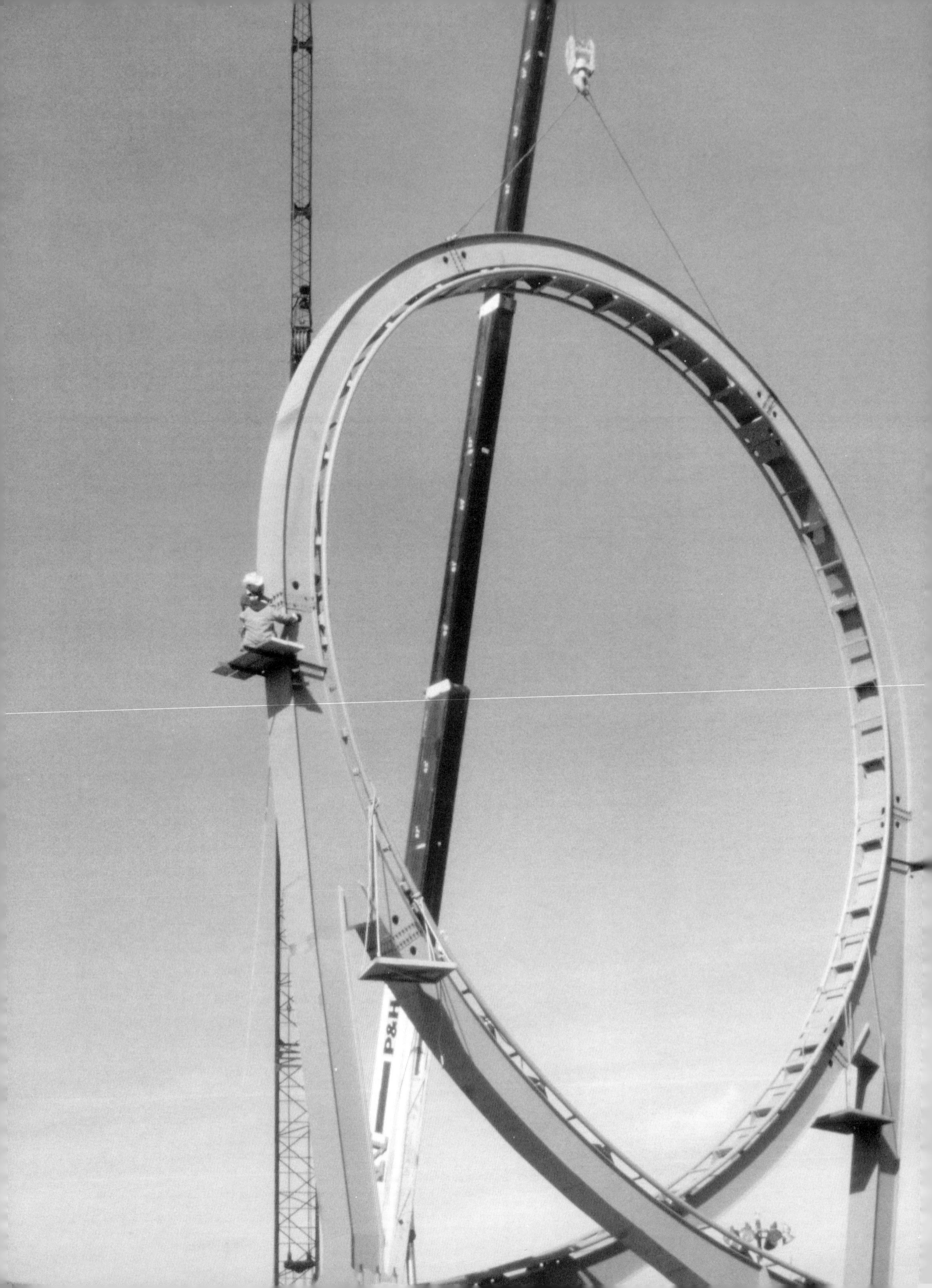
P&H

Bolting the loop together. (At left)
(PHOTOGRAPH BY CHARLES J. JACQUES, JR.)

The Gran Prix with 30 bumper cars was built near Kennywood Boulevard to replace the Skooter.
(PHOTOGRAPH BY CHARLES J. JACQUES, JR.)

The Gulf Oil Company sponsored the Turnpike ride in the early 1980's.
(PHOTOGRAPH BY CHARLES J. JACQUES, JR.)

Occasionally it rains in the summertime at Kennywood.
(PHOTOGRAPH BY CHARLES J. JACQUES, JR.)

The Cuddle Up was placed under a tent from Helios Tension Products.
(PHOTOGRAPH BY CHARLES J. JACQUES, JR.)

the park could easily maintain in-house.) The Laser Loop was really the first of a class of new rides, mostly manufactured in Europe, that were much harder to maintain and in case of a breakdown would be out of service for many days. The electrical department had to learn how to service computers and complex wiring circuits for the first time. But even with all of its drawbacks, the Laser Loop would remain in the park for eleven years, from 1980 to 1990, and although not a favorite of the park maintenance department, it was popular with teenage riders.

In many ways, the Laser Loop was ideal for a park with limited space like Kennywood. The new coaster offered a number of different experiences - including great acceleration (shooting out of the station and reaching a speed of 54 mph in 3.8 seconds), looping, weightlessness, reverse looping, traveling through the station at high speed, and a second moment of weightlessness. The Loop's highest points were 139-and-111-foot inclines at the ends of the rides. The moments of weightlessness on either end made the ride especially appealing.

Harry Henninger, Jr. had to decide where to place the Laser Loop. Management was afraid wherever it would go it

The Racer and Log Jammer stand side by side in the snow awaiting the spring.
(PHOTOGRAPH BY CHARLES J. JACQUES, JR.)

The Windmill in winter.
(PHOTOGRAPH BY CHARLES J. JACQUES, JR.)

would block off a section of the park. Henninger solved this by building the shuttle loop at the front of the park along the pay parking area and then elevating it. This made it possible to build an exciting new entrance to the park which was directly under the coaster's 72-foot high loop without cutting off part of the park. This entrance was so successful it was retained when the Steel Phantom was built and later would serve as Lost Kennywood's main entrance.

The Laser Loop, a shuttle loop coaster, was designed by Reinhold Spieldiener, Swiss engineer, and manufactured by Anton Schwartzkopf in West Germany. Actually the ride was a hybrid, part coaster and part conventional amusement park ride, because it used a flywheel and clutch. Kennywood was the first mid-size park in the United States to purchase a shuttle loop. All of the shuttle loops prior to Kennywood's had been built in major theme parks like Knott's Berry Farm, Astroworld, Carowinds, and Great America. Harry Henninger, Jr. first looked at a shuttle loop at Carowinds near Charlotte, North Carolina, in early 1977, but construction was delayed until 1980 because the section of the park surrounding Noah's Ark had to be completely redesigned to facilitate the new coaster.

Snow blankets Noah's Ark.
(PHOTOGRAPH BY CHARLES J. JACQUES, JR.)

The Casino is used for storing ride cars during the winter.
(PHOTOGRAPH BY CHARLES J. JACQUES, JR.)

Aluminum row boats replaced the old wooden boats on the Lagoon.
(PHOTOGRAPH BY CHARLES J. JACQUES, JR.)

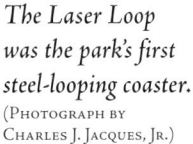

The Laser Loop was the park's first steel-looping coaster.
(PHOTOGRAPH BY CHARLES J. JACQUES, JR.)

Cinema 180, a super-wide motion picture, was presented in a dome adjacent to Noah's Ark in the early 1980's.
(PHOTOGRAPH BY CHARLES J. JACQUES, JR.)

The Loop-O-Plane (foreground) and Roll-O-Plane (background) were placed side by side along the new midway that ran in back of Noah's Ark.
(PHOTOGRAPH BY CHARLES J. JACQUES, JR.)

A new midway was opened along the coaster that connected the Enterprise with the entrance under the Laser Loop. Along the midway, an old refreshment stand, which had been used at the park's Swimming Pool, was remodeled and used for games and refreshments that featured fresh fruits and freshly-squeezed juices. Over the next decade, this midway would be further expanded and developed.

A decidedly low-tech attraction, the ponies, had been moved to the Laser Loop's section of the park when the Log Jammer was built. A decision had to be made whether to leave the ponies underneath the new coaster's highest 139-foot incline. The ponies did not seem bothered by their new neighbor, so they remained but were finally retired after the 1985 season. Ridership had continually decreased and the "unpredictability" of the ponies and their riders was always a concern. Other additions to the park in 1980 included a baseball pitching game that replaced the Gunsmoke shooting gallery. Patrons could see on a digital read-out how fast they could throw a baseball.

To help celebrate the introduction of the new coaster, the American Coaster Enthusiasts (ACE) came to Kennywood in 1980 for their annual convention. Many members fell in love with this traditional park and its coasters. The group voted the Thunderbolt one of its favorite coasters.

Kennywood was still primarily a ticket park in 1980. The park used tickets for school picnics Monday through Saturday in May and June with Pay One Price (POP) of $8 on Sundays. In July and August, POP days were moved to Thursdays and Fridays with the remaining four days being tickets only. The park also added a general admission charge of $1.50 to keep troublemakers out of the park. Carl E. Henninger, chairman of the board, resisted going to pay-one-price, but

The Gold Rusher was the park's new dark ride in 1981.
(Photograph by Charles J. Jacques, Jr.)

Every year a different design was chosen for the park's famous garden clock made from plants and natural materials.
(Kennywood Park)

the competition - Cedar Point, Geauga Lake, and Hersheypark, all of which had adopted some form of it - forced Kennywood to offer more pay-one-price days.

Ride tickets were 20 cents each. The Laser Loop, Log Jammer, Thunderbolt, and non-ride attraction, Cinema 180, required four tickets. Three ticket rides included the Racer, Jack Rabbit, Enterprise, Monster, Gran Prix, Calypso, Sky Diver, Bayern Kurve, and Haunted Hideaway. The rest of the rides were either one or two tickets each.

Riders are spun in two directions at once on the Calypso.
(Photograph by Charles J. Jacques, Jr.)

Even with a broken leg, a Kennywood employee could still sell foam alligators and bug antennas.
(Photograph by Charles J. Jacques, Jr.)

One of the Gold Rusher's cars traveling above the midway before entering the "mine."
(Photograph by Charles J. Jacques, Jr.)

A coyote family inhabited the Gold Rusher dark ride.
(Photograph by Charles J. Jacques, Jr.)

1981 *Panning for gold*

Kennywood's new ride for the 1981 season was the Gold Rusher, a dark ride. "Weather has always been a factor in operating an amusement park," Carl O. Hughes said, "and we were glad to finally get another covered ride; it provides variety to thrill rides and is added protection for rainy days." The Gold Rusher occupied the second floor of the new Sportland Building that housed seven different games on the first floor. The original Sportland Building had been demolished and replaced with a more modern fire-proof building in two phases. First, in 1978, the pylons on the the old Sportland Building were demolished, and a new steel and concrete second floor was built over the existing old wooden building. For the 1978 season the old wooden first floor continued to house games. Then in 1979, the first floor was demolished and replaced by a new steel and concrete one. The park built the new building to house a dark ride on the second floor, but it remained vacant for three years until the Gold Rusher was built.

In its first season of operation, the Gold Rusher loaded from the ground and its riders were carried up a fairly steep incline to the second floor in little four-

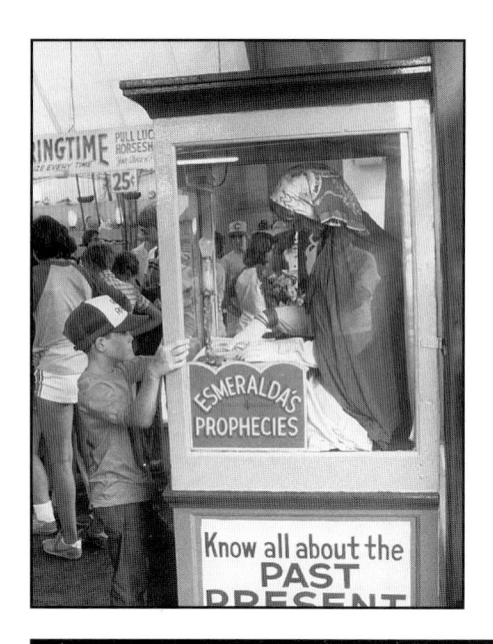

Esmeralda's Prophecies was one of the old-time machines in the Penny Arcade.
(PHOTOGRAPH BY CHARLES J. JACQUES, JR.)

Spider Woman was one of the scenes in the Gold Rusher.
(PHOTOGRAPH BY CHARLES J. JACQUES, JR.)

seat mine cars. However, the little cars were not able to negotiate the hill without constantly breaking down because the grade proved to be too steep. In 1984, stairs were added and the incline track removed. Passengers then climbed stairs to the boarding area, which was built over the midway.

The Gold Rusher was themed by Maurice Ayers, a veteran Hollywood set designer. As ballyhoo for the attraction, he used a waterwheel, sluice, derrick, and several mannequins dressed as miners. Along the Gold Rusher's 550 feet of track "lived" ghosts and skeletons, and bats and coyotes who cooked the "Lone Stranger and Tonto." Other scenes included a charging locomotive, a simulated dynamite explosion that was quickly followed by a waterfall, and the steep descent back to the ride's loading area. The ride's only drawback, after the incline was replaced, was its low capacity. On rainy days or major picnic days, a long line would usually develop.

In 1981, the row boats, which had been on the park Lagoon since the opening of the park, were replaced with new bright yellow paddle boats. Many a Pittsburgher learned the rudiments of rowing in one of Kennywood's row boats. The old boats were often treated like bumper cars with

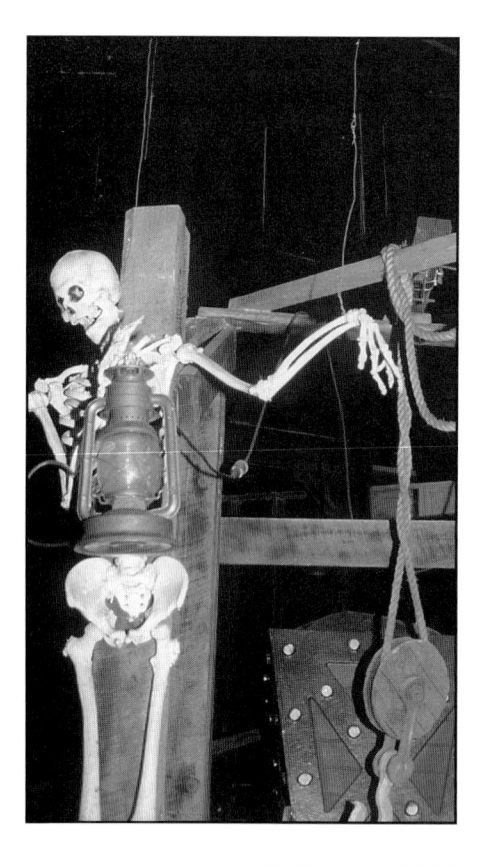

A leering skeleton greeted riders on the Gold Rusher.
(PHOTOGRAPH BY CHARLES J. JACQUES, JR.)

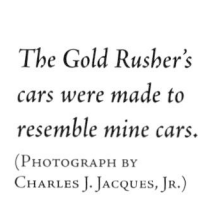

The Gold Rusher's cars were made to resemble mine cars.
(PHOTOGRAPH BY CHARLES J. JACQUES, JR.)

Moonshine Village's hillbilly band was located along the miniature railroad.
(KENNYWOOD PARK)

The Bayern Kurve was so popular that through the years the park owned three different models.
(PHOTOGRAPH BY CHARLES J. JACQUES, JR.)

one group bumping into another or splashing one another. Through the years, the row boats proved to be most popular when the circus acts were performing on the Island Stage. People who wanted to get a close-up view of the performers or who wanted to be seen in front of the Island Stage by friends and schoolmates would wait in line for a boat for the afternoon show. There was an additional charge to rent the new paddle boats, just as there had been to rent the old row boats, but most people felt it was money well spent. The paddle boats offered people a chance to relax in the middle of a hectic day.

Another important ride, the Turtle, was completely rebuilt in 1981. The park spent more than $38,000 rebuilding the Turtle's cars and installing new track. Only a handful of Tumble Bugs, the generic name for Kennywood's Turtle, remained in operation in parks in America. The ride was noisy and hard to maintain, and many parks removed it for those reasons, but Kennywood was willing to maintain the ride and the noise was not a factor because the park located the ride in an ideal spot - at the end of the park with the Thunderbolt as its only close neighbor.

Kennywood offered a sweet promotion on August 14, 1981, when the park, along with the Clark Candy Company, made the world's largest candy bar, a huge Clark Bar. Ann Hughes, publicity director of the park and wife of park president Carl O. Hughes, remembered that the candy got so hard that the park employees had to cut it with a hacksaw. The park and candy company hoped to get into the Guiness Book of Records. Newspaper accounts of the size of the bar varied. Some reports indicated it was 15 feet long while others said it was 12 feet long. It weighed approximately 2,000 pounds and was the equivalent of 19,000 regular size or 32,000 small size candy bars.

There was a small grease fire on the Jack Rabbit in 1981. No real damage was done, and it was out of operation for only an afternoon. That same year, more than 30 percent of the Little Dipper was

A live monster show on the Garden Stage at Kennywood.
(PHOTOGRAPH BY CHARLES J. JACQUES, JR.)

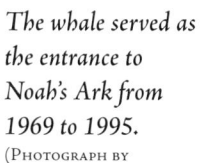

The whale served as the entrance to Noah's Ark from 1969 to 1995.
(PHOTOGRAPH BY CHARLES J. JACQUES, JR.)

rebuilt and painted white. The greening of the park continued with the planting of 62 large shade trees.

During December 1981, drivers along Kennywood Boulevard were treated to a new sight as Kennywood placed lights in the shape of a Christmas tree inside the Laser Loop's loop. This tradition continued until the Laser Loop was removed; then the tree was placed on the lift hill of the Steel Phantom.

1982 *A forty-five-foot swing ship takes to the sky*

In 1982, the Pirate, a major new ride, a 45-foot swing ship, was purchased from Huss of West Germany. The new ride was placed near the Enterprise and again added excitement and flash to the front of the park. The Pirate was a modern computerized version of an old, turn-of-the-century swing ship ride. (The turn-of-the-century version was powered by two brawny men.) Kennywood's ship was powered by electric motors which controlled tires that would first push the ship higher, and then help bring it to a stop. At night, covered with thousands of lights, the ride was spectacular.

The book, *Kennywood: Roller Coaster Capital of the World* by Charles J. Jacques,

The Pirate, a 45-foot long swing boat, was introduced in 1982.
(PHOTOGRAPH BY CHARLES J. JACQUES, JR.)

The Penny Arcade was rebuilt in 1982, and for one season it had a wooden front with a coin and the words Penny Arcade on it.
(PHOTOGRAPH BY CHARLES J. JACQUES, JR.)

Fishing in the fish tank was the most popular game for younger children.
(PHOTOGRAPH BY CHARLES J. JACQUES, JR.)

Distortion mirrors were added to the Ship's Wharf area in 1982.
(PHOTOGRAPH BY CHARLES J. JACQUES, JR.)

Jr., was first published in 1982. It helped to focus the attention of Pittsburgh on the history of the park. For the first time, many park patrons realized what a treasure they had in their midst.

In 1982, members of the National Carousel Association came to ride the park's Dentzel Carousel. The carousel preservation group presented Kennywood with a plaque for preserving an important part of American history. Many members of the carousel group got to meet Tony Sacramento, Kennywood's long-time carousel operator, for the first time. Tony had just celebrated his 65th birthday on "his" carousel. He told a newspaper reporter he "didn't want to work in no mill, so I took a job with Kennywood." At first, he worked the pony track and the Laff-in-the-Dark, before taking over the Merry-Go-Round in 1946. Sacramento believed the Carousel was the park's most important ride. "Without this Merry-Go-Round, it's not a park," he said. "It's a ride for everybody, whether one or ninety."

The old wooden Penny Arcade building, with its pseudo-modern, pseudo out-of-this-world front, was demolished at the end of the 1981 season and replaced with an all new steel building. The park, as it did with so many of its structures (like the Sportland Building and Island Stage), replaced the old structure with a new building that was built on the same location, was about the same size, and was used for the same purpose - in this case, as an arcade. Many guests thought the Arcade building had just gotten a new wooden facade. The following season (1983), the wooden facade was replaced with a glass front.

In 1982, new coaster trains were purchased for the Racer from the Philadelphia Toboggan Company, Lansdale, Pennsylvania. Each of the new trains, two red and one blue, cost more than the whole Racer coaster cost to build. The new trains featured electronic lap bars and seat dividers. Two of the old coaster cars were donated to the Pittsburgh History and Landmarks Foundation. A third car was later given to the Western Pennsylvania Historical Society and is on display in the Senator John Heinz History Center.

Trying to ring the bell on the Hi-striker.
(PHOTOGRAPH BY CHARLES J. JACQUES, JR.)

CHAPTER 4

1983-1984 Idlewild and More

The Most Beautiful Theme Park in America

A new member of the family

Kennywood dramatically changed its course in 1983 when it purchased neighboring Idlewild Park. Up until that time, Kennywood's management had concentration solely on running its lone operation - the big park in West Mifflin. Over the years, Kennywood had received other offers to purchase amusement parks, but management had always declined, feeling it should devote full attention to its one park.

Therefore, when the *Pittsburgh Post Gazette* announced on January 28, 1983, that "Kennywood Park Corporation has bought Idlewild Park, Story Book Forest, the Timberlink Golf Course, and Steak-Out Restaurant in Westmoreland County," it was a big surprise to people who lived in western Pennsylvania, even to those who followed Kennywood closely. Although no price was announced, a deed was recorded by the Westmoreland County Recorder of Deeds indicating a price of $1,800,000 for the land, with another deed for Story Book Forest showing an additional consideration of $225,000.

Idlewild, which got its start as a railroad park in the nineteenth century, was much smaller than Kennywood. The

Sign at the entrance to Idlewild Park.
(JIM FUTRELL COLLECTION)

Aerial photograph of Idlewild, Loyalhanna Creek, Lake St. Clair, and Lake Bouquet circa 1920.
(IDLEWILD)

54

Early rustic automobile entrance to Idlewild.
(CHARLES J. JACQUES, JR. COLLECTION)

A crowd in front of the new Skooter building watching free entertainment at Idlewild.
(CHARLES J. JACQUES, JR. COLLECTION)

Ligonier Valley Rail Road track through a portion of Idlewild Park.
(JIM FUTRELL COLLECTION)

park had about ten times the acreage of Kennywood, but only a fraction of it had ever been developed. It was located thirty miles from West Mifflin on the Lincoln Highway, Route 30, in Westmoreland County, Pennsylvania. Idlewild, which sat on the Chestnut Ridge of the Allegheny Mountains near Ligonier, had a more natural setting.

The week before Thanksgiving in 1982, Carl O. Hughes, president of Kennywood, left on a three-week trip to Southeast Asia. It had become a running gag between Harry Henninger, Jr., general manager, and Hughes, that every time Hughes took a vacation, Henninger took advantage of his absence to buy something new for the park. Upon returning home, Hughes asked Henninger, "Well, what did you buy this time?" "How about Idlewild," Henninger replied with a big grin.

Kennywood's management had talked for several years about the possibility of purchasing Idlewild. Bill Henninger, Kennywood's vice president and head of the refreshment company, was especially eager to make an offer. It was no secret that Idlewild had been up for sale. Several parties, including Cedar Point and the Art Rooney family, had looked into the possibility of buying the park. Kennywood's purchase was more to

Gasoline-powered launch on Lake Bouquet with the new Swimming Pool in the background.
(CHARLES J. JACQUES, JR. COLLECTION)

Lion facade on the Great Pavilion that was built before the turn of the century.
(PHOTOGRAPH BY BETTY JACQUES)

protect its own territory than any thoughts management might have had about developing the park.

Idlewild and Kennywood were similar in some ways and totally different in others. Ironically, both were founded by the same wealthy banking family, the Mellons of Pittsburgh. Founded by Judge Thomas Mellon in the late 1870's, Idlewild was much older than Kennywood. The park really grew out of an effort to revive a failed railroad enterprise in 1877. The railroad, the Ligonier Valley Rail Road Company, had been organized to run between Latrobe and Ligonier, but the narrow-gauge line had never been built. Apparently Judge Mellon did not want to buy the railroad's assets and right-of-way, but three of his sons, Richard, Thomas, and Andrew, who were all in their twenties, convinced him that the railroad might become a paying proposition.

Actually, the railroad had little chance of succeeding without Judge Mellon's "ace in the hole," a site along the right-of-way that had been used for church camp meetings since before the Civil War. Mellon was familiar with the site since he had grown up on a farm near Ligonier before moving to Greensburg and later to Pittsburgh. Judge Mellon was able to

The Great Pavilion was used for dancing and picnicking and could hold more than 1000 persons.
(PHOTOGRAPH BY CHARLES J. JACQUES, JR.)

The octagon carousel structure was built by T. M. Harton of Pittsburgh at the turn of the century.
(CHARLES J. JACQUES, JR. COLLECTION)

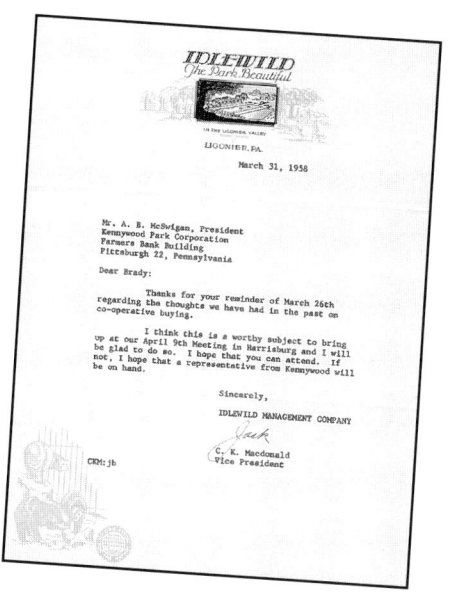

Row boats on Lake St. Clair at Idlewild.
(CHARLES J. JACQUES, JR. COLLECTION)

Crowds on the grounds at Idlewild in the 1930's.
(IDLEWILD)

Idlewild's Swimming Pool was 80 by 200 feet in 1932.
(CHARLES J. JACQUES, JR. COLLECTION)

lease the camp grounds on the northern side of Loyalhanna Creek from William Darlington in 1878. Darlington placed one condition on Mellon; that "no timber or other trees are to be cut or injured." The Mellon family developed the rustic camp grounds into Idlewild Park.

Judge Mellon then had his three sons build the railroad. He was not sure they could complete the job, since his sons had little experience in business, but Richard supervised the construction, which included overseeing some rough construction workers, while Andrew ran the financial end. Thomas helped out where needed. Shortly after the line was completed, the narrow-gauge railroad was widened so that trains from connecting railroads could use the track to bring picnickers to the park.

The August 6, 1891, *Idlewild Lutheran* reporting on the Lutheran reunion at Idlewild, showed how close the Mellons' ties to the park were:

Each succeeding year, the thousands would increasingly gather, until we were forced to pity the overdone Superintendent of the Ligonier Valley Railroad [George Senft], who had at times to hold his breath and wonder what it all meant and where in the world the immense crowds of happy people had all come from! But George Senft is still alive and as busy as ever working up the interests, the enterprises and pleasures of the people along the Loyalhanna Valley, making Idlewild the radiating center of pleasure united with success.

By his side, as the unyielding support, stands Thomas A. Mellon, the modest, quiet, unassuming, kind-hearted "Tommy Mellon," the son of the energetic, wide-awake Judge Mellon of Pittsburg, who counsels, advises, and endorses the good plans of Mr. Senft for the advancement and success of the Ligonier Valley

Landscaping made Idlewild one of America's most beautiful amusement parks.
(IDLEWILD)

Railroad. By common parlance and affection, we all call him "Tommy Mellon," for his kindness and modesty have drawn to him hosts of friends.

George Senft, who became superintendent of the railroad in 1881, was also related to Judge Thomas Mellon. He was married to Kizzie J. Negley, who was the niece of Sara Jane Negley, Judge Mellon's wife. Prior to working for the railroad, Senft was a cashier for T. Mellon and Sons, bankers.

With popularity came some problems. In the August 5, 1891, *Ligonier Echo*, Idlewild's management warned patrons to be on the look out for pickpockets. "We would advise our people to keep a lookout for these vultures and scavengers of humanity who lurk about all large gatherings. Next Thursday when you go to the Lutheran Picnic, take no more money with you than you will really need and then watch that. We are informed that a number of people were robbed at both the U.P. and U.H. picnics last week. So watch your pocketbook if you are so lucky as to have one!"

When Kennywood was founded in 1898, Idlewild was already in its 19th season. Idlewild's attractions included a steam-driven Merry-Go-Round built by T.M. Harton, a bicycle track around Lake Bouquet, hiking trails on an island in the center of the lake (where the Swimming Pool was later built), tennis courts, fishing in Loyalhanna Creek, row boats on Lake St. Clair, and swan boats and naphtha (gasoline powered) launches on Lake Bouquet. There was a Women's Cottage, Dining Hall (with a capacity of one thousand), and the Great Pavilion. All of these structures are still in use at Idlewild.

At the turn of the century, Idlewild often competed with Kennywood for church and industrial picnics and family reunions. Neither of the parks served liquor. While Kennywood soon expanded, adding new rides including the latest in roller coasters, Idlewild remained primarily a rustic park whose chief appeal was its location in the mountains with its clear air and clean streams. At a time when most people did not travel great distances, a day trip to Idlewild was exciting and different.

Idlewild retained its rustic style through the 1920's. Since the park did not have any electricity, it had to close at sunset and could not add new rides like the circle swing, the Whip, Caterpillar, Tumble Bug, and roller coaster, which required electricity. The park did not

Children's rides were slowly added in the 1930's and 1940's creating a Kiddieland.
(CHARLES J. JACQUES, JR. COLLECTION)

Idlewild added a miniature train in 1939 that traveled around Lake St. Clair.
(PHOTOGRAPH BY CHARLES J. JACQUES, JR.)

A Ferris Wheel at Idlewild Park.
(PHOTOGRAPH BY CHARLES J. JACQUES, JR.)

In the 1950's Idlewild had a tram to carry passengers around the park.
(IDLEWILD)

A clown and drum announced Kiddieland in the 1950's.
(CHARLES J. JACQUES, JR. COLLECTION)

Children on a Roto Whip.
(CHARLES J. JACQUES, JR. COLLECTION)

even have a sewage system and was forced to use outhouses. Idlewild was also facing competition from newly created national and Pennsylvania parks. If Idlewild was to survive, it had to change.

Thomas Mellon, a grandson of Judge Mellon and son of Andrew Mellon, realized that the days of privately-owned, rustic parks were over, so he formed a partnership called the Idlewild Management Company with Clinton "C. C." Macdonald, an experienced amusement park man, who owned and operated a traditional amusement park, Rock Springs Park, near the Ohio River in Chester, West Virginia.

The Macdonald family, which in addition to C. C. Macdonald included his son Jack and his wife Grace, took over day-to-day operation of the park. Electricity was brought to the park. The new management company immediately replaced Harton's Merry-Go-Round with a new Philadelphia Toboggan Company Carousel (PTC #83). In 1932, the Mellons built a new 80-by-200-foot Swimming Pool with a sand beach that cost $75,000. Without the Mellons' participation, Idlewild could not have been redeveloped during the Great Depression.

Soon other new rides and attractions

followed: a Penny Arcade, Kiddie Auto Ride, Custer Car ride, a portable Whip, a Pretzel-type dark ride called the Rumpus, and a Ferris Wheel. During the winter of 1937-38, C. C. Macdonald had Herbert P. Schmeck, chief engineer of the Philadelphia Toboggan Company, design a junior coaster, Rollo Coaster. The Macdonalds erected a small saw mill near the site of the new coaster and milled the lumber for the ride. The 900-foot coaster used the natural terrain with the high points being located on top of a ridge and the trip back located in a valley. The small coaster featured a wonderful swoop-turn, although the highest drop was only twenty-seven feet.

A 4,000-foot-long miniature railroad, called the Idlewild Express, was added in 1939. The gasoline-powered trains were purchased from the Dayton Fun House Corporation, Dayton, Ohio. The park's old portable Whip was replaced by a newer, park model Whip.

World War II hit Idlewild hard. The park experienced staffing problems; it was dificult to hire people to work in the park, and there was a continual turnover of employees. Train travel became uncertain, and railroads stopped offering excursion fares. Tires and gasoline were rationed. The situation went from bad to worse in 1943 when the government banned pleasure driving to amusement parks, and the Macdonalds were forced to close Idlewild for the duration. There was even a question of whether the park would reopen, but C. C. Macdonald was determined to operate it after the war.

In 1946, just as C. C. Macdonald was preparing the park for its post-war opening, a terrible fire destroyed the

Idlewild's dark ride, the Rumpus, was destroyed by fire in 1946.
(CHARLES J. JACQUES, JR. COLLECTION)

The Rollo Coaster (roller coaster) was built during the winter of 1937-38.
(IDLEWILD)

The Doodlebug was the nickname of the last gasoline coach to operate on the Ligonier Valley Rail Road and also a children's ride in Idlewild's Kiddieland.
(PHOTOGRAPH BY CHARLES J. JACQUES, JR.)

Rumpus dark ride and Laffing Sal mechanical lady. If not for the fast work of Macdonald and other employees, more rides and buildings would have been destroyed. Slowly, the park revived, and new rides were again added.

In 1951, the Mellons sold their interest in Idlewild to their longtime partners, the Macdonald family. By the 1950's group picnics had generally abandoned the railroad as a means of getting to the park, and the Mellons decided to close down the railroad. In its final few years, the Ligonier Valley Rail Road was reduced to operating a single gasoline coach, which local people called the "Doodlebug." A steam train full of railroad enthusiasts made its final trip to the park on June 22, 1952. Most of the railroad's right-of-way was then sold to the state so Route 30 could be made into a four-lane highway.

A storied forest

With the coming of the baby boom in the 1950's, Idlewild expanded its Kiddieland, adding one or two new rides a year. In 1954, the Macdonalds built a new attraction for children, Story Book Forest, to complement their existing park. The nursery rhyme-themed park was the idea of Dick Macdonald, who ran it for many years, while Jack Macdonald continued to run Idlewild. The 17-acre attraction was a collection of 15, life-sized displays of famous nursery rhymes complemented by employees dressed in costumes. The Macdonalds decided to operate Story Book Forest and Idlewild as separate attractions. Each had its own entrance, charged its own admission, and had its

Entrance to Story Book Forest - "The Land of Once upon a Time."
(Idlewild)

Humpty Dumpty before he fell off the wall was one of Story Book Forest's original displays.
(Photograph by Betty Jacques)

Train signs from Story Book Forest.
(Photograph by Charles J. Jacques, Jr.)

Jack-in-the-Box in Story Book Forest.
(PHOTOGRAPH BY CHARLES J. JACQUES, JR.)

A dragon in Story Book Forest that had been used on a float in one of Kennywood's Fall Fantasy Parades.
(PHOTOGRAPH BY CHARLES J. JACQUES, JR.)

own parking lot. Story Book Forest proved to be an instant success, drawing 84,000 customers its first season. The Macdonalds soon found that Story Book Forest drew from a much wider area than Idlewild and attracted many young families. Unfortunately, because of the dual admission policy, many visitors to Story Book Forest never went into Idlewild.

To celebrate America's Bicentennial in 1976, the Macdonalds created the Historic Village at Story Book Forest. The Village had five little shops around a grassy quadrangle; a larger general store; and a restaurant, the Feed Box. C. S. Macdonald, vice president of the park and son of Jack Macdonald, had hoped to expand it to 30 units over a five-year period, but it never was profitable enough to warrant the expansion. Perhaps the Village's biggest problem was its location; it was built about a half mile from Idlewild at the far end of the Story Book Forest parking lot.

By 1980, the Macdonalds owned and operated Idlewild Park, Story Book Forest, Timberlink (a par 55 18-hole golf course), The Historic Village, Steak-Out Restaurant, and Frontier Zoo. Each was offered as a separate attraction, each had its own separate employees, and each attraction was run by a different member of the Macdonald family.

Sometimes this fragmentation caused conflicts - like when patrons were warned they could not park in Story Book Forest's parking lot and walk into Idlewild Park. This was because Story Book Forest offered free parking while Idlewild charged $2. Therefore, people who wanted to go from Story Book Forest to Idlewild had to drive out onto Route 30 to get to the other park.

By the late 1970's Idlewild's attendance had stagnated at between 200,000 and 250,000 per year. The Macdonalds had to expand or sell out, and in 1983 they decided to sell to Kennywood.

Guinevere's Castle in Story Book Forest was removed in 1997.
(IDLEWILD)

Jack and Jill after they fell down the hill.
(PHOTOGRAPH BY CHARLES J. JACQUES, JR.)

Costumed balloon seller in Idlewild.
(IDLEWILD)

On the Olde Idlewild stage performers entertained all ages.
(PHOTOGRAPH BY CHARLES J. JACQUES, JR.)

There is a seat for little children beside the old woman who lived in the shoe.
(IDLEWILD)

Keith Hood was park manager from 1983 to 1995.
(PHOTOGRAPH BY CHARLES J. JACQUES, JR.)

Upgrading the neighborhood

Following the purchase, Carl O. Hughes said, "Anything we do will be in keeping with the philosophy the Macdonald family has so carefully followed. That is providing refined recreation in a natural setting." Using the same strategy they had used so often at Kennywood, Hughes and Harry W. Henninger, Jr. made changes without making them look like changes. One of the easiest was to integrate Story Book Forest into Idlewild. A few visitors complained that all they wanted to do was visit Story Book Forest and they had to pay to park and it cost more, but the majority of guests were happy because they thought they were getting two attractions for the price of one. Next, Henninger and Hughes had the utility and sewer lines relocated and buried. They brought in a new park manager, Keith Hood, who had worked for Camden Park in West Virginia. He was an excellent manager who could get the most out of Idlewild's employees. Hood would remain manager until 1995. Later, new attractions, rides, and even whole new sections were added to the park.

Henninger and Hughes wanted to add something new immediately at

A slide in Jumpin' Jungle.
(Photograph by Charles J. Jacques, Jr.)

The entrance to Jumpin' Jungle in Idlewild Park was built in 1983.
(Photograph by Charles J. Jacques, Jr.)

Jumpin' Jungle has ropes to swing on.
(Photograph by Charles J. Jacques, Jr.)

A huge rope ladder leads to a three-story tree house in Jumpin' Jungle.
(Photograph by Charles J. Jacques, Jr.)

Jumpin' Jungle's ball crawl holds more than 180,000 green, blue, and yellow plastic balls.
(Photograph by Charles J. Jacques, Jr.)

One of the residents of Hootin' Holler' in Idlewild Park was the Old Timer, Steve Tomasic of Smithton.
(Idlewild)

Potato Patch employee at Idlewild carved "I love the Patch" in a spud.
(Photograph by Charles J. Jacques, Jr.)

Idlewild, but it had to be something that "fit in." It was too late to order a new ride or attraction, so a children's playground that originally had been intended for Kennywood was diverted to Idlewild. The attraction, called Jumpin' Jungle, helped to fill in the gap that existed between Idlewild and Story Book Forest. Jumpin' Jungle was just the first in a long line of new names and attractions that would soon be added to Idlewild's map.

Hootin' Holler' was Harry Henninger's idea. It was created by moving the buildings that had been located in The Historic Village into the gap that remained between Jumpin' Jungle and Idlewild. In addition to the buildings from the Village, other old structures from the park were remodeled and used. An old park maintenance building became the Wild Horse Saloon. Hired as the first Mayor of Hootin' Holler' was the "Old Timer," as he called himself, Steve Tomasic of Smithton. A real character in every sense of the word, the bearded Old Timer and his quilt-making wife, Eunice, were fixtures for many years in the themed town. Tomasic was no stranger to Hughes and Henninger. He was a Fall Fantasy Parade regular, for years playing everything from a pirate and prospector to a moonshiner and blacksmith.

A country and western performer in Idlewild's Hootin' Holler' who doubled as the sheriff.
(IDLEWILD)

Dancers in Hootin' Holler'.
(IDLEWILD)

In 1984, Mother Goose was moved from Kennywood to Story Book Forest.
(IDLEWILD)

A train robbery on the Loyalhanna Ltd. miniature railroad at Idlewild Park.
(IDLEWILD)

Water slides in Idlewild's H2OhhhZone.
(IDLEWILD)

Hughes and Henninger continued to renovate Story Book Forest's old displays while adding new ones. Mother Goose, which topped Kennywood's Kiddieland rest room for many years, was moved to Idlewild and became a display in Story Book Forest. A dragon, which had been used as a float in a Fall Fantasy became another display in the Forest.

Idlewild's Swimming Pool was renovated and updated. The Pool received a new filtration system. A wonderful little water park called H2OhhhZone was created. Bill Henninger supervised the addition of four water slides, which changed the whole atmosphere. Later, a children's area called Little Squirts was added close to the main Pool.

Aerial view of Idlewild's Swimming Pool, water slides, and surrounding lakes.
(IDLEWILD)

Wild Mouse, which was added in 1993, is Idlewild's most thrilling ride.
(PHOTOGRAPH BY CHARLES J. JACQUES, JR.)

Idlewild's Philadelphia Toboggan Company Carousel (PTC #83) was restored by park employees Ed Ostroski and Rosemary Overly. The Carousel's 48 horses and two chariots were carefully stripped down to the wood and painted in authentic carousel colors. Each horse took between 30 and 35 person hours to complete. During the winter of 1990, two horses were "rustled" off the park's carousel, but they were later safely recovered.

The children's ride section was moved from the northern side of Loyalhanna Creek to the southern side and was redesigned. New rides were added, and it was renamed Raccoon Lagoon. The park's appeal to young families was greatly enhanced by the addition of Mister Rogers' Neighborhood of Make-Believe in 1989. Fred Rogers, who created the ideas

Philadelphia Toboggan Company Carousel #83 was completely restored by Idlewild.
(PHOTOGRAPH BY CHARLES J. JACQUES, JR.)

The children's ride area was moved across Loyalhanna Creek and renamed Raccoon Lagoon.
(PHOTOGRAPH BY CHARLES J. JACQUES, JR.)

Rafters Run uses rafts so riders are permitted to wear regular clothes.
(PHOTOGRAPH BY CHARLES J. JACQUES, JR.)

Ricky the Raccoon was one of Idlewild's costumed characters.
(IDLEWILD)

King Friday's Court in Mister Rogers' Neighborhood of Make-Believe.
(IDLEWILD)

When the Hanneford Circus performed at Idlewild in 1996 and 1997, families got a chance to ride an elephant.
(PHOTOGRAPH BY CHARLES J. JACQUES, JR.)

Trolley to Mister Rogers' Neighborhood of Make-Believe.
(IDLEWILD)

Mud volleyball was a new activity for teenagers at Idlewild.
(IDLEWILD)

and characters on his public television show, *Mr. Rogers' Neighborhood*, helped with the development of the new attraction. Rogers, who grew up in Latrobe, visited Idlewild as a child and was excited about helping the park develop the attraction. Rogers wrote the script and provided the characters' voices. Johnny Costa, musical director of Rogers' TV show, arranged the music.

Harry W. Henninger, Jr. told the *Pittsburgh Business Times* in March 1990 that attendance was approximately 200,000 when Kennywood took over Idlewild, but by 1990, the attendance had reached 400,000. Henninger said "while Idlewild's former management had tried to compete with Kennywood, current

Idlewild refreshment stand at night.
(PHOTOGRAPH BY CHARLES J. JACQUES, JR.)

An Octopus and Ferris Wheel are located in the Olde Idlewild section of the park.
(PHOTOGRAPH BY CHARLES J. JACQUES, JR.)

management [Kennywood's] focused on making the two separate attractions complementary, not competing, by targeting them to different market segments."

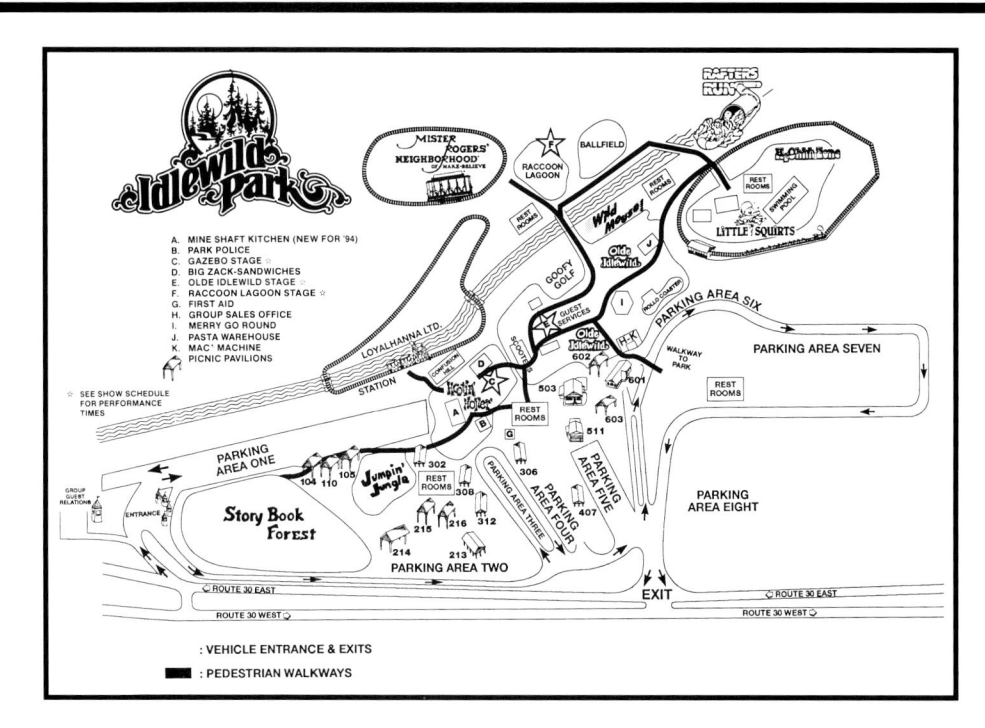

1983 "I'd rather play Cleveland" Jack Lambert said.

Though the newest member of the family, Idlewild, required a great deal of attention, Hughes and Henninger did not neglect their primary attraction at Kennywood. No new major rides were added at Kennywood in 1983, but the park's advertising agency, MARC & Co., created an award-winning TV advertisement for the Thunderbolt and other coasters featuring Pittsburgh Steeler linebacker Jack Lambert. The ads had Lambert in pads, helmet, and Steeler jersey daring to ride Kennywood's roller coaster.

In the ads, Lambert, playing himself, a veteran football star, had his eyes wide open in disbelief and fear as he endured the acceleration, drops, and turns of Kennywood's coasters. The plot line was that Lambert would rather play the Cleveland Browns than ride the park's coasters. By the end of the commercial, Lambert obviously wanted no more as he sat on his helmet and yelled "I'll get you!" The commercials reinforced Kennywood's

In 1984, Kennywood's award-winning TV commercial featuring Pittsburgh Steeler Jack Lambert.
(KENNYWOOD)

68

Kennywood's Arcade received a new glass front in 1983.
(Photograph by Charles J. Jacques, Jr.)

Kennywood continued to offer circus and high wire acts in the 1980's.
(Photograph by Charles J. Jacques, Jr.)

reputation as the "Roller Coaster Capital of the World."

It took over 12 hours of shooting to complete the 30-second ad and Lambert had to endure over 30 separate rides on a steamy, hot day. Lambert was grateful to be allowed to wear his helmet and shoulder pads on the coasters. "I thought that if I fell, I'd survive," he said.

In 1983, Kennywood built new ticket booths on the parking lot side of the entrance tunnel, while guest relations and turnstiles were placed on the park side of the tunnel near the Turnpike. Later the park would moved everything across the road.

Kennywood bought a caterpillar train

The Dipper roller coaster's final season was 1984.
(Photograph by Charles J. Jacques, Jr.)

The Dipper was removed in August 1984 to make room for the Raging Rapids.
(Photograph by Charles J. Jacques, Jr.)

ride with whistles and lights for Kiddieland. Noah's Ark and Le Cachot received a number of new stunts. The new arcade building received a Golomb glass front. The park started to accent its historic background when it added an antique ice cream parlor with a marble counter and old style fixtures near Noah's Ark.

1984 The year of the swingers

Kennywood entertained over one million visitors for the first time in 1984. It was an increase of almost 125,000 from the previous year. Carl Hughes, president of Kennywood, told the *Pittsburgh Press* there were more people coming to Kennywood because the park was attracting many more groups. Through the years, the park lost almost all of its large industrial picnics as heavy industries in Pittsburgh either went out of business or were downsized. However, there were now many more small businesses, and Kennywood was able to add more of these each year to its picnic calendar. To accommodate these new groups, Kennywood continued to build new picnic shelters in the 1980's.

Two swing rides, which would become favorites of park visitors, were added by Kennywood for 1984. The

A Wave Swinger was purchased by the park in 1984.
(Photograph by Charles J. Jacques, Jr.)

Wave Swinger was a high-tech version of the old chair plane ride. It telescoped into the air and then tilted after it was in the air. Its lighting was spectacular and was featured in WQED's documentary, *Kennywood Memories*, shot several years later. The Wave Swinger was located between Noah's Ark and Le Cachot and replaced the Monster.

The second swing, the Swing Around, replaced the unpopular Ranger, which had been leased and lasted only one year (1983). The Ranger had an action similar to the Pirate except that it turned its riders completely upside down. This happened so slowly, however, that it proved painful to the riders. The Swing Around was removed after only one season, but later was brought back to replace the Monster over the Garden Stage. Both swing rides were made in West Germany; the Wave Swinger was manufactured by Joseph Zierer and the Swing Around by Huss.

Kennywood's refreshment company ended a long-established policy of selling refreshment tickets for food purchases. People were no longer willing to accept the inconvenience of purchasing refreshment tickets to buy food and drink. (There are countless stories of people who were unfamiliar with the park and who waited in line for a long time only to find out they needed refreshment tickets to buy food; people who had a lot of ride tickets but were one 10-cent refreshment ticket short when they made their order; or people who left refreshment tickets at home, forgetting to bring them to the park.) In 1984, Bill Henninger converted all of the refreshment stands entirely to cash and refreshment tickets were discontinued.

The lift hill of the Log Jammer.
(Photograph by Charles J. Jacques, Jr.)

The Log Jammer was one of the few log flumes that featured a speed drop in midcourse.
(Photograph by Charles J. Jacques, Jr.)

70

Kenny Kangaroo celebrated his 10th birthday in 1984.
(Photograph by Charles J. Jacques, Jr.)

The park's first Swing Around was located in the spot later occupied by the Wonder Wheel.
(Photograph by Charles J. Jacques, Jr.)

The Ranger was in the park for only one year (1983).
(Photograph by Charles J. Jacques, Jr.)

Kenny Kangaroo, the official mascot of the park, celebrated his 10th birthday in 1984. The Kenny costume was usually worn by women. In 1984, they were Sharen Ruscak, Mitzi Marsh, and Tina Kashlak. The costume consisted of four pieces - head, body, feet, and gloves. The women all agreed the toughest part of their job was the heat. "It is unbearable," Ruscak said, "but as the summer wears on, you get used to it." Kenny walked, rode, played, and entertained "his" way through the park every day from noon until 8 p.m. Ruscak figures she easily walked 15 to 20 miles a day. Generally, when one woman was in the costume another was acting as spotter for her, making sure that no one took advantage of Kenny's lack of sight and mobility.

Shortly before Labor Day in 1984, the Dipper junior roller coaster was cut down so that it could be removed from the park. The coaster's removal prompted rumors of an accident, but that was not the case. The space was needed for the park's new multi-million-dollar white water rapids ride. Also removed for the water ride was the Starvue Plaza, which had replaced the park's first bandstand in 1962.

"You will get soaked."
(CHARLES J. JACQUES, JR.
COLLECTION)

CHAPTER 5
1985-1986
Raging Rapids

You will get soaked

Carl O. Hughes, president of Kennywood, announced a new water raft ride to park employees in his 1984 Christmas letter:

> Let me fill you in on what spring has in store for Kennywood. Most obvious, as you can tell by the trails of mud, there's the new, white water raft ride—Racing Waters [Later its name was changed to Raging Rapids]. It's the first to be built in the Northeast United States.

Harry W. Henninger, Jr. often liked to recite the old amusement park proverb, "you should never purchase a new ride without putting your seat [or words to that effect] in it." Every year in November, Carl Hughes, Harry Henninger, Bill Henninger, and others from Kennywood would attend the trade show of the International Association of Amusement Parks and Attractions looking for new rides. But they would never consider buying a ride - especially a multimillion dollar one - without trying it out first. In 1984, the park was looking for a new ride and leaning towards a water ride because the Log Jammer had been so successful. Taking to heart the old quote about riding

The Raging Rapids, Kennywood's white water rapids ride, was built in 1985.
(Photograph by Charles J. Jacques, Jr.)

Placing artificial rocks along the channel of the Raging Rapids.
(Photograph by Charles J. Jacques, Jr.)

a ride before buying it, Harry and Bill Henninger, and even Carl Hughes, got thoroughly soaked that summer trying out rapids rides. In the end, they all agreed that Kennywood should build a white water rapids ride.

Harry W. Henninger, Jr. was put in charge of the development of the new ride. Financing was easy (if raising four million dollars is ever easy) because of the park's success with its new rides and increased cash flow. However, the engineering and technology required to build and operate a rapids ride would prove to be much more troublesome.

Henninger's first problem was where to put the new ride without disturbing too much of the existing park. Picnic areas were too important to sacrifice. Henninger finally decided the rapids should be built in the northeast corner of the park. Although the ground dropped off sharply there, it was still usable. The primary drawback to the development of the site was that it would require razing both the Dipper coaster and Starvue bandstand. The advantage was the ride would be located on the perimeter of the park at the opposite end from the Log Jammer. "The Raging Rapids would draw visitors away from the more congested center of the park to a part of the park

Harry Henninger supervised the construction of the Raging Rapids.
(Photograph by Charles J. Jacques, Jr.)

Carl Hughes helped to clean up the park in the spring of 1985.
(Photograph by Charles J. Jacques, Jr.)

that was little used," Henninger said. Later he would find that building the ride also required lifting part of the Thunderbolt coaster so the water ride could run underneath it.

During the summer of 1984, Henninger visited Kings Dominion, Doswell, Virginia, with Peter Schnabel of Intamin, a ride manufacturer, to look at a raft ride in operation. Afterwards Henninger wrote Schnabel, "while I was very impressed, I also have great fears that Kennywood may not be able to afford the initial price and installation or, more particularly, the on-going maintenance and utility costs." Henninger requested information on the pump sizes required, and the ground space and reservoir square footage needed for the ride. He examined both a four-passenger and a six-passenger ride, and he decided to go with the six-passenger model even though it cost a half-million dollars more.

That summer, both Hughes and Henninger visited Kings Dominion again to ride the park's six-passenger rapids. Later Henninger wrote Kings Dominion, "If your weather has been anything like ours these last two weeks, your white water raft ride must be doing gangbusters! By the way, in that ours is opening next summer, the high temperature will

The opening day crowd waiting for the first ride on the Raging Rapids.
(PHOTOGRAPH BY CHARLES J. JACQUES, JR.)

The loading platform of the Raging Rapids.
(PHOTOGRAPH BY CHARLES J. JACQUES, JR.)

Building the Raging Rapids lift hill under the Thunderbolt coaster.
(PHOTOGRAPH BY CHARLES J. JACQUES, JR.)

probably be 55 degrees." Henninger, like most people in the outdoor amusement industry, was superstitious about the weather, and he never liked to predict good weather.

Raging Rapids was manufactured by Intamin, Inc. of Zurich, Switzerland. Each white water rapids ride built was different because it was designed and engineered for the terrain and space available. Kennywood's topography, which dropped sixteen feet in a very tight space, helped to make the ride extra special. Henninger compared the Raging Rapids to "a ride down the Youghiogheny River rapids at Ohiopyle."

The new ride's six-passenger rafts were loaded from a revolving platform. The rafts were nine and one-half feet in diameter, and each was placed in the middle of a large inner tube. As each raft was released from the moving loading platform it would enter the current and quickly bounce along the walls of the channel encountering water obstacles like waves, dips, and plenty of white water on the way.

Raging Rapids was powered by three 200-horsepower pumps that sent more than 110,000 gallons of water per minute through the channel, which created a swift current. Patrons were warned "you will get soaked," and most would. As the channel broadened into two "lakes," waves reached three feet in height and tossed the riders around. At the end of the ride, each raft was carried up a 118-foot conveyor belt made of wooden slats and built underneath part of the Thunderbolt, back to the loading station. The ride contained a total of 725,000 gallons of water. In addition to the raft course, there was an 800,000-gallon reservoir where water was stored when the ride was not in use. Three thousand yards of concrete and 40,000 square feet of manmade rock were used in building the ride.

As late as the 1960's, Kennywood's visitors were not used to getting wet when they came to the park. In the 1950's and 1960's, The Old Mill had a small water curtain that made it look as though the passengers were going to get wet when the boat went underneath, but the device was set to turn off as a boat approached. Occasionally, the water curtain would not turn off and a small amount of water would spray the passengers. When this happened, the park office would receive complaints from patrons who got wet. Even the Log Jammer, built in 1975, was designed to direct the spray outward and away from its passengers at the bottom of the last drop. If anyone got wet on the Log Jammer (or The Old Mill), it was usually from being splashed by fellow passengers.

The Raging Rapids was Kennywood's first ride designed to get its passengers wet. Younger riders seemed to love it and older passengers usually tolerated the water. Families would bring a change of clothes, rain gear, or have bathing suits on under their clothes.

Shortly before it opened, Carl O. Hughes said that he hoped the new ride would be worth the trouble and money needed to build it and would help boost attendance by 100,000 visitors. While the Laser Loop appealed more to teenagers, the Raging Rapids was a ride that the whole family could ride together.

Within a month of its opening, Kennywood had to shut the Raging Rapids down because of major mechanical problems. "Just about anything that

Aerial view of the Raging Rapids with the Thunderbolt in the foreground.
(Photograph by Charles J. Jacques, Jr.)

Three rafts negotiate the turbulent waters.
(Photograph by Charles J. Jacques, Jr.)

A six-passenger raft rises and dips along the waterway.
(Photograph by Charles J. Jacques, Jr.)

could go wrong has gone wrong," said Richard Henry, the ride superintendent of the park. All three 200-HP pumps broke down at once and they had to be sent to Florida by charter jet to be rebuilt. Some oil leaked into the water, and the park had to learn how to remove oil from water. Three gearboxes malfunctioned. "It was just an unbelievable nightmare," Henry said. In the end, the park was forced to replaced all three pumps with new submersible propeller pumps.

Once the ride reopened, Harry W. Henninger, Jr. found out this ride was more like a trip down the Youghiogheny than he thought it would be. In May, a rider, who apparently panicked, fell into the water while trying to leave a raft in the middle of the course. The other passengers in his raft also jumped out. No one was seriously injured, but the ride was closed to review its operation.

According to Rich Henry, the Raging Rapids was unique among the park's attractions. "Every other ride that Kennywood has is on a fixed track," he said, "but the 'Rapids' is a free-floating ride." People were not used to a ride that did not always do the same thing. A passenger who was not familiar with the action of the ride might panic when the boat started careening from side to side hitting the channel walls.

A gate system, designed by Harry Henninger, was installed about midcourse in the ride that could be opened and closed to start and stop the rafts and maintain the desired distance between them. A spotter was placed along the channel to monitor the course. The employee had a public address system so he or she could instruct riders who might

A waterfall soaks passengers on the Raging Rapids.
(Photograph by Charles J. Jacques, Jr.)

Cope and Lambert riding the waves.
(Kennywood)

Jack Lambert, Myron Cope, and a TV crew filming the Raging Rapids commercial.
(Kennywood)

need help. Although the rafts traveled in only two and one-half feet of water, the current and velocity tended to create problems. Through the years the ride was further fine-tuned. The channel was narrowed in several places by adding wooden posts to prevent a raft from running into the raft in front or in back of it. Riders have also become more experienced and know what to expect on the Raging Rapids.

No two trips down the 1,650-foot Raging Rapids were the same, and the new ride soon became a favorite of patrons on hot summer days. Passengers were never sure how their raft would turn and how it would bounce off the sides of the channel. This was determined by the weight of the passengers, how that weight was distributed, and at what angle the raft entered each section of the ride. Until the ride was over, the question remained - who would get really soaked?

Coping with success

Next, Kennywood had to sell the new ride to the public. MARC & Co., the park's advertising agency, suggested a campaign with Pittsburgh Steeler linebacker Jack Lambert, who had starred in the park's coaster commercials the

Yoi!
The commercial Pittsburgh has been waiting for starts today!

Can Myron cope with Kennywood's new Raging Rapids? Will it dampen the spirits of Jack Splat? Find out today when a new Kennywood commercial created by MARC Advertising rages onto the screen.

MARC ADVERTISING
Four Station Square, Suite 500, Pittsburgh, PA 15219. (412) 562-2000
MARC and Company, Inc.

(Kennywood)

previous year, and WTAE sports talk show host, Myron Cope. The park agreed to go with Lambert and Cope. Since a television spot was needed before the Raging Rapids was opened, it was shot in April at Kings Dominion. The commercial was created by Ed Fine of MARC and directed by Rip Charbonnet.

Ron Cook, a writer for the *Pittsburgh Press*, who accompanied Lambert and Cope to Kings Dominion described the shooting of this commercial in his article "The Odd Couple - Lambert and Cope Take A Ride On The Wet Side," which appeared in the *Press* May 5, 1985.

> The day the television commercial was to be shot was damp and cold, but by 11:00 a.m. the sun came out. Myron Cope, looking dapper in a tan raincoat, blue dress shirt, and yellow paisley tie, opened the commercial standing in front of a surging waterfall. Behind him was Jack Lambert in his Steeler uniform looking every inch a mean grizzly NFL veteran.
>
> "Yoi! I can't believe it. Jack Splat is really going to ride Kennywood's new Raging Rapids," shouted Cope.

The Calypso.
(Photograph by Charles J. Jacques, Jr.)

Myron gets a bath.
(MARC Advertising)

"And guess who's coming with me, Myron," said Lambert.

Cope played his part to the hilt; his face showed all the terror of one not accustomed to such a wet ride. The production crew loved it as Lambert grabbed Cope by the shoulders and yanked him out of the picture to begin the wild, wet water ride.

Cope played the role of the petrified passenger perfectly. He wore a yellow rain hat and swimming mask with a snorkel and squeezed the life out of a large, yellow rubber ducky inner tube. Lambert also appeared to be frightened at first, but he loosened up as the ride continued. He pushed Cope away, who clung to him for protection.

After the 13th ride, Cope confided "I gave it the bawling act pretty good out there, but I didn't even have to act. "It's miserable. I'm so cold I can't even hear the falls because my teeth are chattering," he said.

Lambert felt he owed some payback to Cope, who as color analyst for the Pittsburgh Steelers' radio network, regularly reported Lambert's

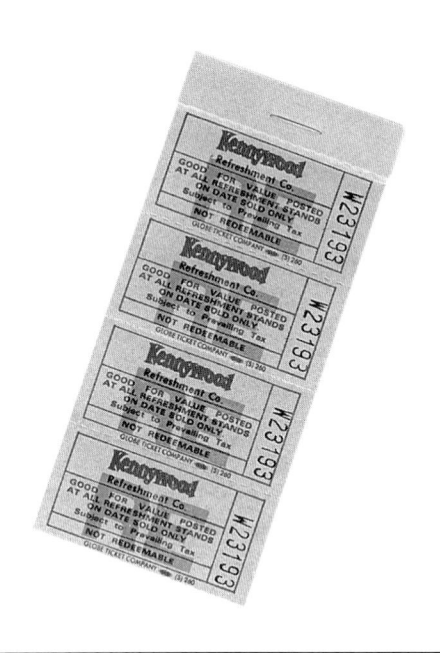

The Laser Loop remained popular through the 1980's.
(Photograph by Charles J. Jacques, Jr.)

misdeeds on the football field. Lambert was almost gleeful when he asked Charbonnet, "Is this the part where I get to dump the water on Myron's head? All right! I've been waiting 11 years for this," the line backer said.

"If he gets too much pleasure out of it,' Cope quipped, 'I'll step on his [often injured] left big toe."

For the final scene, the two were back in front of the waterfall. Cope looked as though he had been through a washing machine, his tie was loose and over his shoulder, his shirt collar was turned up, his raincoat was disheveled and his hair was standing on end. He and Lambert were dripping wet.

"Good thing I brought along my Terrible Towel," said Cope.

"It sure is Myron!' said Lambert.

Lambert dumped a helmet full of water on Cope's head as the commercial ended. He did it eight times, smiling more devilishly each time."

Lambert and Cope's ride on Kennywood's Raging Rapids was the hit of the summer. It was the talk around town and thousands of people headed out to Kennywood to try out the new ride.

Kennywood's Super Round-Up was later moved to Idlewild.
(Photograph by Charles J. Jacques, Jr.)

80

"Modern" Racer front at night.
(Photograph by Charles J. Jacques, Jr.)

The Enterprise.
(Photograph by Charles J. Jacques, Jr.)

1985 Adjusting the Rapids

Carl O. Hughes did not get his 100,000 visitor increase in 1985 for two reasons; the Raging Rapids was down too many days as the park made adjustments, and the Laser Loop was also out of action at the end of the season with a worn out clutch. But the park did have an increase of more than 60,000. The Raging Rapids was everything that Kennywood hoped it would be, and it was worth the soakings that the Henningers and Hughes and Lambert and Cope took.

The Casino Restaurant, one of the park's original buildings, received a major overhaul and was renamed "The Patio Cafe." After 85 years, waitress service was eliminated in favor of one large and more functional cafeteria. It offered a scramble-serve system that proved to be very successful.

Two games were introduced by the park in 1985; the Tin Can Alley and Jumping Frogs (called Frog Bog). To win a prize in Frog Bog, the customer had to make a little, rubbery frog go into a dish of water by striking a lever with a mallet. In Tin Can Alley, a line of brightly-colored trash cans was programmed to open in varying patterns for a brief time. The contestant's job was to toss balls into

The tradition of a floral calendar continued into the 1980's.
(Photograph by Charles J. Jacques, Jr.)

the cans before the lids closed.

Carl E. Henninger, chairman of the board of Kennywood Park, died May 21, 1985. Henninger helped the company grow from a single trolley park, which operated on a leased site, to a well-managed, financially stable multi-million dollar corporation that owned two amusement parks, Kennywood and Idlewild.

1986 - The park's largest wheel

The Wonder Wheel debuted at the park in 1986, and it was the largest Ferris Wheel the park had ever installed. Over the years, the park had a number of different Ferris Wheels; usually they were of the smaller, portable variety. In the 1960's, the park even operated two Eli wheels side by side. The Wonder Wheel was 85-feet tall and had 24 gondolas, each holding six passengers. The wheel, which was placed along the Lagoon, featured computer-controlled lighting that reflected in the water at night.

Junior bumper cars were added in Kiddieland for youngsters six to ten years of age. Since its previous Kiddie Whip had been destroyed in the fire that had started in the Ghost Ship dark ride in 1975, the park had been looking for a replacement. Kennywood was finally able to purchase a Kiddie Whip at an auction held in 1986 when Paragon Park, Hull, Massachusetts, closed.

Raging Rapids was made both wetter and drier in 1986. A triple waterfall was added that cascaded down a man-made mountain 25 feet high. A huge pump projected 3,500 gallons of water a minute over the mountain. Two "pop up" geysers, controlled by a park employee, were also added to the ride. For adults and others who did not like the wetness, the park added a new observation deck located between the ride and the park's miniature railroad.

Early in the 1986 season, Kennywood announced that the park was discontinu-

The Wonder Wheel was added in 1986.
(Photograph by Charles J. Jacques, Jr.)

82

The Casino, one of the park's original buildings, at night.
(PHOTOGRAPH BY CHARLES J. JACQUES, JR.)

The Wave Swinger is beautifully lit at night.
(PHOTOGRAPH BY CHARLES J. JACQUES, JR.)

ing a free gate to become a "pay-one-price" (POP) park. The last non-pay-one-price admission day was June 25, 1986. Kennywood felt that a one-pay system would help it control the gate better and discourage troublemakers from entering the park.

Every year the park would rebuild sections of its three wooden roller coasters. In 1986, the Jack Rabbit, designed by John A. Miller in 1920, celebrated its 65th birthday (actually the coaster's 66th birthday). Even the Laser Loop got a new coat of paint.

Souvenirs were becoming more important to the park. In 1986, Ken Garrett, manager of the games department, introduced the park's first walk-in gift shop, located across from Fascination.

The Raging Rapids had done a terrific job of attracting new people to the park. As hard as it was to believe, America's greatest picnic park now needed more picnic shelters to accommodate the groups that were coming. According to Carl Hughes, "the need for more picnic space was critical, but it's a nice problem to have." To meet this growing need, the park's maintenance staff built a new picnic pavilion behind the Turnpike ride.

National Historic Landmark plaque.
(PHOTOGRAPH BY CHARLES J. JACQUES, JR.)

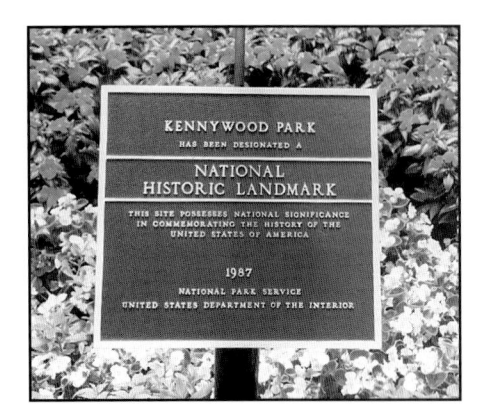

CHAPTER 6

1987 Historic Kennywood

Statue of George Washington in Kennywood Park by Mary Ann Spanagel.
(PHOTOGRAPH BY CHARLES J. JACQUES, JR.)

In 1987, James Charleton, historian for the United States Department of the Interior, unveils the National Historic Landmark plaque.
(PHOTOGRAPH BY CHARLES J. JACQUES, JR.)

"Who would have thought it?"

Although "What's new at Kennywood this year?" might be the most frequently asked question, another question often asked is "Why are there so many historical markers, plaques, and displays around the park?" The answer is simple, if not always apparent; Kennywood is one of the most historic sites in Pennsylvania. The park is one of only six National Historic Landmarks in Allegheny County, Pennsylvania, recognized by the United States Department of the Interior. (The others are Point State Park and the Fort Pitt Blockhouse; the Smithfield Street Bridge; the John Neville House in Heidelberg, significant in the Whiskey Rebellion; Henry Richardson's great architectural masterpieces, the Allegheny County Courthouse and Jail; and the Oakmont Country Club.)

In the 1980's, the National Park Service conducted a program to identify, designate, recognize, and protect recreational sites of national significance. Carl O. Hughes, newly-elected chairman of the board, heard about the program and thought Kennywood should be included. "Perhaps some people are surprised Kennywood is considered historically significant," Hughes said, "but the park

84

The death of General Edward Braddock when he was purported to have said, "Who would have thought it?"
(CARNEGIE LIBRARY OF PITTSBURGH)

shows the other side to the steel mills and industries. It shows what people did for fun and recreation. There have been some changes over the years, but it is really interesting watching people ride our Carousel, just like their parents or even grandparents rode it seventy years ago."

Braddock's defeat

Long before Kennywood came into being, the river and cliff just below the park played a part in one of the most important battles of the French and Indian War. In an attempt to regain control of the fork of the Allegheny, Monongahela, and Ohio rivers, the British sent Major General Edward Braddock and his army of 1100 men to the region. George Washington, a young colonel in the Virginia Militia, led a small detachment of Colonials that accompanied General Braddock's army. After crossing the Allegheny Mountains, Braddock's army traveled down the Youghiogheny River, forded the Monongahela (which was shallow enough in the summer months before dams and locks were built), and marched up the Duquesne-Kennywood side of the river. The soldiers stopped to regroup at a spring at the foot of the Kennywood Bluff.

Major General Edward Braddock.
(CARNEGIE LIBRARY OF PITTSBURGH)

Braddock's Crossing historical marker is located along Kennywood Boulevard.
(PHOTOGRAPH BY CHARLES J. JACQUES, JR.)

On July 9, 1755, with drums beating and flags unfurled, Braddock's army recrossed the Monongahela, turned left, and continued the march to Fort Duquesne. General Braddock had been fearful that the enemy might attack his force while it was divided crossing the river, but the French and Indians were delayed and so the battle took place on the gentle, but steadily sloping upward ground across the river from Kennywood on what today is Braddock and North Braddock. The French and Indians, with a much smaller force, seemed to have little chance of winning, but they routed the larger, better equipped British Army. General Braddock was mortally wounded and carried from the field. A few days later he died, but not before murmuring to a trusted aide, "Who would have thought it?"

From the very beginning, Kennywood Park had a sense of its own history. A brochure for the 1902 season refers to Braddock's Spring, where Braddock's Army was refreshed before the battle, as a site to be viewed and enjoyed. Looking for a season-ending attraction in 1928, Kennywood advertised a spectacular pageant with "exact scenery and settings honoring the men who fought in Braddock's defeat." However, for some unexplained reason, the pageant was never held.

James Van Trump of the Pittsburgh History and Landmark Foundation and Tony Sacramento at the dedication of a plaque honoring the park's Carousel in 1977.
(Richard L. Bowker Collection)

A topiary garden was located next to the Carousel Pavilion.
(Photograph by Betty Jacques)

Braddock's Army was again recognized in 1964 by the Pennsylvania Historical and Museum Commission when it erected a roadside marker commemorating Braddock's Crossing on the southern most point of Kennywood's property along Kennywood Boulevard. Three years later, in 1967, Kennywood erected a cameo scene of Braddock along its miniature railroad. The display featured life-sized figures of the French and Indians firing from behind trees and bushes at the trapped British and Colonials. The scene included wagons and other implements, and wounded and dying soldiers were strewn about the battlefield. The park added audiovisual effects with smoke, fire, and the sounds of muskets as part of the presentation.

Birthdays are important

It was only natural in a business where so many amusement parks did not survive more than a few years that Kennywood would start celebrating its own birthday. Shortly after the turn of the century the park started mentioning how many seasons it had been in operation. In 1931 the park built a huge plaster "birthday cake" to celebrate its 33rd birthday. One additional candle was added to the cake for many years.

For its Fiftieth Anniversary in 1947, Kennywood produced a booklet which gave a fascinating history of the land when the Kennys owned it. Under the title, "Faith is the substance of things hoped for ...," the story told of Thomas Kenny leaving his home in Chester County, Pennsylvania in 1818 and choosing a site opposite Braddock's Field as a site for his business and family. A thickly-wooded tableland grew into a gathering place for Kenny's family and their friends. Soon people came considerable distances by

86

A tiger and a lion are on the Dentzel Carousel.
(Photograph by Charles J. Jacques, Jr.)

The Carousel was completely restored in 1976.
(Kennywood)

The Carousel manufactured by William Dentzel Company in 1926.
(Photograph by Charles J. Jacques, Jr.)

Kennywood's historic Carousel.
(Photograph by Charles J. Jacques, Jr.)

In 1983, Arthur P. Ziegler, Jr., president, Pittsburgh History and Landmarks Foundation, presents a plaque to Kennywood recognizing the Casino's historic status.
(The Daily News)

horse and buggy, steamboat, or ferryboat to enjoy the beauty and friendliness of a day at Kenny's Grove. Later heirs of Thomas Kenny made clearings among the oaks and maples for a quaint, rustic dance pavilion and picnic shelter house. On moonlight nights, many hayride parties traveled the old Braddock Road with "Kenny's" as their destination. After the quadrilles and waltzes came corn-popping and marshmallow-toasting in the lamplighted grove.

The park's Dentzel Carousel is honored

James Van Trump, vice president and director of research of the Pittsburgh History and Landmarks Foundation, presented Kennywood with a plaque recognizing the fiftieth anniversary of the park's Dentzel Carousel in 1977. The William Dentzel Company of Philadelphia actually was commissioned to build the carousel for the Sesquicentennial Exhibition, which was held in Philadelphia in 1926. Dentzel did not get the Merry-Go-Round done on time, and he sold the beautiful four-row machine to Kennywood the following year. The park built a new Carousel Pavilion, installed the old band organ, and the new Dentzel Carousel has operated there ever since.

On February 8, 1982, Richard M. Scaife, of the Pittsburgh History and Landmarks Foundation, notified Bill Henninger, vice president of Kennywood and head of the refreshment company, the foundation had awarded Kennywood's Casino a plaque on the basis of its architectural significance. Arthur P. Ziegler, Jr., president of the Foundation, presented a plaque to the park marking the Casino Restaurant as a historical site. It was at the dedication ceremony that Ziegler mentioned to Hughes about the National Park Service study of recreation sites as possible candidates for National

John R. Graff, executive director of the International Association of Amusement Parks and Attractions, spoke at the dedication of the Kennywood Park historical marker.
(Photograph by Charles J. Jacques, Jr.)

Historic Landmarks. Carl Hughes later recalled, "I thought, there's not much chance of that happening to Kennywood, but I followed it up."

A national treasure

An exchange of correspondence between the park and James Charleton, National Park Service historian for the U.S. Department of the Interior, started the process. Charleton had been working on a study of properties for sports and recreation for possible landmark status. Buildings had to be more than 50 years of age and well preserved. The authenticity and antiquity of the buildings, rides, and attractions were important.

The nomination was made through West Mifflin. Mayor Peter Richards said "I am pleased with the consideration being given the park, and that Kennywood has always been an asset to the community."

Mr. Charleton, who visited the park in December 1984, admitted the process was "rather difficult" but added even a nomination was an honor for Kennywood. "It's a very select company even in terms of applying for the designation," he said. The park was nominated for the following reasons:

Frank S. Beal of the Pennsylvania Historic and Museum Commission unveils the new historical marker on August 25, 1992.
(Photograph by Charles J. Jacques, Jr.)

Pittsburgh History and Landmarks Foundation official Dr. A. G. Van Dusen presents Harry W. Henninger, Jr., president of Kennywood Park, an Award of Merit in December 1993.
(Pittsburgh History and Landmarks Foundation)

Kennywood's miniature railroad was from the New York World's Fair of 1939-40.
(KENNYWOOD)

Carl and Ann Hughes at the Kennywood Park dedication ceremony in 1992.
(KENNYWOOD)

Kennywood symbolizes Twentieth Century American culture. The park includes rides from several generations, each providing a clue to what people of that era did for fun.

Kennywood also displays the artistry of the century in the rides built by skilled craftsmen, many of whom were immigrants.

The park has retained many of its early attractions that now are virtually endangered species.

The Racer roller coaster, with its twin tracks, and Noah's Ark are the only two of their kind remaining in the United States. The Old Mill and the Jack Rabbit roller coaster, with its double dip, are rare. Other historically significant rides include the Merry-Go-Round, Auto Race, and Turtle [Tumble Bug].

It took almost three years, but finally in March 1987 Kennywood was notified it had been named a National Historic Landmark. The park received the award from Secretary of the Interior, Manual Lujan, and Director of the National Park Service James Ridenour, because

Kennywood's Noah's Ark, built in 1936, is the only remaining ark in America.
(Photograph by Charles J. Jacques, Jr.)

Kennywood was "the best example of the old trolley parks." At the unveiling of the National Historic Landmark plaque, Charleton said "only well preserved sites are ever considered for landmark status. Rundown areas or demolished buildings, no matter how glorious they once were, are never in the running." Kennywood has retained so much of its past while prospering in the present. The original 1898 Carousel Pavilion and the Casino Restaurant still stand from the park's first days. Rides that pleased generations of fun-lovers are in the same spanking-new condition as the park's most modern roller coaster. Hughes was happy that the park received the award. "Naturally, we're delighted," he said. "It's exclusive company."

Only one other amusement park was given landmark status. Playland Park, which is located in Rye, New York, and owned by Westchester County, was recognized as an outstanding example of an art deco - 1920's style park.

The Pennsylvania Historical and Museum Commission further honored Kennywood Park when it dedicated a state historical marker near the park's entrance on August 25, 1992. This marker recognized the founding of Kennywood by the Monongahela Street Railway Company in 1898. Present at the

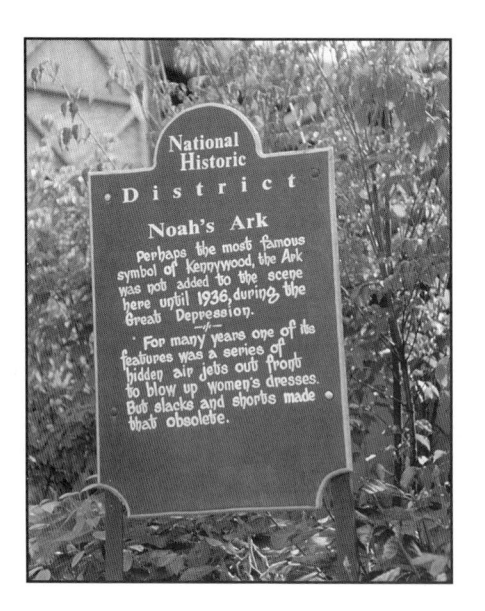

Although alterations have been made through the years, the ark remains the park's most recognizable symbol.
(Photograph by Charles J. Jacques, Jr.)

Animals looking out the windows of Noah's Ark have been an important part of the attraction's ballyhoo for younger children.
(Photograph by Charles J. Jacques, Jr.)

A Jack Rabbit sign has always been on the front. The most recent sign has a neon outline.
(PHOTOGRAPH BY CHARLES J. JACQUES, JR.)

The Jack Rabbit was designed by John A. Miller, one of America's greatest coaster designers.
(PHOTOGRAPH BY CHARLES J. JACQUES, JR.)

In 1951 the Jack Rabbit received new coaster cars from the Philadelphia Toboggan Company.
(PHOTOGRAPH BY CHARLES J. JACQUES, JR.)

Children look forward to their first ride on the Jack Rabbit.
(PHOTOGRAPH BY CHARLES J. JACQUES, JR.)

The Jack Rabbit is one of the few remaining "ravine" coasters in the world.
(PHOTOGRAPH BY CHARLES J. JACQUES, JR.)

dedication of the marker were Arthur P. Ziegler, Jr., president, Pittsburgh History and Landmarks Foundation; John Graff, executive director of the International Association of Amusement Parks and Attractions; and Frank S. Beal of the Pennsylvania Historical Museum Commission.

Carl O. Hughes said the effort to preserve Kennywood's heritage was also a smart business decision. "Had we modernized, Kennywood would have been a small player in a big market. So,

> **Kennywood**
> is pleased to announce the designation
> of its amusement area as a
> *National Historic Landmark*
> by the National Park Service and
> U.S. Secretary of Interior Donald P. Hodel.

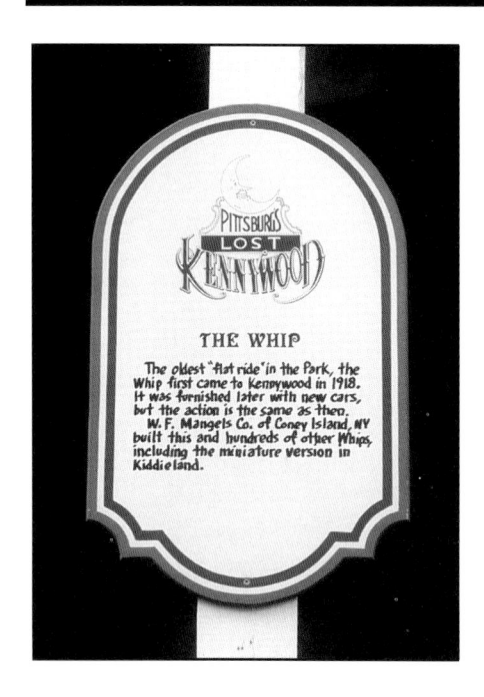

THE WHIP

The oldest "flat ride" in the Park, the Whip first came to Kennywood in 1918. It was furnished later with new cars, but the action is the same as then. W. F. Mangels Co. of Coney Island, NY built this and hundreds of other Whips, including the miniature version in Kiddieland.

The Whip was housed in a steel building from the late 1920's to 1994.
(PHOTOGRAPH BY CHARLES J. JACQUES, JR.)

The park has had a Whip since 1919.
(KENNYWOOD)

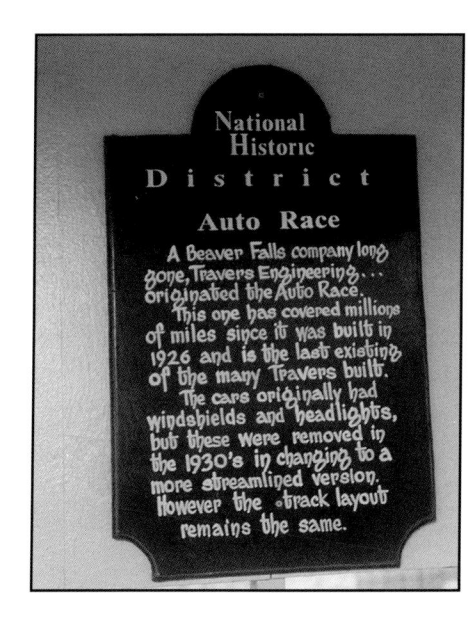

The Auto Race, built in 1930, is the only remaining one in America.
(PHOTOGRAPH BY CHARLES J. JACQUES, JR.)

The Turtle, a/k/a the Tumble Bug, throws its riders together.
(PHOTOGRAPH BY CHARLES J. JACQUES, JR.)

The Turtle was such a noisy ride that the park placed it in a ravine adjacent to the Pippin coaster (later the Thunderbolt).
(PHOTOGRAPH BY CHARLES J. JACQUES, JR.)

for competitive reasons, we decided to sell the park as an alternative - a historic, traditional family park. And anyway, our patrons are so loyal that if we did change, we'd probably suffer economically."

In 1987, a new raised-brick display area of flowers and shrubs was built for the Centennial Timepiece. The old-fashioned Victorian display was located near the Merry-Go-Round. The centerpiece was an 1890 street clock manufactured by Canterbury International, Sherman Oaks, California that cost $22,700.

The timepiece in Centennial Square was later replaced by the statue of George Washington.
(Photograph by Charles J. Jacques, Jr.)

Mary Ann Spanagel's George Washington being transported to Kennywood.
(Photograph by Mary Ann Spanagel)

George Washington returns

After a 238 year absence, George Washington returned to Kennywood Park in the form of a nine and one half-foot, 1500 pound bronze-coated statue. The statue of the 23-year-old colonel was dedicated on Flag Day, June 14, 1993. The statue replaced the 1890 street clock. Franklin Regional Pep Band played "Hail to the Chief" at the unveiling. Carl O. Hughes, who enjoys studying local history, did the most of the research for the project.

Mary Ann Spanagel created the statue with the help of her sister Tracy Simmen and David Schremp. Although not a park employee, Spanagel had built floats for the Fall Fantasy Parade for many years. The trio worked on George Washington for nearly three months. The statue is made of fiberglass and foam and is covered with a bronze patina. "Working on George was a different challenge. There was a lot of fuss over every little part of it [the statute}," Spanagel said]. She used a sculpture in Braddock, Pennsylvania, as her inspiration. She did not copy it but consulted other history books to give the statue its own unique flavor. "Mr. Hughes wanted a Washington with his saber raised, so I depicted him as a dynamic, striding Washington," Spanagel said. "It was an honor to do such a huge piece of work for Kennywood, not to mention that it is of George Washington," she said.

Perhaps a devoted Kennywood patron, after looking at the statue of George Washington and reading all of the historical markers, plaques, and displays around the park, might find himself or herself echoing General Braddock's final words, "Who would have thought it?"

Sign, British flag, and statue of George Washington mark the spot where General Braddock camped in 1755.
(Photograph by Betty Jacques)

The Musik Express was purchased by the park in 1987.
(Photograph by Charles J. Jacques, Jr.)

The Pagoda Refreshment Stand replaced the Tower Refreshment Stand in 1987.
(PHOTOGRAPH BY CHARLES J. JACQUES, JR.)

Hand-carved dragons, which had been on the front of The Old Mill boats, were used to decorate the Pagoda.
(PHOTOGRAPH BY CHARLES J. JACQUES, JR.)

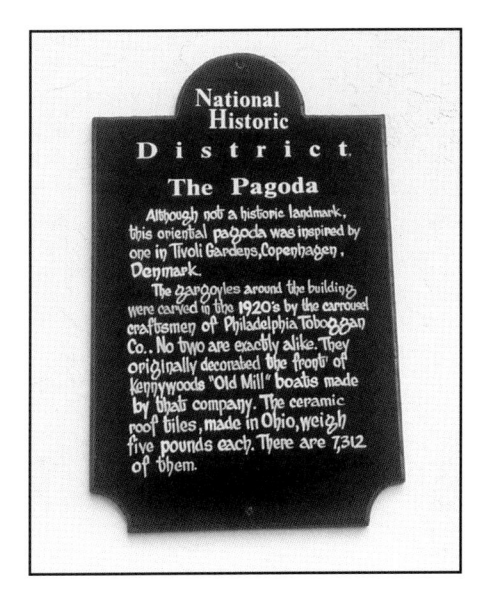

1987 A Touch of Tivoli

When Kennywood decided to replace the Tower Refreshment Stand, which was the home of the park's first public address system, "Voice of Kennywood," as well as a refreshment stand, Harry and Bill Henninger, and Carl Hughes contacted Al Filoni, noted Pittsburgh architect, to design the new structure. When Filoni asked them, "What sort of look do you have in mind?" Hughes thought for a minute and answered, "How about a pagoda?" Before his death a few years earlier, Carl E. Henninger said he wanted to build a pagoda like the famous one in Tivoli Gardens, Copenhagen, Denmark. Kennywood's Pagoda Refreshment Stand, which is decorated with dragons that had adorned the front of Kennywood's Old Mill boats in the 1920's and 30's, was built in 1987.

Other improvements included a new miniature golf course under the Laser Loop, Dumbo the elephant ride in Kiddieland, landscaping on the old golf course location, and a Musik Express, which bounced passengers to the beat of top forty hits.

The Laser Loop provided some excitement in 1987 when its train got stuck on a level section about ten feet above ground. The 26 riders had to be removed by ladders. A bolt from the ride's pusher bar had come loose, and the train did not have enough momentum to make it backwards through the loop to the loading station. After repairs were made, the ride reopened the following day.

The park's advertising campaign for 1987 used a top-40 hit song from the 1960's, "Palisades Park" with new "Kennywood Park" lyrics. It was then released as a two-minute single and sold at the park and National Record Mart stores with all proceeds going to help Pittsburgh's Children's Hospital.

The Musik Express was a thrill ride that ran forward and backward.
(PHOTOGRAPH BY CHARLES J. JACQUES, JR.)

CHAPTER 7

1988
Kennywood Memories

Oh those dancing eyes

Every summer since 1899, people around Pittsburgh, Pennsylvania, have been going to an amusement park called Kennywood. Kennywood has been a place for picnics, for music, for all sorts of rides, and especially for several of the world's greatest old wooden roller coasters.

Over the years, Kennywood has seen lots of good times. Sitting high on a bluff above the Monongahela River, it's outlasted most of the heavy industry that originally brought fame and fortune to the valley. Kennywood's charms and thrills have made it an important part of the Pittsburgh summer.

When you go to Kennywood, you can't see it all. You don't see what goes on behind the rides. And when you're trying to taste all the kinds of Kennywood cuisine, you don't stop to think of all the history that's made this place such an extraordinary Pittsburgh institution. And maybe you've never been there on Italian Day. It doesn't matter.

Cameraman Al Rosen and sound engineer Radar Long (at right) film riders on the Log Jammer (at left).
(WQED)

Rick Sebak, producer of the award winning documentary Kennywood Memories.
(WQED)

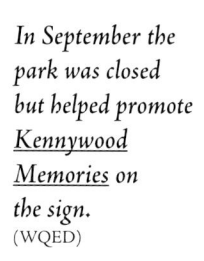

If you've ever been there, you know the best things you take with you when your parents force you to leave at the end of the night are memories.

So begins Rick Sebak's award-winning, documentary, *Kennywood Memories,* which he produced in 1988 for WQED-TV, Channel 13, Pittsburgh's widely respected public television station.

The one-hour program about the history and special appeal of Kennywood was an early part of WQED-TV's ongoing *Pittsburgh History Series* and is still considered by many its best. The program won a number of awards including the Golden Quill Award for outstanding documentary and the Ed King Memorial Golden Quill for Outstanding Broadcast Journalism. It was a top finalist in the 1990 Houston Film Festival and was nominated by NATPE (National Association of Television Program Executives) for its prestigious Iris Award for excellence in television.

Kennywood Memories was written by Rick Sebak, who also narrates the show. Sebak's program is built around a one-day visit to Kennywood, starting with maintenance crews in the morning and then wandering through the park during

In September the park was closed but helped promote Kennywood Memories *on the sign.*
(WQED)

97

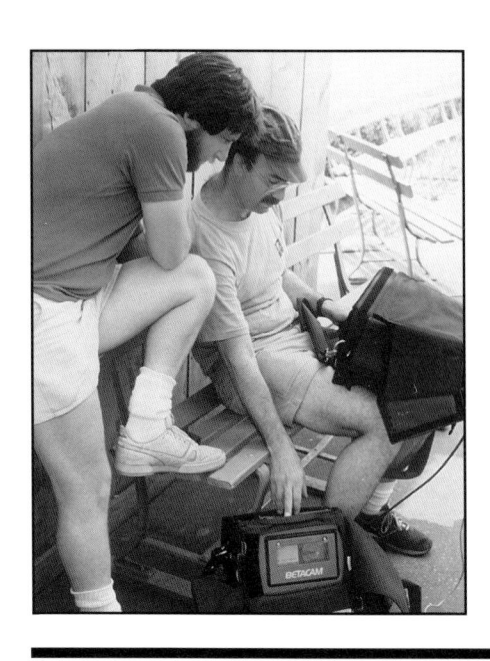

Rigger Barry Kessler and cameraman Al Rosen check some of the footage on location.
(WQED)

Shooting the Laser Loop from Shorty's Miniature Golf Course.
(WQED)

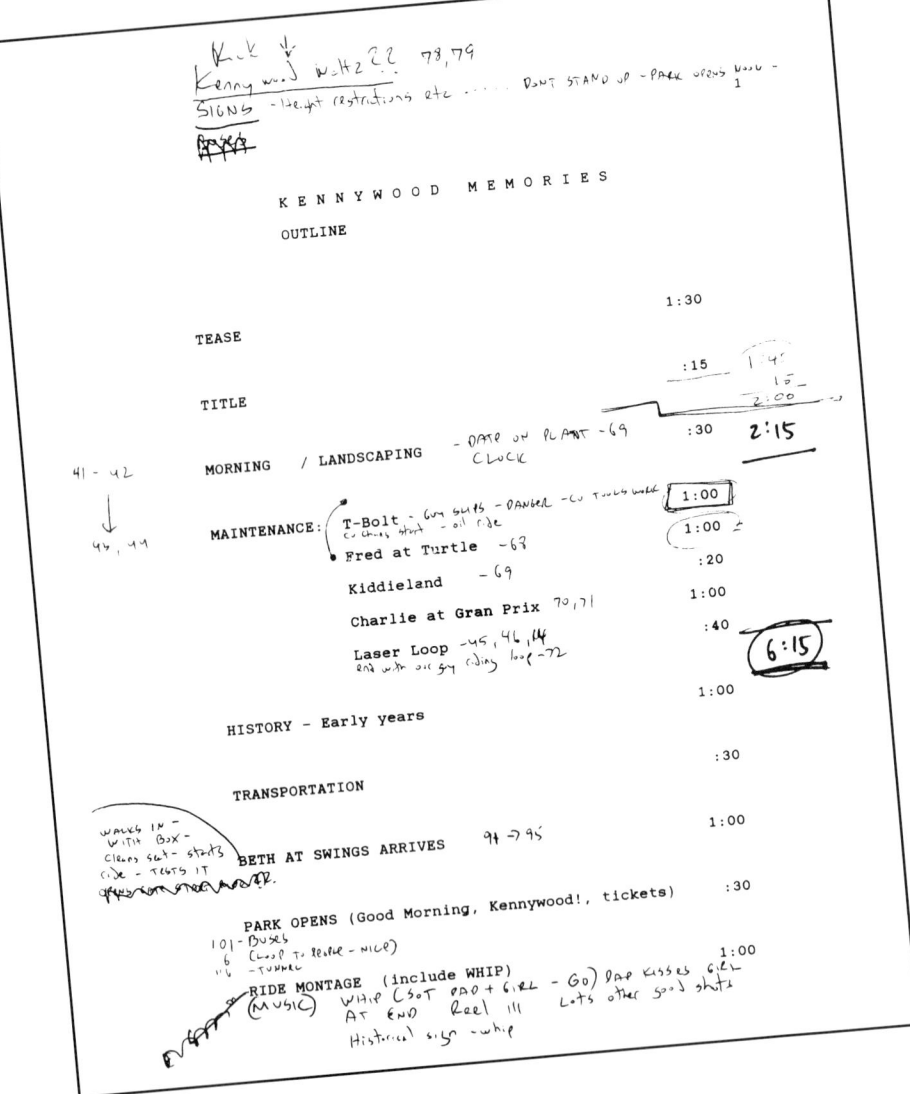

Page one of Sebak's outline with some notes and estimated running times.
(WQED)

the day. Through the memories of workers and park visitors, the history of Kennywood unfolds. It is like following a wonderful storyteller with 90 years' worth of tales of the past who meets and talks with lots of people in the present. The sun sets and the lights come on. Finally, it is dark, and the park closes, leaving the audience wishing there was more.

The program is fun for lots of reasons. Structurally it is almost perfect. Sebak's pacing and editing are superb; he mixes facts and trivia; he uses interviews and narrative, weaving all of this together with wonderful historic and current footage of Kennywood. Sebak also cuts quickly from old black-and-white footage of a coaster to bright color tape of the park. His choice of music helps capture the feeling of Kennywood, especially in the footage after dark where Allen Rosen's photography mixes with the dreamy quality of old standards that seem to give the park a timeless quality.

Kennywood Memories first aired on WQED-TV on Wednesday, September 28, 1988, and was repeated on Saturday, October 1. The response was immediate and very positive, and the show quickly became one of the most popular documentaries ever aired on WQED. APS, the American Program Service, which

Al Rosen, who initially refused to go on the Laser Loop, shoots it from a safe distance.
(WQED)

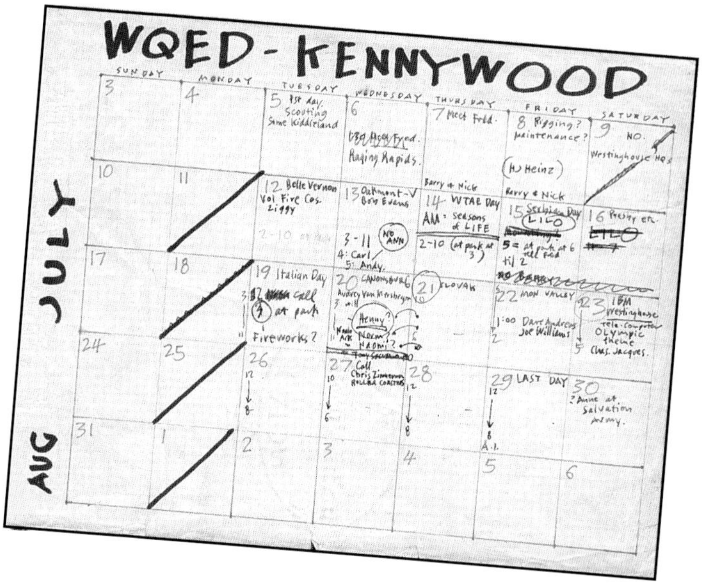

Sebak's scheduling calendar.
(WQED)

distributes public television programming nationwide, picked up *Kennywood Memories*, and programmers at over one hundred public television stations eventually carried the documentary. Sebak said, "I sometimes think it airs more often in Maryland and Florida than it does here [in Pittsburgh]."

Starting in 1990, WQED Video began selling home-video cassettes of the show. (Because of music rights, some of the original soundtrack had to be changed, and two short "new scenes" that appear only on the tape were added.) By 1997, more than 15,000 copies of the tape had been sold.

Sebak always felt Kennywood Park would be an unbeatable topic for a documentary. "Any kid who grew up around Pittsburgh knows Kennywood is a great once-a-year experience, an unforgettable place," he said. Upon graduation from the University of North Carolina at Chapel Hill in 1976, he considered going to the film school at the University of Southern California and wrote on his application he hoped someday to do a film about Kennywood Park.

Instead of graduate school, Sebak got a job at the South Carolina Educational Television Network, (SCETV), where he worked from 1976 to 1987. Then Nancy Lavin offered him a job at WQED's newly-reorganized Local Programming Department. At his job interview, Sebak told her that he would like to do a program about Kennywood Park. She, a non-native born in New York and schooled in California, was a bit skeptical but said they would talk about it.

In the spring of 1988, Sebak saw two of Robert Qualters' prints from a series of paintings called "Kennywood Memories" in the window of the Marcus Gordon Gallery on South Craig Street in Oakland. Although Sebak was just thinking

Sebak, Cowboy Joe, and Nancy Lavin, executive producer of <u>Kennywood Memories</u>.
(WQED)

99

Kenny Kangaroo greets young visitors.
(WQED)

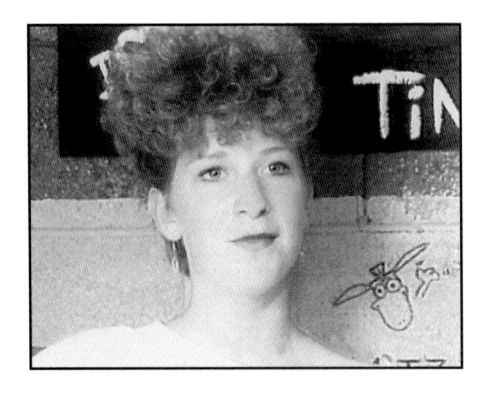

about the show at that point, he called Qualters and asked if they might be able to use one of those paintings on a poster if WQED did a program about Kennywood. Qualters agreed; Sebak also asked him if WQED might use "Kennywood Memories" as their title too. Qualters said the phrase, "Kennywood Memories," actually came from those small pressed-metal souvenir coins that people used to make in the Penny Arcade at the park. Later, Qualters' voice was used in the program reminiscing about the Buck Rogers-like airplanes.

In June 1988, after Sebak finished "The Mon, The Al, and the O," a WQED program about Pittsburgh's three rivers, Nancy Lavin said, "Let's start your Kennywood program." Sebak then contacted Andy Quinn, who was marketing director at the park, and asked about possibly shooting a documentary at Kennywood. Quinn, who did not know Sebak at all, was agreeable and told him to get in touch with Ann Hughes, publicity director and wife of Carl O. Hughes, Kennywood's chairman of the board.

How it was made

Sebak and his crew started shooting July 5, 1988, and worked at the park Tuesday

Lighting director Jim Bruwelheide, Al Rosen, and Radar Long shoot the Wave Swinger.
(WQED)

Radar Long, sound engineer, takes a break.
(WQED)

100

Ann Hughes chauffeurs Al Rosen in Norman Sweich's golf cart.
(WQED)

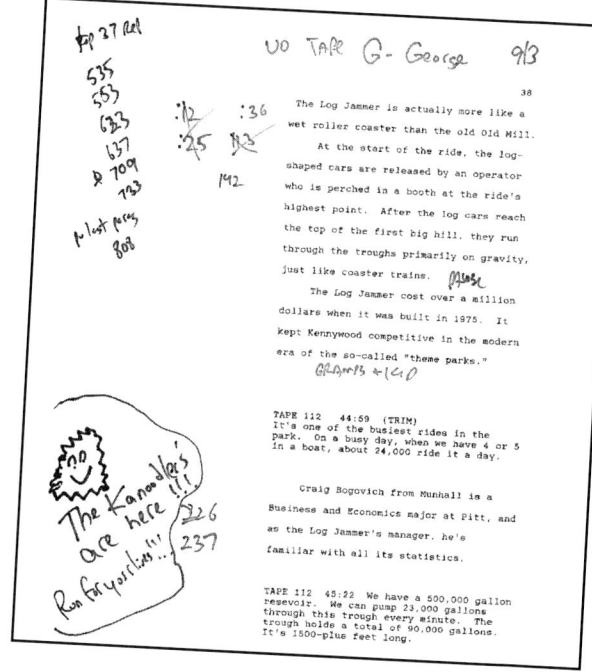

Sebak's script with some of Al Rosen's comments.
(WQED)

Nancy Lavin and Joe Abeln, lighting director, share a corn dog.
(WQED)

through Friday (and occasionally on Saturdays) through July. Altogether they shot 130 20-minute tapes of the park and in addition were able to obtain some historic film footage that they transferred to tape. The final shooting ratio was about 50:1, or 50 hours of tape for the final one hour program.

Each morning Sebak and the crew would park the WQED van by the Guest Services Building and transfer their equipment to Norm Sweich's golf cart. Sweich, who worked in group sales, lost the use of his cart for the whole month. July was a hot dry month, and the crew soon found out they really needed the cart to carry the camera and other heavy equipment around the park.

Back at the station, people were curious about the project. They razzed Sebak, "Oh, going to Kennywood again? Hard work, eh?" He responded, "Yes, hard work. But someone has to do it." Sebak feared burn-out with a solid month of shooting, but the crew never got tired of the park. There were always new surprises and adventures and plenty of people to interview. They also never got tired of corndogs and french fries.

101

Al Rosen.
(WQED)

Ann Hughes, Kennywood's publicity director, accompanied the WQED crew everywhere.
(WQED)

WQED'S crew

Al Rosen shot and edited the program. He was a very talkative cameraman and a good editor. Some of the nice surprises in the finished show were his. Rosen did not like roller coasters and dreaded going on the Laser Loop. The camera was usually strapped on Rosen rather than on a "mount" because Sebak liked the slightly wobbly effect more than the ultra-smooth look that came from mounting the camera on the train itself. Barry Kessler, a WQED crew member who had worked on some amusement park commercials, came along to help the crew work out the best way to secure the camera to Rosen on various rides.

Ann Hughes, Kennywood's publicity director, worked with the crew nearly every day. Sebak said that Ann Hughes was extremely helpful and soon became just "one of the guys." Jim Bruwelheide helped with lighting and grip work during the shooting. Bruwelheide was a great practical joker and liked to trap Sebak in funny situations. One day Sebak got the ride operator on the Raging Rapids to soak Bruwelheide, Rosen, and Ann Hughes as they floated by. When Bruwelheide found out that Sebak had requested the soaking, he told Sebak that Ann Hughes was really mad, and that "she

Barry Kessler helps Al Rosen get the camera in position for a reverse angle shot on the Thunderbolt.
(WQED)

Filming the Thunderbolt from another angle.
(WQED)

Radar Long recording at the Wave Swinger.
(WQED)

Sebak points to a section of track the crew had walked earlier that day.
(WQED)

The Kiddie Caterpillar.
(WQED)

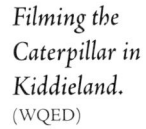

Filming the Caterpillar in Kiddieland.
(WQED)

was going to get to the bottom of this!" Sebak fell for Bruwelheide's story and was ready to apologize to Hughes when Bruwelheide admitted Ann Hughes really was not upset, but he just wanted to watch Sebak squirm.

Nick Tallo was lighting man on most of the shooting days. Tallo hated roller coasters and would not ride one during the shooting. However, he did walk to the top of the Thunderbolt and all the other rides. Nick also told Sebak about Italian Day at the park, and Nick's mom appears in the documentary.

Radar Long, sound engineer on the Kennywood shoot, was amused when Sebak stopped outside the Log Jammer and decided to interview some of the St. Athanasius altar boys from West View on their church's picnic day. Radar (his real name, not a nickname) grew up in Philadelphia and, by coincidence, had gone to grade school at another St. Athanasius School there. Of course, he identified with the pack of confident young men ("Chase after girls," one of the altar boys says as they get on the Wave Swinger, "that's what we basically do.") but Long said he never knew Kennywood as a kid. Nevertheless, while working in the park that summer, he often called his parents in Philadelphia, and his mother, a

The Racer.
(WQED)

native of Duquesne, Pennsylvania, shared many of her own childhood memories of the park with him. "Kennywood's definitely part of our family's memories," Long said.

Sebak's job as producer was to keep the crew working and on schedule. This was not always easy when almost everyone in the park was relaxing and having a good time on those hot July afternoons. Rick also conducted all the interviews and tried to make sure his crew got enough new footage of the park. Although a producer technically heads up the project, Sebak will gladly tell you that sometimes the producer's job is to get the coffee and donuts or corn dogs and french fries.

Old footage was harder to find. Rick Sebak likes to tell the story of his good fortune on one of the last days of shooting when a gardener came up to talk with Ann Hughes and Sebak was asking her "for about the millionth time" about the possibility of finding some old movies of the park. The gardener said, "Oh, you know there's a big box of old movies in the basement of the Administration Building. I can show you." It was a forgotten treasure chest of fantastic old films (mostly 35mm clips that had been used as short subjects in old neighborhood cinemas), and that box contained beauti-

Rosen shoots the Racer as it approaches the brake run.
(WQED)

ful old vintage moving images that were incorporated into the show. Most of the old film was black-and-white, but some was color (including several scenes of roller skating bears and other performers). The other major source of old film was from the collection of Charles J. Jacques, Jr., who years before, had transferred rare

Sebak in his office at WQED.
(WQED)

Radar Long recording Beth Snodgrass, assistant ride operator of the Wave Swinger.
(WQED)

Al Rosen and Nick Tallo check the script of <u>Kennywood Memories</u>.
(WQED)

Sebak found Laffing Sal still laughing in the train station.
(Photograph by Charles J. Jacques, Jr.)

early footage from the 1920's and 1930's from nitrate stock to safety film. There is no question the moving pictures (some slowed slightly to achieve a more dreamy effect) added depth and evocative power to the program.

Shortly after Carl Hughes saw *Kennywood Memories* for the first time, he wrote Margot Woodwell, station manager of WQED, that he was thrilled with Sebak's documentary. "Your people worked so hard in the intense heat of the past summer and spent so much obvious talented effort on the studio production, that they deserve every bit of praise I know will be coming to them," he wrote.

Sebak's memories

Sebak's favorite memory of the park is of the big fat laughing lady who used to be outside the Laff-in-the-Dark ride. "I remember staring at her when I was a little kid and watching her shake," he said. To Sebak's astonishment, he found the old girl was still working and laughing at Kennywood. She had just been moved to the ticket booth for the miniature railroad. "She was exactly as I remembered her from my childhood," Sebak said. So he included her and her unforgettable laugh in the final program.

Gino Chamboredon before he climbs the Laser Loop.
(WQED)

Real people

Perhaps what gives *Kennywood Memories* a unique sense of perspective is the people (both workers and park visitors) who appear in it. There is Gino Chamboredon hanging out the front of the train on the Thunderbolt to oil the track or slipping on the wet wooden surface of the Thunderbolt. Charlie Lyons philosophizes about the park while working on the bumper cars. People honestly express opinions, like Amy Winters, who makes corn dogs but would never eat them. Naomi Jones, the star of the lost and found department, remembers "When I first started here, this was a mud hole. It wasn't paved. When it rained, everybody was mud from head to feet."

Isabel Snyder brings the sheet music her mother, Margaretha Scandroli, wrote and dedicated to the park in 1899. Her mother's picture is on the cover of the sheet music. Beth Snodgrass, Wave Swinger operator, watches out for her riders with those beautiful dancing eyes. She cleans and tests the ride in the morning, and then the boys from St. Athanasius make her remember her "younger days" when she would "hang out at Kennywood, and you know, we would watch guys."

Isabel Snyder, whose mother Margaretha Scandroli wrote the "Kennywood Park Waltz."
(WQED)

The Wave Swinger has to be watched so swings don't get tangled.
(WQED)

Oh, those dancing eyes, Beth Snodgrass.
(WQED)

Al Rosen, Beth Snodgrass, and Jim Bruwelheide at the Wave Swinger.
(WQED)

It's heart

Shortly after the documentary was first shown, Jane Kaiser wrote Sebak "I taped the program to send to my sister in Connecticut. She says she comes to Pittsburgh every summer to visit me, but I know she comes to visit KENNYWOOD. We've had such good times, and your program just reinforced what a wonderful place Kennywood Park is. Pittsburgh is so lucky to have such an old-fashioned amusement park."

Mary Jane Smoley wrote, "My family and I watched *Kennywood Memories* on Channel 13 two weeks ago and it was so wonderful. I taped it for my children (ages 6 and 3). We play the tape at least once a day. My oldest child quotes from the tape in his daily conversation."

"But it wasn't just the memories. I actually felt as I did then."

" I have seen my own children grow up with Kennywood and hopefully will see my grandchildren enjoy it too."

"There were tears in my eyes as your beautiful special on Kennywood Park came to a close," wrote Margie Sullivan. "You did such a fantastic job recreating the feelings of Kennywood through the interviews and film. It brought back fond memories of my childhood; riding the train and looking for my parents' picnic table; and watching my mother sitting in Kiddieland passing out tickets and gossiping with old friends and neighbors. It brought back the crazy teen years and the matching Kennywood outfits. But it wasn't just the memories. I actually felt as I did then... I have seen my own children grow up with Kennywood and hopefully will see my grandchildren enjoy it too."

"My family and I watched "Kennywood Memories" and it was so wonderful. We play the tape at least once a day."

1988 French Fry Capital of the World

In addition to being "The Roller Coaster Capital of the World," Kennywood might also be called "The French Fry Capital of the World." More than 277,000 pounds of fresh potatoes were used by The Potato Patch during the 1988 season. To complement the fries, the refreshment department added fried German bologna with green peppers and onions and Philly Beef and Cheese sandwiches.

Kennywood installed a new fountain

"My sister in Connecticut says she comes to Pittsburgh every summer to visit me, but I know she comes to visit Kennywood."

"Pittsburgh is so lucky to have such an old-fashioned amusement park."

Skee ball alleys in the double decker refreshment building.
(PHOTOGRAPH BY CHARLES J. JACQUES, JR.)

Jim Bruwelheide and Kenny Kangaroo with a WQED cap, as the shooting comes to a close.
(WQED)

made with imported tile called the Fantastic Fountain in the section formerly occupied by the park's miniature golf course. The fountain was especially beautiful at night when a synchronized light and water show took place which featured pulsating jets of water and colored lights that kept beat to music. To give it the right setting 20-foot high evergreens were planted behind it.

In 1988, Kennywood reintroduced the Rotor after a 16-year absence. It was the third Rotor the park had operated. According to Rich Henry, director of operations, "The Rotor was gone long enough and it was popular enough to bring it back." The new steel and fiberglass model, manufactured by Chance Manufacturing Company, of Wichita, Kansas, sent riders spinning in a circle at approximately 30 miles per hour. Once the Rotor reached top speed, the floor was lowered, leaving the riders pinned to the walls because of centrifugal force. For the weak of stomach, the ride offered a spectator area. It was erected between the Gran Prix and the tunnel entrance into the park.

Flying Carpet, a German ride themed as an experience right out of the Arabian nights, was the 1988 season's other new ride. The ride simulated a weightless, free-falling feeling similar to the Pirate ship. A maximum of 40 passengers were swung slowly back and forth, higher and higher, until they were sent sailing over the top, but riders were never turned upside down. As Ann Hughes put it, "It's one of those rides where your stomach is there, but you don't know exactly where."

To make way for the new rides, some rides were removed including the Super Roundup and the Calypso. The Bayern Kurve was also retired after a 16-year run, but the park immediately started looking for a new one. The Mini Scooter bumper cars for children were moved to Kennywood's sister park Idlewild.

In 1988, members of the National Carousel Association returned to the park and gave an outstanding achievement award for preserving the antique wooden carousel to Kennywood's Carl Hughes. The carousel group was again entertained by Tony Sacramento, who presided over the carousel and who enjoyed giving his own fanciful history of the horses. According to Sacamento, one horse used to belong to the queen of Egypt, another to one of Julius Caesar's lieutenants, and the four horses of the Apocalypse were there too, without their riders (except perhaps after hours).

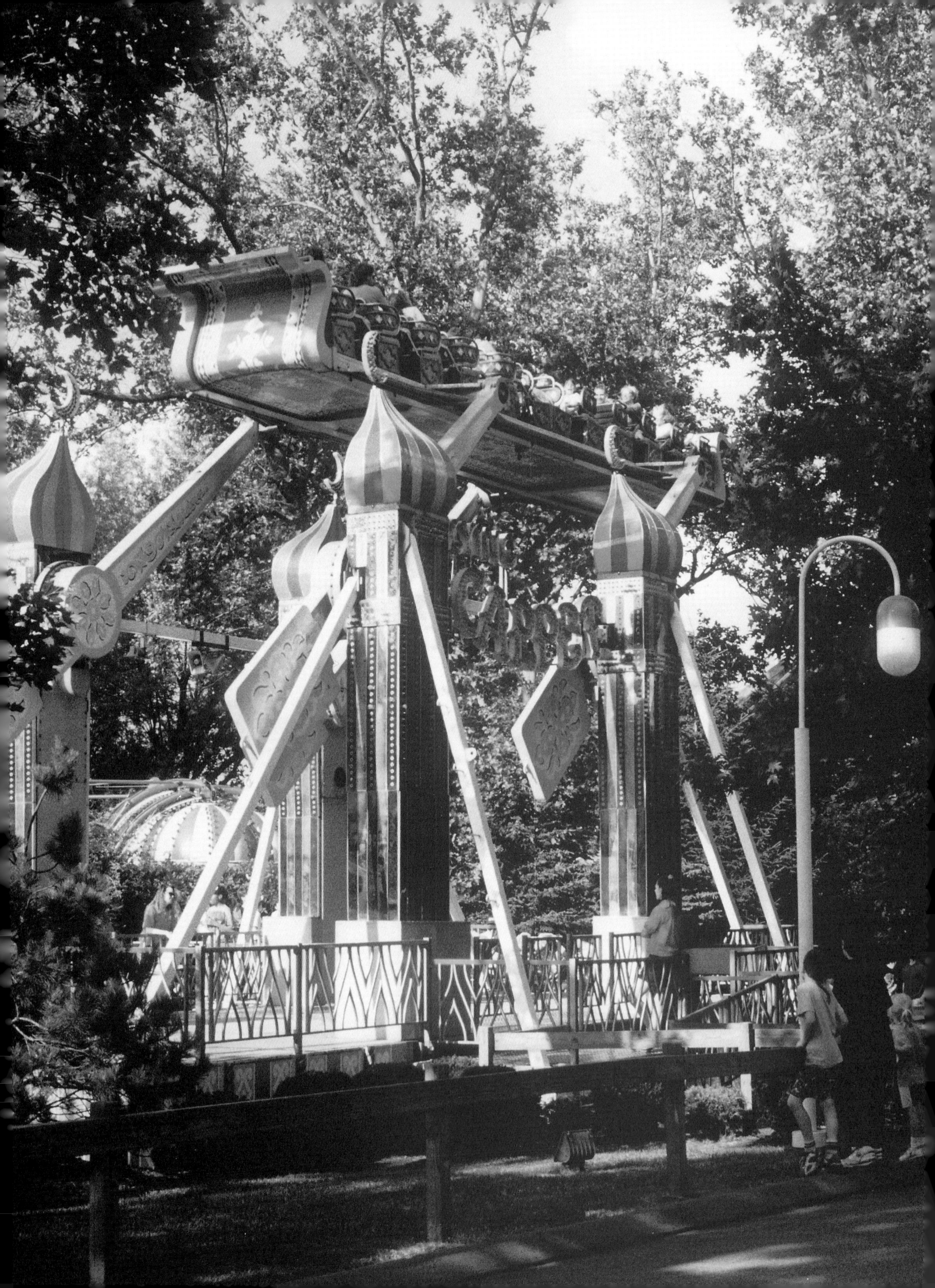

(At left)
The Magic Carpet was one of Kennywood's new rides in 1987.
(Photograph by Charles J. Jacques, Jr.)

Kennywood Memories was first shown at the Fulton Theater in downtown Pittsburgh on September 22, 1987.
(WQED)

An out-of-park experience

Every spring Kennywood puts out over 400 yellow arrows showing the way to the park. The signs have become Kennywood's out-of-park trademark. Rich Henry said "People do rely on the signs. If one disappears, we start getting calls." At the end of the season, all of the signs are returned to the shop where about one-third of them are repainted every year. The painting is done by Jerry Lisanti, Jr., a painter who works in the park's sign shop. He and other maintenance employees are warmed by a potbelly stove in which old lumber from the Racer is used as fuel.

Once the park closes for the season, Kenny the Kangaroo often has to share his home with wild animals like raccoons, rabbits, squirrels, and even deer. Five deer climbed up the bluff from the Monongahela River and stayed for a few days in 1988.

A new Rotor from Chance Manufacturing was added in 1987.
(Photograph by Charles J. Jacques, Jr.)

CHAPTER 8
1989-1990 *Sandcastle*

Does Pittsburgh need a waterpark?

One blazing hot summer day in 1987, with attendance down at Kennywood, Harry W. Henninger, Jr., 40-year-old president of the park, asked himself, "Does Pittsburgh need a waterpark?" Henninger, whose first job at Kennywood was as a lifeguard at the park's old Swimming Pool, remembered how jammed the Pool was on a 90-degree day. The Swimming Pool did big business and was crowded on really hot days, while the rest of the park languished. "People like water and water rides like the Raging Rapids," Henninger mused, "then, why not a waterpark?"

A few days later, as the heat spell continued, Henninger mentioned his "waterpark idea" to Carl Hughes. Looking out over the Monongahela River from Hughes' three-story house on Mount Washington, the two men could see hundreds of pleasure boats on the river. Whether it was the heat or the activity on the river, they both agreed that a waterpark sounded like a good idea.

Waterparks had come into their own in the 1980's. In the 1960's and 1970's, so called waterparks sprang up near any body of water, but usually they were little more than glorified water slides. This all

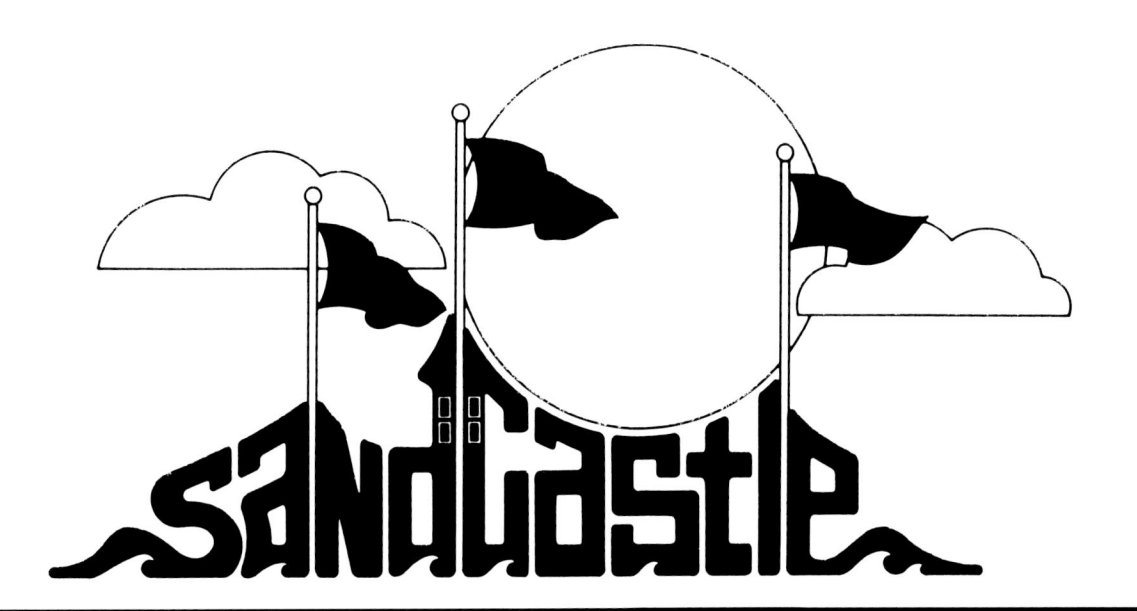

Sandcastle

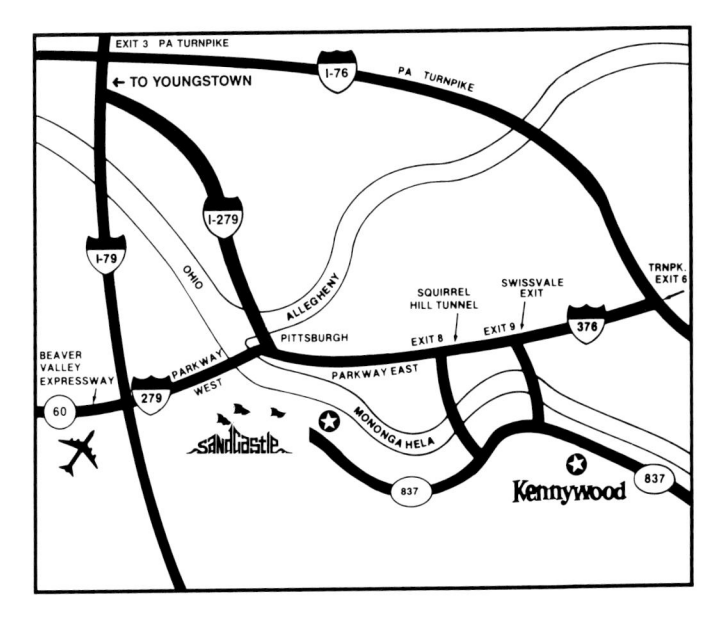

Aerial view of the Splashdown slide area at Sandcastle.
(PHOTOGRAPH BY CHARLES J. JACQUES, JR.)

changed in the 1980's. New waterparks were entire complexes often containing pools, lazy rivers, slides, children's activity areas, other water attractions, food and drink areas, games, and souvenir shops. Even Disney, Busch, and Six Flags owned waterparks.

There had been a huge Swimming Pool at Kennywood for many years, but by the 1970's, the Pool was technologically outdated and losing money. It would have cost hundreds of thousands of dollars to have the Swimming Pool upgraded, so in 1973, the Pool was closed and filled in. Ten years later, when Idlewild Park was purchased, Kennywood found itself with another old swimming pool. Idlewild's Pool also required extensive renovation and it also was losing money. Kennywood's board of directors at first thought about closing it, but Bill Henninger, vice president of Kennywood, and a member of the board, thought it was worth saving. He talked his cousin, Harry Henninger, Jr. and Hughes into saving it. They decided to add some water slides while the Pool was undergoing renovation. Thus Idlewild's H2OhhhZone was born. It was a beautiful little waterpark. The "Zone" was an immediate success and attracted many new visitors to the park. There was some fear that the weather was not warm enough for a waterpark, but the H2OhhhZone proved that western Pennsylvania's climate could support such an attraction.

Where should the waterpark go?

"Yes," Harry Henninger thought, "Pittsburgh does need a waterpark," but where should it go? Hughes and Henninger agreed that it should not be at Kennywood, because the park did not have enough room for slides, pools, and the extra parking that a complex would require. They also did not want crowds of people walking around Kennywood in

Construction of the quarter-mile-long boardwalk at Sandcastle.
(SANDCASTLE)

Sandcastle's entrance and turnstiles under construction.
(SANDCASTLE)

bathing suits.

A search of vacant properties away from the urban areas turned up a couple of interesting locations, but Henninger had another idea. Each Sunday morning during the summer of 1987, Henninger would drive along the river valleys in western Pennsylvania looking for possible sites for a waterpark. For more than a century, the steel industry from McKeesport to Pittsburgh had owned the banks of the Monongahela River. But following the Second World War, these mills closed one by one until by the 1980's, all that remained were abandoned plant sites up and down the Monongahela River.

The biggest problem, Henninger found, was not the lack of riverfront property - there was lots of it - but access. High walls had been erected along the river, and abandoned industrial property tended to be ten or more feet above the water. Railroads too were strung out up and down the river valleys, thereby creating another major impediment to access and development of a waterpark.

The search finally paid off, and the answer was much closer to Kennywood than anyone would have thought. Located halfway between downtown Pittsburgh and Kennywood Park, along the Monongahela River, was property

Lightning Express speed slide at Sandcastle.
(PHOTOGRAPH BY CHARLES J. JACQUES, JR.)

Thunder Run's landing pool at Sandcastle.
(PHOTOGRAPH BY CHARLES J. JACQUES, JR.)

owned by USX, formerly called United States Steel Company. Part of the property was an undeveloped jungle of greenery just above the water level. This meant a waterpark could have easy boat access to the river. Subsequent investigation showed that the property had once been part of the mammoth Homestead Steel Works, which had been demolished, and USX was interested in selling it. Community activists wanted a new steel mill, but Hughes and Henninger, using all of their skills of persuasion, convinced them that a waterpark would be an acceptable development for part of the site. They argued that it would serve the recreational needs of the community, and it would offer summer employment to hundreds of students from the valley.

Next, Harry Henninger had to persuade members of his own board of directors that a waterpark in an old mill town like West Homestead was a good idea. So Henninger set up a visit to the proposed site. Carl Hughes recalled the first time Kennywood's board of directors looked at the site. "Just imagine six men of various ages and physical condition, dressed up in suits, crawling over railroad tracks, around fences and down a steep dirt path into an almost impenetrable jungle. We had to follow a modest trail

Construction of a slide tower at Sandcastle.
(SANDCASTLE)

that fishermen used until we finally arrived at the muddy edge of the Monongahela. The board found something we had never thought would be there - a terrific view - serene water - and directly across the river, a green tree-covered hillside, which would never be developed. One board member was so overwhelmed by the scene that he blurted out 'It's beautiful,'" Hughes recalled.

Kennywood immediately went into negotiations with USX to purchase 42 acres of the old mill site, and the sale was completed on December 5, 1987. Kennywood now owned acreage that stretched for nearly one mile along the riverfront. When the property was finally surveyed, it was discovered that the site actually contained 67 acres because over the years, sediment left by the river floods had accumulated and built up a delta.

Picking a name for the new park

A team of Kennywood employees was set up to help pick a name for the new park. But as things often turn out, a preliminary name was needed to organize the new corporation before the team had finished its work. While visiting the corporate attorneys' offices in downtown Pittsburgh, Carl Hughes was asked by one of the attorneys for a name for the new company. On the wall in back of the attorney was a picture of a child playing on a sand beach, so Hughes answered, "How about Sandcastle?" So the name was adopted for organizational purposes.

Later, the Kennywood team chose Splashdown as the name for the new waterpark. However, by that time, the name Sandcastle had been given to the media to describe the project, and it was feared that a name change would suggest that the original park idea had been scrapped and something new substituted. So Sandcastle became the official name for the park. The name Splashdown was not completely discarded but was used for the

Access to the boardwalk from the landing pools.
(PHOTOGRAPH BY CHARLES J. JACQUES, JR.)

Sandcastle's first logo.

The Lazy River under construction. (SANDCASTLE)

water slide section of the new park.

Although many waterparks featured wave pools as their primary attraction, Henninger and Hughes felt that Sandcastle should not have a wave pool because Allegheny County already operated several. Instead of a wave pool, they decided to build a number of different kinds of water slides. Slides had proven to be very popular at Idlewild, and the two men felt that additional slides would help draw people to the new park; Sandcastle might be called the "Water Slide Capital of the World."

Sandcastle had many different kinds of water slides. They branched out in all directions from five large towers, each offering a different experience, from the usual trip downward in just bathing suits to slides in one-or-two-person inner tubes. The tallest were three speed slides. The largest, a giant speed slide, was 85 feet tall and 250 feet long. The rider glided down a gradual slope for 25 feet, then dropped a steep 60 feet. Each channel had a double dip. Deceleration was in four inches of water. There were two slightly smaller speed slides, each 250 feet long that started 60 feet above the ground, with gradual slopes, then a 50-foot drop. These slides were called body slides because tubes or mats were not used.

Other slides featured "sky ponds," or elevated shallow pools where riders in inner tubes could mingle and rest before deciding to drop further. Two were shotgun slides where riders went down a 25 foot fiberglass cylinder on their backs. These slides ended above a 14-foot deep pond where riders experienced an eight-foot free fall drop. Three slides started from a 50 foot tower; two from 46 feet. The new slides were given names like Thunder Run, Bermuda Triangle, Tuber's Tower, Cliffhangers, and Lightning Express.

Cascade, a company from Georgia, designed the slides, and W. Thomas Borellis, a Pittsburgh landscape architect, did the original layout for the complex. A Fayette County firm, T. C. Shallenberger Construction of Connellsville, built the landing pools, the Lazy River, and the kiddie-sized Tadpool.

For Harry and Bill Henninger and Carl Hughes, Sandcastle was a first. They had built new sections in Kennywood and Idlewild, but they had never developed a whole new park from conception through construction to opening.

The boardwalk runs under the water slides at Sandcastle. (PHOTOGRAPH BY CHARLES J. JACQUES, JR.)

Monongahela River flooded Sandcastle during construction in the spring of 1989.
(SANDCASTLE)

The Monongahela has repeatedly flooded the park.
(SANDCASTLE)

The Mon is not always nice

In October 1988, construction started on Sandcastle. The first phase, which cost seven million dollars, was scheduled for completion in early June 1989. (The original master plan called for two additional phases to be built over five years.) First, seven miles of railroad track had to be removed from the site. Next, the contractors were forced to work through the winter whenever the temperature was above 32 degrees pouring concrete for the Lazy River and footers and pools for the slides.

In the spring of 1989, the weather and the Mon virtually conspired to halt construction on the new park. Sandcastle was built on two levels. The lower level or delta level lay only eight feet above the river. All the attractions on this level like the Lazy River, water slides' landing pools, beach, and children's play area and pool were supposedly in a five-year flood plain (a level area near a river or stream that would flood about every five years).

The upper level, located 25 feet above the river, was completed on time and on budget. It contained the turn-of-the-century entrance gate, and the 1800-foot long boardwalk with a row of food shops, souvenir stands, arcade, and a bathhouse.

During the spring, the Monongahela River repeatedly flooded the lower level. It was the wettest spring on record in western Pennsylvania, and work came to a complete stop. The completion date was pushed back by heavy rains and the flooding. Every step taken was in mud. Construction timetables were rendered obsolete, and costs were driven up. Carl Hughes lamented, "When we bought the land from USX in 1987, we were told to expect flooding every five years. So far this spring, we've been flooded three times."

Opening day was moved back to July 1, but with more river flooding, it became obvious that even that date was too optimistic. With one eye on the sky, Henninger and his crew worked sixteen-hour days for months trying in vain to meet the July 1 opening date. They missed it by just sixteen days.

At last, opening day

Sandcastle opened on July 17, 1989, without much fanfare. Workers were still putting the finishing touches on the park when it opened. The day was cool and gloomy, but Harry Henninger put on his bathing suit to try the new water slides. Very few people showed up that first day although the number of people who claimed to have been there will probably grow over the years. Building Sandcastle had been a backbreaking struggle because of having to clean up after each flood.

"Missing the opening date was expensive," Carl Hughes commented. "Just missing the Fourth of July holiday cost us about 25,000 people, which translated into $300,000 in lost revenue," he said. To save time, Sandcastle's

Thunder Run tube slide at Sandcastle.
(PHOTOGRAPH BY CHARLES J. JACQUES, JR.)

Tube sliders on the boardwalk in front of Splashdown.
(PHOTOGRAPH BY CHARLES J. JACQUES, JR.)

A slow float on the Lazy River.
(PHOTOGRAPH BY CHARLES J. JACQUES, JR.)

employees were trained at Kennywood and were ready to go on opening day. "We wanted to give them some experience at an entertainment complex prior to the park's opening," Harry Henninger said.

Although Sandcastle was built in the heart of an old river town, West Homestead, once visitors were inside the park, only the green of grass and trees, the colors from the boardwalk's buildings and slides, and the mirror-like finish of the river were visible. Pittsburghers had no real problem with the location, but they did have a problem with Sandcastle's one dollar parking fee that was quickly eliminated. Perhaps, they were too used to "free parking" at Kennywood.

Maybe Pittsburgh needed a waterpark, but at times during the spring, Harry Henninger was not sure that he had chosen the right spot for it. Even before the park was opened, the beach was down-sized. Henninger commented, "You realize that if you put sand down there [on the lower level] it's going to be mud after a flood, and that's a very expensive proposition, so we've reduced the amount of sand."

The first phase did not include an adult-sized swimming pool. The closest thing was the 1,400 foot Lazy River, which was a waterway three feet deep and 13 feet wide that carried passengers in inner tubes. For children there was a small pool called Tadpool. On the few hot days that summer, employees found, to their dismay, adults would literally crowd children out of the small pool.

The water slide areas were busy, but there was almost no interest in the lower level, where the Tadpool, Lazy River, and small beach area were located. "Ninety percent of the attractions were from the

The Lazy River entrance.
(Photograph by Charles J. Jacques, Jr.)

Sandcastle's Lazy River is one-quarter-mile-long.
(Photograph by Charles J. Jacques, Jr.)

Speeding up the boardwalk past shops and Crab Apple Jack's.
(Photograph by Charles J. Jacques, Jr.)

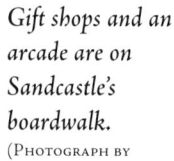

Gift shops and an arcade are on Sandcastle's boardwalk.
(Photograph by Betty Jacques)

beginning of the food buildings [on the boardwalk] to the slides, and the whole other area of development was a wasteland. No one was there," Henninger recalled.

On bright sunny days, Sandcastle came alive, but the park often closed on rainy days. On damp, gloomy days, the place was almost a ghost town. Henninger and Hughes felt the park had to broaden its appeal to draw and hold larger crowds.

A mid-course correction

At the end of Sandcastle's first season, it was obvious changes had to be made. It was important to attract more adults and families and make the park less of a teenage - water slide park. One of the first things to go was the advertising slogan, "Water Slide Capital of the World." Attendance had reached only 85,000 during the rain-shortened first season, and even though the park lost money, Henninger and Hughes knew that they would have to spend more money making the changes necessary to attract people.

Over the years, Kennywood Park had become less weather sensitive. Most people who went to Kennywood booked in advance and most members of the group would show up regardless of the

The Lazy River runs along the Monongahela.
(Photograph by Charles J. Jacques, Jr.)

weather. People also had become less concerned about showers, since they were going to get soaked on the Raging Rapids. However, Hughes and Henninger soon found out Sandcastle was extremely temperature and even sunshine sensitive. If the sky looked gray or if the temperature was not warm, people just would not come.

Kennywood reluctantly spent another half million dollars on Sandcastle for the 1990 season. In an attempt to develop a more balanced park, Club Wet, an outdoor riverside play area for adults,

120

One of Sandcastle's three hot tubs.
(Photograph by Charles J. Jacques, Jr.)

River City is Sandcastle's eating, entertainment, and dancing pavilion.
(Photograph by Charles J. Jacques, Jr.)

Riverfront volleyball.
(Photograph by Charles J. Jacques, Jr.)

was developed. In the park's original master plan, an adult area was to be built at the opposite end of the property from Sandcastle's entrance, but management decided that it should be built on the lower level near the existing attractions and near the front gate.

The sand beach, which by this time had all but disappeared, was replaced with an 8,000-square-foot, adult-oriented, activity pool called Moonlight Bay. This pool went from ankle-deep to four feet of water. The park found that four feet was a good depth for adults to socialize without getting really wet. For those who wanted to get completely drenched, Moonlight Bay offered a 20-foot long waterfall along one of its sides. Other grown-up amenities in the area included two 35-person hot tubs called Hot Tootsie, a concrete and wooden deck area for lounging, a barbecue pit, volleyball courts with four California-style sand courts, a 50-slip dock area, and a bar. This new area was also used on Friday and Saturday evenings.

As a revamped and revitalized Sandcastle prepared to open for its second season, Harry Henninger conceded, "it is time to see if Pittsburgh's first waterpark would sink or swim." The second season's numbers proved to be

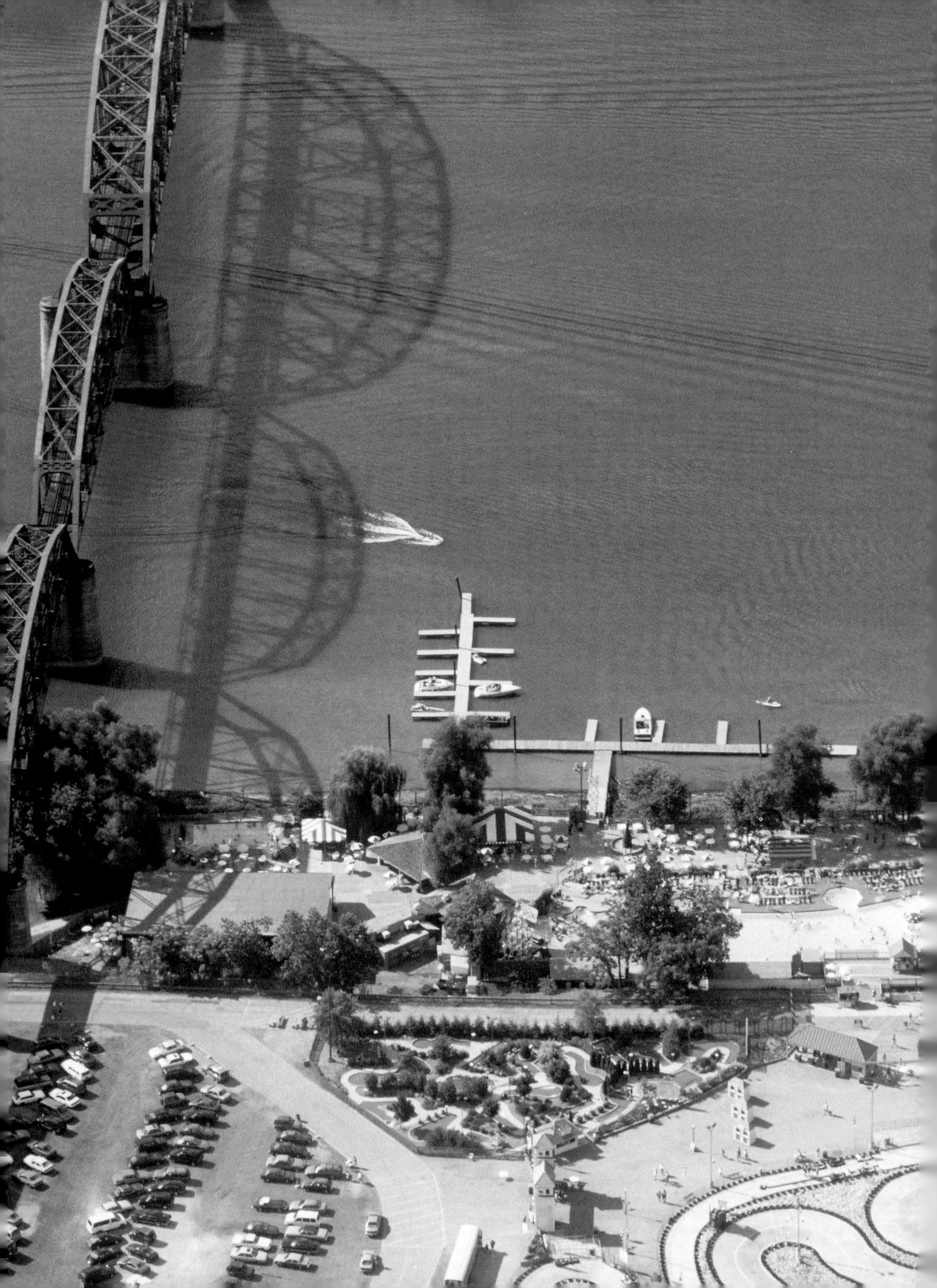

Aerial view of the Monongahela River, railroad bridge, and the park. (At left)
(PHOTOGRAPH BY BETTY JACQUES)

Oasis Miniature Golf at Sandcastle was added in 1993.
(SANDCASTLE)

Formula One Speedway at Sandcastle was added in 1993.
(PHOTOGRAPH BY CHARLES J. JACQUES, JR.)

Heading home.
(PHOTOGRAPH BY CHARLES J. JACQUES, JR.)

much more on track. Park employees had gained important experience on how to operate a waterpark, and the weather was more favorable.

With the success of the new adult section, the following year (1991) Sandcastle augmented the area with another hot tub, this one billed as the "world's largest hot tub." The new tub measured 36 feet by 18 feet. Perhaps the park went a little overboard in saying, "throw a hot tub party and bring 100 friends along." (The hot tub might accommodate 100 people, but they had better be close friends.) Club Wet was further expanded in 1992 with a covered, colorful dance area called River City. DJs performed Thursday through Monday at River City. The following year a 16-screen Super Video Wall was added to the area.

Also in 1992 some non-water activities were introduced. Bungee jumping was offered in the parking lot on Fridays and Saturdays through the summer. A total fall of 110 feet made it "Pittsburgh's Highest Jump." A golf driving range and softball batting cages were offered by the park for only one season. However, none of these attractions helped much when Pittsburgh experienced its first sub-90 degree summer in over fifteen years.

Sandcastle added more land-based attractions in 1993: a speedway ride called Formula One, which featured gas powered sports cars driven over a quarter mile track; a children's version of the track for six to nine-year olds; and an 18 hole miniature golf course and arcade outside the gate. Adding these non-water attractions almost guaranteed that the summer would be one of the hottest on record. Attendance soared at Sandcastle. Under the headline "Steam-bath sizzlers," the *Pittsburgh Post-Gazette* reported, on July 6, 1993, "Sandcastle was so inundated with people that it was forced to close its doors between 1:30 and 2 p.m. yesterday as thousands crowded onto the grounds."

Scott Mackay, manager of Sandcastle, told Johnstown's *Tribune-Democrat*, one way to avoid long lines was to pay close

On the boardwalk at Sandcastle.
(Photograph by Charles J. Jacques, Jr.)

Wet Willie's Water Works is a children's play area at Sandcastle.
(Photograph by Charles J. Jacques, Jr.)

Wet Willie's under construction in the spring of 1994.
(Sandcastle)

attention to the weather. "When you have a couple of days of bad weather and then you get the first nice one, that's the day to be here," Mackay said. "Because it's usually the second or third day before things start to really pick up."

The kids got another play area, Wet Willie's Water Works, which was added in 1994, and the boardwalk was extended to provide access. Wet Willie's was a jungle gym play area with water fountains and slides. It had a play island in the center of a 95-by-100-foot, 50,000-gallon swimming pool. The pool, with depth graduated from zero at the edge to 18 inches in the center, had slides, fountains and valves all operable by children.

Sandcastle actually had two boardwalks. The first and longest was located from the front gate to the Riverplex area and ran parallel to the river on the upper level for more than 1,800 feet. Then there was a shorter, one-third-as-wide walk, which extended under the trees along the shore of the Monongahela River. It connected the park's picnic catering area, marina, sand volleyball courts, and Club Wet, and offered a wonderful view of the Mon.

After the water slides and other family amusements closed, Sandcastle operated an after-hours night spot in the 1990's. The Sandbar nightclub was open Thursdays through Sunday nights. Sundays was an under 21 night. But night time entertainment was a fast-changing scene in Pittsburgh, and after three years of increases, the attendance suddenly dropped sharply.

In 1995, Sandcastle unveiled Riverplex (riverfront entertainment complex). It contained a 400,000 square-foot festival plaza with an adjacent 4,500-seat, state-of-the-art concert amphitheater that could be used for either concerts or festival events. The facility had a 40-by-40-foot stage. Riverplex's main asset, when compared to similar facilities in the area, was its location along the Monongahela River.

Riverplex amphitheater at Sandcastle.
(Photograph by Charles J. Jacques, Jr.)

At Kennywood, Kenny Kangaroo likes the design on the floral clock.
(Kennywood)

Children and adults can experience Wet Willie's together.
(Photograph by Charles J. Jacques, Jr.)

The first show in the new amphitheater was Hootie & the Blowfish. It was a sellout, and a documentary on the group was filmed during the concert. Riverplex had its own entrance and parking area. The new area was another way of increasing revenues that were not as dependent on the weather. It was also a way of introducing concert-goers to the waterpark.

From the beginning, there were a number of nay-sayers who said that Pittsburgh did not need a waterpark. Harry Henninger would just sit back and smile, remembering the large crowds at Kennywood's old Swimming Pool on 90-degree days. In the end, timely hot weather and careful diversification showed that he was right - Pittsburgh really did need a waterpark.

1989 Back to basics – picnics, picnics, and more picnics

In 1989, the wettest spring in western Pennsylvania's history, which had knocked Sandcastle for a loop, hit Kennywood hard too. However, as the season progressed, Kennywood made a dramatic comeback in attendance and revenue. There were three reasons for the recovery: the absence of a July-August heat wave, the best group picnic bookings ever, and the first Labor Day weekend in three years without any rain.

For the 1989 season, Kennywood added a Swing Around atop the Garden Stage. (An earlier Swing Around had operated at Kennywood for one season in 1984.) This replaced the Monster, which was moved to a spot behind the park's

Safety City, a new attraction for children, was added in 1989.
(Photograph by Betty Jacques)

Le Cachot, a dark ride, was themed by Bill Tracy of Stone Harbor, New Jersey.
(Photograph by Charles J. Jacques, Jr.)

4x4 trucks are used in the Safety City attraction.
(Photograph by Charles J. Jacques, Jr.)

A Swing Around was placed atop the Garden Stage in 1989.
(Photograph by Charles J. Jacques, Jr.)

office. The new Swing Around was purchased from Huss of Germany.

Safety City, a new attraction for children, was located in Kiddieland. It did more than entertain; it also helped teach safety to children. Small 4x4 trucks, which were manufactured by Venture Rides of South Carolina, traveled through a miniature town that resembled Pittsburgh, complete with bridges, street signs, traffic signals, and other landmarks.

Kennywood began marking its historic rides and "Historic Districts" with green and white plaques. People enjoyed the park's old rides, but as Rich Henry, the park's director of operations, said, "A lot of parks are taking their old rides out because of the problems in getting parts. If a ride breaks down, it is very expensive to have a single part made." Kennywood thought it was worth the trouble and additional expense. An example of the park keeping its history alive was the antique Wurlitzer band organ on the Dentzel Carousel. Every spring, the park had to pay an expert to overhaul and tune the organ, which was built in 1916.

The American Coaster Enthusiasts visited the park again and voted it the "Best Overall Amusement Park." Kennywood was also voted by the coaster club's members (in a tie with Worlds of

Le Cachot is a leading example of fun house design.
(Photograph by Charles J. Jacques, Jr.)

Trying to escape from Le Cachot.
(Photograph by Charles J. Jacques, Jr.)

Coaster fans still rate the Thunderbolt one of the best coasters in America.
(Photograph by Charles J. Jacques, Jr.)

Lift hill on the Thunderbolt.
(Photograph by Charles J. Jacques, Jr.)

Fun, Kansas City, Missouri) the "Most Courteous Personnel, of all parks, not just in the United States, but in the World."

Carl O. Hughes reminded senior management what Carl E. Henninger had pounded into him over the years, "Nobody *has* to come to Kennywood." Hughes wrote in his 1989 annual report:

> When I began at Kennywood full-time, Frank Danahey, the man I succeeded, told me: "Look after the school picnics; they're Kennywood's meat and potatoes. Whatever we get in July and August is gravy."
>
> Disney's well-accepted management seminars emphasize company traditions as one of the three key elements in personnel training. Well, no park has a school picnic tradition like Kennywood, and lest anyone forget, we have carefully nurtured it. As a matter of fact, we have increased the number of school picnics each year since the late 70's.
>
> I can well remember Brady McSwigan saying in frustration some 30 years ago "This has become nothing but a school picnic park." If Brady had lived another 10 years, he would have put even more emphasis on that statement. Because that was the period when we lost the huge industrial picnics that were so big, there was only one each Saturday in July and August. Truly two-thirds of our business was done by July 4.
>
> That has particular significance in the current sales pictures, because for the first time (1988 and even more so in 1989) we have more visitors after June 30 than up to then! Truly a historic turn-around, even if aided by the wet spring this year.

Every year Kennywood adds some new games to the arcade.
(Photograph by Charles J. Jacques, Jr.)

The Great Balloon Race was added in 1990.
(Kennywood)

The Racer's new front was a restoration of its original 1927 design.
(Photograph by Charles J. Jacques, Jr.)

The Parachute Drop was added in Kiddieland in 1990.
(Kennywood)

1990 The Racer gets a new-old front

Park maintenance was the key word for 1990 while the park prepared for a major steel coaster the following year. Sections of the Log Jammer trough were replaced at a total cost of $62,453. The Lagoon Bridge was rebuilt in steel under the direction of Fred Weber. Kennywood had decided to "restore" the Racer front to its original look, as shown in old photographs. Dave Moll, the park's talented carpenter foreman, was given the task. After tearing off the porcelain facade that had been added in 1960, Moll found the 1946 front and behind that, in typical Kennywood fashion, was the original front about 90 percent intact. It required just minor repairs to restore the 1927 look. The refreshment and games buildings next to the Racer, originally constructed in the 1920's, were razed and replaced with new fire resistant structures. R & R. Creative Designs, Inc. of Anaheim, California, designed new fronts that captured the look of the 1920's.

The Parachute Drop, the biggest - at least tallest - kiddie ride Kennywood ever owned, was purchased in 1990. The ride took passengers up and then gently brought them down. It replaced the Mini-Caterpillar train, which was sent to Idlewild. Parents were permitted to ride with their kids, a first for Kennywood's Kiddieland. The Monster was replaced by The Great Balloon Race, manufactured by Zamperla. What the park lost in thrills by removing the Monster, it gained in beauty with The Great Balloon Race. The new ride held 32 riders in baskets under brightly colored "balloons" that lifted into the air and slowly rotated. The Great Balloon Race, which had special lighting, was particularly spectacular after dark.

In 1990, Carl O. Hughes, chairman of Kennywood, was named to the International Association of Amusement Parks and Attractions' Hall of Fame.

Removing the Laser Loop in 1990.
(KENNYWOOD)

He was the only living member inducted in the first group of seven inductees. Hughes had served as the association's president in 1974 and was recognized for helping bring amusement parks from all over the world into the organization.

Saying good-bye to the Laser Loop

The Laser Loop was counting down its 11th and final season of operation in 1990. It was announced early in the season the shuttle loop coaster would be replaced by a new steel coaster. Rich Henry, director of operations, and his maintenance crew, were not sad to see the Laser Loop go. "It's a maintenance headache," Henry said. The coaster's computer program often shut the ride down. "Our electronics department went from being electricians to technicians in that era. We had to go to school for it," Henry acknowledged. The ride was also costly to maintain because the parts had to be purchased from the German firm that manufactured the coaster. Just one month before the ride was removed, the Laser Loop's clutch went bad and had to be replaced. New clutch plates alone cost Kennywood more than $14,000. However, the Laser Loop had carried more than 12 million riders in its 11 seasons of operation at Kennywood.

In July 1990, the name for the new coaster, Steel Phantom, was announced. To get a head start on construction, the park started clearing the ground and excavating immediately. Visitors riding the Thunderbolt could follow the construction of the Steel Phantom all summer long.

It is a tradition at Kennywood that the senior management takes one last trip before any ride leaves the park. So late Labor Day evening 1990 each management employee, from the chairman of the board on down, took one last ride on the "Loop." In spite of its shortcomings, the shuttle coaster had served the park well.

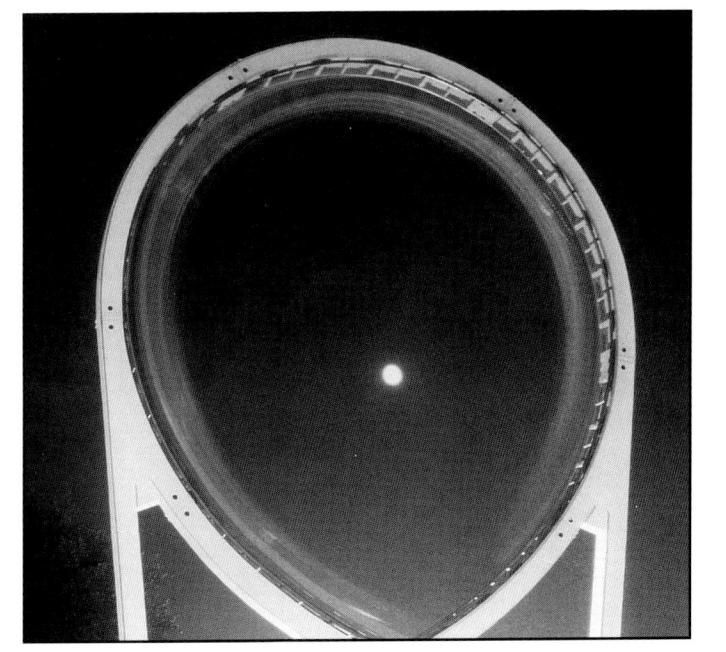

The Laser Loop was sold to La Feria Chapultepec Magico, a park in Mexico City, and reopened in 1994.
(PHOTOGRAPH BY KEN SIMMONS)

The Laser Loop served the park well.
(KENNYWOOD)

The Phantom, Ann Hughes, at the Steel Phantom's opening.
(PHOTOGRAPH BY PAUL L. RUBEN)

CHAPTER 9

1991-1994
The Steel Phantom

Indisputably unique

With the opening of the Steel Phantom on May 10, 1991, Kennywood added to its claim as the "Roller Coaster Capital of the World." In addition to its three classic wooden roller coasters, the park now had one of the top steel roller coasters in the world. What made the Steel Phantom extraordinary was that like the legendary Thunderbolt, the steel coaster fully used Kennywood's unique terrain and location.

The park's new $4.5 million coaster offered the usual thrills and excitement of the other top ten steel coasters, and then added an ingredient that no other park could match - its setting of rugged cliffs and valleys. The Steel Phantom dropped 28 passengers at a time over a bluff into a ravine where they streaked through the Thunderbolt's structure toward the Monongahela River at 80 mph and then brought them all back alive, turning them upside down four times and finishing with a fast return to the loading station.

Kennywood chose to build a steel coaster for two reasons; it already had three exceptional wooden roller coasters, and second, the park wanted to do some things it could only do with a steel structure. Using steel permitted the park to construct a coaster that went much higher and then much lower than any wood coaster. It also permitted the use of more critical angles that enabled Kennywood to better utilize the space available.

The Steel Phantom offered much more than the Laser Loop. The new coaster was higher and longer and had more loops and much bigger drops. With two trains, it could carry many more passengers per hour at much higher speeds. The maintenance department was happy because the new coaster was more reliable than the Laser Loop since it used a simple chain lift and gravity.

The Steel Phantom was what Kennywood needed to compete with major theme parks like Cedar Point, Kings Dominion, The Old Country, and Kings Island that had developed and exploited bigger and faster steel looping coasters in the 1980's. Most of these steel coasters were merely a series of elements (drops, loops, corkscrews, etc.) strung together so it was hard to tell one from another. The Steel Phantom was indisputably unique.

The Steel Phantom's spectacular first drop.
(PHOTOGRAPH BY CHARLES J. JACQUES, JR.)

(Above)
A huge crane was needed to build the Steel Phantom.
(Photograph by Charles J. Jacques, Jr.)

The Steel Phantom under construction.
(Photograph by Charles J. Jacques, Jr.)

Although the new coaster was much larger than the compact Laser Loop, Harry W. Henninger, Jr, as if by some feat of magic, was able to fit The Steel Phantom into the limited space available. Nothing had to be removed except the Laser Loop and a few holes from the park's miniature golf course. Henninger often had to do more manipulating when bringing in a smaller ride. However, using the valley behind the Thunderbolt necessitated moving 12,000 cubic yards of dirt and required drilling hundreds of extra test holes down along the face of the bluff before footers could be constructed. Henninger somehow built a huge coaster

A hill on the new coaster takes shape.
(PHOTOGRAPH BY CHARLES J. JACQUES, JR.)

A train climbs the hill leading to the ravine drop.
(PHOTOGRAPH BY CHARLES J. JACQUES, JR.)

with drops of 155 feet and 225 feet and 3,000 feet of track without ruining Kennywood's delightful family-park feeling. Although the Steel Phantom's first and second hills were imposing, thereby giving the park a new skyline, the rest of the coaster seemed to blend in inconspicuously. The Steel Phantom quickly became the park's dominant signature ride.

Henninger admitted that removing the Laser Loop was a difficult decision for him. It was his own favorite ride, as well as that of his twelve-year-old son, Bradley. "My son was ready to kill me when we made the decision to take it out," he admitted, "I will miss the 0 to 54 miles per hour in three seconds acceleration of the aircraft-carrier-like start. It [the Laser Loop] filled a need when it was installed. Now the technology has advanced to the state where we can do new things."

With delight, Henninger described how and why the Steel Phantom was developed:

> The Laser Loop's appeal was never as broad as I had originally envisaged. The reason, I believe, is that the launch of the shuttle loop, the visual impact, was so startling that many people shied away from it. People

Waiting in line for the Phantom.
(PHOTOGRAPH BY CHARLES J. JACQUES, JR.)

The boomerang loop.
(PHOTOGRAPH BY CHARLES J. JACQUES, JR.)

132

The Steel Phantom's first drop starts high above Kennywood Boulevard.
(PHOTOGRAPH BY CHARLES J. JACQUES, JR.)

who would ride the Thunderbolt, with its hidden dips, would not go on the Laser Loop, even though the Thunderbolt was a much more exhilarating, vigorous ride. That taught me a lesson. One of the things that we tried to do with the Steel Phantom is hide everything. We've got a lot hidden. [So much was hidden that a sign had to be added at the entrance warning visitors the Phantom was a physically-demanding ride.]

Everybody that comes into the park sees the first drop - it's right off Kennywood Boulevard. It is extremely dramatic to watch, but that's only 155 feet. Just a few years ago if you said a coaster was 155 feet high people would have thought you were crazy. Now it's only 155 feet, on a curve at a 60-degree bank. I mean, have we lost our minds or what?

That's only the appetizer; the greatest thrill, the main course, occurs after you get to the bottom of that 155-foot drop. When you come off the first drop, you shoot along at ground level, about 150 feet at very high speed, then go back 115 feet in the air. This is needed to reduce the velocity to a very realistic set-up speed for what follows. We set up the turn of about 26 degrees leading to the big drop. You go down straight as an arrow. About three-quarters of the way down we start to twist the train through the Thunderbolt structure, setting up for this high speed turn of 180 degrees. You're doing 80 miles an hour on a 63-degree bank six inches off the ground the whole way around the 180-degree turn. There's nothing like it in the world.

A loop is the first element after coming out of the ravine.
(PHOTOGRAPH BY CHARLES J. JACQUES, JR.)

Henninger knew that the park was not large enough to afford to make any mistakes in building the new multi-million-dollar coaster. "Kennywood always has to be more astute with its picks than the large theme parks. We can't afford to make a mistake," he explained. It would have been safer to build this megacoaster on level ground in case it had to be moved or sold, but the Steel Phantom is so much better because it was designed for use in only one place on earth - Kennywood.

"If you know a little bit about roller coasters, you can do a center line [layout] and basic profile," Henninger said. He wanted to use the ravine, and he also thought about having the Steel Phantom cut through the Thunderbolt in the ravine. Henninger found that a 47-degree straight line would go down through the Thunderbolt, and then he worked backwards to lay out the rest of the coaster. It was a great layout for a fantastic coaster, but it was extremely hard to build. The Steel Phantom required 160 footers, some requiring 6,000 pounds of reinforced steel and 35 cubic yards of concrete.

Henninger spent many months mentally designing the new coaster; then he rode coasters in the Sun Belt parks.

The souvenir shop for the Steel Phantom.
(Photograph by Charles J. Jacques, Jr.)

Finally, he spent what little precious time off he had during the summer traveling to northern parks. The idea for the Phantom's first hill came from a section of the Shockwave Coaster at Six Flags Great America near Chicago. "It has this tremendous flying turn, the first turn, and first drop and I thought that was exhilarating. I just went 'holy smoke,'" Henninger said. "The first element I loved was the sweeping first drop." Previously most steel coasters had tried to mimic wood coasters, but they could not do it. They had to find their own personalities, and Henninger thought that by the early 1990's "steel coasters had finally come into their own."

"Five years ago," Henninger said, "if you had said roller coasters are going to go over a 200-foot drop, I would have said no, our technology hasn't reached that." Now incredible 200-foot drops are possible. The Phantom's second hill, amazing in height and speed, is similar to the Thunderbolt's legendary last hill with both coasters' deepest drops sharing the same ravine. Henninger added a loop to replace the one lost with the dismantling of the Laser Loop, plus a boomerang (two upside-down turning loops) and half a corkscrew. The Steel Phantom retained a rapid entry into the station, again bor-

In the boomerang curve.
(Photograph by Charles J. Jacques, Jr.)

Expectant riders on the Phantom's lift hill.
(Photograph by Charles J. Jacques, Jr.)

The Steel Phantom cuts through the Thunderbolt.
(Kennywood)

Free circus acts continue into the 1990's.
(PHOTOGRAPH BY CHARLES J. JACQUES, JR.)

Under the Phantom is Shorty's Miniature Golf Course.
(PHOTOGRAPH BY CHARLES J. JACQUES, JR.)

rowed from the Laser Loop.

Ron Toomer, president of Arrow Dynamics Inc., worked with Harry Henninger, Jr. on the final design. Toomer, a mechanical engineer, drew the plans for the Steel Phantom, and then turned them over to engineers who used computers to work out the mathematics that determined the exact angles of the track. The Phantom then was fabricated by Arrow Dynamics in Utah and shipped in sections to the park. The Phantom, unlike the Laser Loop, is a true roller coaster - propelled by gravity and carried along by momentum, not motors. The cars are pulled up the first lift by a chain and propelled by gravity the rest of the way. The placement of features like loops and lifts helps control the speed and pacing.

Corkscrew and boomerang turns are usually found near the end of a ride when a lot of energy has already been expended because the cars must slow down to about 40 miles per hour as they enter these turns. Engineers try not to subject riders to more than three and one-half times the force of gravity because some people might pass out or feel uncomfortable. After the Steel Phantom was opened, computer analyses showed the coaster was going "just too fast." Toomer was brought back in to slow it down. The ride was completing its 3,000-foot run in one minute forty seconds - five seconds faster than it should. Brakes were mounted on the track where the Phantom entered the boomerang, loop, and corkscrew area to slow it down.

When asked what F. W. Henninger might think about the Steel Phantom, Henninger replied that his grandfather would be just as proud of the Phantom as he was of the first coaster he helped build, the Speed-O-Plane, which went 20 miles per hour in the dips, but 20 miles an hour was "pretty darn exciting" for 1910. "Today, technology allows us to do what they couldn't do 80 years ago," Henninger commented.

Henninger took a chance, again

Eating at the Potato Patch.
(PHOTOGRAPH BY CHARLES J. JACQUES, JR.)

Harry W. Henninger, Jr. helped design the Steel Phantom.
(PHOTOGRAPH BY CHARLES J. JACQUES, JR.)

risking one of the park's prime attractions, the Thunderbolt. This was the second time that Henninger modified the Thunderbolt to build something new. (The first time was when he built the final ascent of The Raging Rapids under the Thunderbolt's structure.) Cutting through the Thunderbolt added an important element to the Phantom and made the Thunderbolt even more exciting.

Construction supervision for the Steel Phantom fell on the shoulders of Rich Henry, the park's operations supervisor. Known fondly as "Richie Rabbit" because his first job at the park was working on the Jack Rabbit, Henry later became its manager for a few seasons. Henry's job was made even more difficult when Harry W. Henninger, Jr. suffered a heart attack in October 1990. The two of them had worked as a team lining up the project, which was now well underway. Henry had to go the rest of the way alone. Henry and John Lane, the field engineer from Arrow Dynamics who had been on the job for months as the manufacturer's trouble shooter, took the first ride in the front seat of the new coaster. Their reaction was "Wow!"

The name Steel Phantom was chosen by employees of the park. In a contest for a name for the new coaster, it easily won by a margin of three to one over the next closest challenger. The name was not chosen to pay homage to the steel industry as most current Kennywood employees could not remember when steel mills dotted the Monongahela River Valley.

American Coaster Enthusiasts enjoy the new coaster

American Coaster Enthusiasts (ACE) held their annual convention (Coaster Con 14) at Kennywood from June 16 to 20, 1991. Nearly 800 people, some from as far away as California, Washington, and Hawaii, visited the park to try the new coaster. It was the third visit to the park by the coaster group. Randy Geisler, from St. Paul, Minnesota, and a past president of the organization, said, "Kennywood is regarded as one of the finest places on earth for coasters. The Thunderbolt has long been considered one of the top ten coasters in the country, and there's the Steel Phantom, The Racer, The Jack Rabbit, and 40 other rides that make the park worthwhile." Geisler observed that "coasters provide an inexpensive, two-minute adventure that combines the sensations of sky diving, bronco busting, and bobsledding." ACE members immediately noticed that the tunnel had been removed from the Thunderbolt, while a tunnel was put back on the Jack Rabbit. (Originally the Jack Rabbit had a tunnel.) The tunnel was removed from the Thunderbolt to give people more opportunity to watch the Steel Phantom plunging down through the Thunderbolt's structure.

The Great Balloon Race.
(PHOTOGRAPH BY CHARLES J. JACQUES, JR.)

Selling fudge in the double-decker refreshment building.
(PHOTOGRAPH BY CHARLES J. JACQUES, JR.)

The Tri-Star.
(PHOTOGRAPH BY CHARLES J. JACQUES, JR.)

The Phantom's first drop.
(PHOTOGRAPH BY CHARLES J. JACQUES, JR.)

1992 Kennywood may be closed, but it is far from dead

The off season sometimes seems as busy as the regular season to Fred Weber, who heads the park's maintenance staff. Weber works from an office in the park's maintenance building, which is located behind the Racer. His staff consists of ten carpenters and 15 mechanics. Kennywood's maintenance crew handles a wider range of equipment than the normal manufacturing plant. Weber, who started with the park in 1955, feels that working at Kennywood helps keep him young. "These young people really keep you going. It's a blessing in disguise," he says.

During the winter, the refreshment operation run by Bill Henninger drops back to three full-time employees. His staff is responsible for all of the food and other supplies like paper products and batteries used in the park. According to Henninger, "The amusement park business is constantly changing, and it is important to keep an eye on new trends." If Henninger is thinking about introducing a new food line, he often tests the idea out first on his wife, Barbara. "If she does not like it, then chances are, it will not be successful," said Henninger. In 1992, he remodeled the old Fountain Stand (named after a soda fountain that was there for many years) into a food court. Called Carousel Court, the new food operation was housed in the park's first Merry-Go-Round Building.

In 1992, Kennywood added the Tri-Star, a ride manufactured by Huss Trading Company of Germany. It was placed near the entrance to the Steel Phantom. The ride had three arms with seven cars attached to each. All of the arms rotated simultaneously to create a complete whirlwind effect. The ride did not prove to be very popular because of its isolated location and was removed after only one season.

Walkway leading to the park's entrance tunnel.
(PHOTOGRAPH BY CHARLES J. JACQUES, JR.)

Ken Garrett's favorite game.
(PHOTOGRAPH BY CHARLES J. JACQUES, JR.)

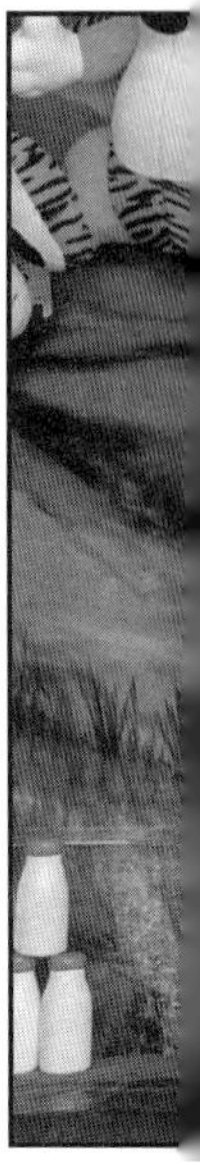

Games Manager Ken Garrett.
(PHOTOGRAPH BY CHARLES J. JACQUES, JR.)

A major change took place in 1992 when all parking was moved across Kennywood Boulevard from the park. This was done for safety reasons and to make more land available for future development. Over the years Kennywood had received some complaints about letting people, especially those with young children, cross the busy highway. The park moved thousands of yards of earth to create a new tiered parking area. An escalator (or People Mover as it was called) was added to help people get to the second level. Total parking spaces were increased by 1,000, which management at first thought would be enough but soon proved to be inadequate. The former pay parking lot of four and one-half acres was earmarked for future expansion of rides, games, and amusements.

Kennywood now had only one entrance: through a new landscaped entrance plaza, down into a tunnel under Kennywood Boulevard, and into the park. The tunnel was originally built for the convenience of trolley passengers, who had to cross the trolley lines and the road at the turn-of-the-century. Over the years the tunnel had been lengthened and modernized. All visitors now had to enter through turnstiles located across the highway from the park. The Group Sales office was moved across the road into a new building designed to look like an old inter-urban railway station. The old-fashioned-looking building, which included Guests Relations, in addition to the sales office, featured a clock tower, shingle and brick exterior, glass block windows, and a roof with patterns made from different colored shingles. For added security at night, metal sliding doors could be pulled down over the doors into the building.

The Guest Services Building.
(PHOTOGRAPH BY CHARLES J. JACQUES, JR.)

The People Mover.
(PHOTOGRAPH BY CHARLES J. JACQUES, JR.)

Scene on the miniature railroad depicting the Homestead steel strike.
(PHOTOGRAPH BY CHARLES J. JACQUES, JR.)

1993 Heading off gang-related violence

In an effort to head off any gang-related violence, Kennywood officials reluctantly begin using metal detectors in 1993. The park also banned shirts bearing vulgar or suggestive slogans. "We have a reputation as a place for clean family fun, and we wanted to prevent any problems before they happened," community affairs director Andy Quinn said. "People don't need to be subjected to that kind of stuff on a fun day with their families." Quinn said the park officials were spurred by reports of gang-related clashes at other urban amusement parks around the country.

The Enterprise was removed for a year and replaced by the Wipeout, which simulated the motion of the ocean. Each car held four people who sat face to face as the ride dipped up and down and side to side. The Wipeout, designed and built by Chance Rides of Wichita, Kansas, was done in hot pinks and covered with lights.

The hillbillies that populated the end of the train ride for 11 years were replaced with scenes depicting Pittsburgh history. Mary Ann Spanagel of Indiana, Pennsylvania, who had made floats for Kennywood's Fall Fantasy for 27 seasons,

Enjoying the Kiddie Whip.
(PHOTOGRAPH BY CHARLES J. JACQUES, JR.)

Kiddie Cadillacs.
(PHOTOGRAPH BY CHARLES J. JACQUES, JR.)

TV crew films Mary Ann Spanagel in front of her representations of ethnic pride.
(Mary Ann Spanagel collection)

Joe Magarac being transported to the park.
(Mary Ann Spanagel collection)

Joe Magarac.
(Photograph by Charles J. Jacques, Jr.)

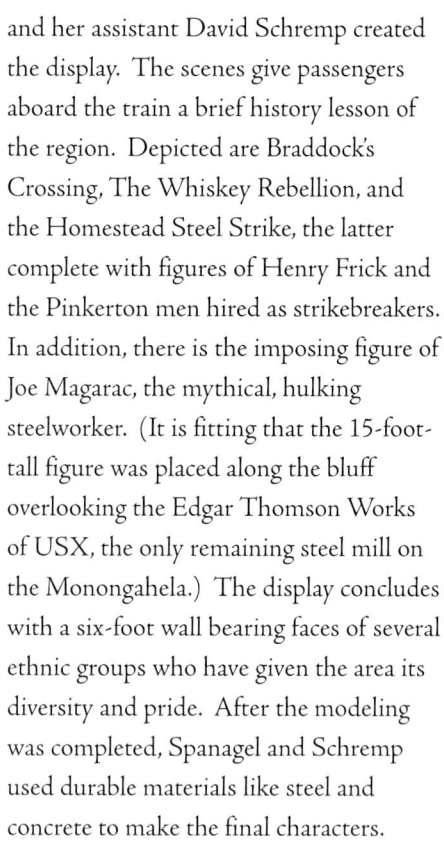

and her assistant David Schremp created the display. The scenes give passengers aboard the train a brief history lesson of the region. Depicted are Braddock's Crossing, The Whiskey Rebellion, and the Homestead Steel Strike, the latter complete with figures of Henry Frick and the Pinkerton men hired as strikebreakers. In addition, there is the imposing figure of Joe Magarac, the mythical, hulking steelworker. (It is fitting that the 15-foot-tall figure was placed along the bluff overlooking the Edgar Thomson Works of USX, the only remaining steel mill on the Monongahela.) The display concludes with a six-foot wall bearing faces of several ethnic groups who have given the area its diversity and pride. After the modeling was completed, Spanagel and Schremp used durable materials like steel and concrete to make the final characters.

The Patio Restaurant, which was called the Casino in 1898, was refurbished and renamed the Parkside Terrace. The building, dating from the park's opening, was repainted. Inside the restaurant, with its exposed wooden beams and a tin ceiling, the sandwich and salad section was expanded. New, brightly-colored striped awnings, tables and chairs, and brickwork were added to the enlarged patio. The refreshment stand across from

Guessing your weight is a popular tradition.
(PHOTOGRAPH BY CHARLES J. JACQUES, JR.)

Games are big money-makers for the park.
(PHOTOGRAPH BY CHARLES J. JACQUES, JR.)

Cool monkeys.
(PHOTOGRAPH BY CHARLES J. JACQUES, JR.)

Toy soldiers guard Kiddieland.
(PHOTOGRAPH BY CHARLES J. JACQUES, JR.)

Paddle-boating on the Lagoon.
(PHOTOGRAPH BY CHARLES J. JACQUES, JR.)

An Amish family attends the Grand Victorian Festival.
(PHOTOGRAPH BY CHARLES J. JACQUES, JR.)

the Jack Rabbit was given a new look. Bill Henninger's refreshment operation introduced a drink named Kenny's Koolers, a fruit punch drink, named for the park's mascot.

The park finally gave up trying to establish a new entrance to Kiddieland. A calendar, which spelled out the day in flowers, had been placed in the middle of the old Kiddieland entrance, but people would not accept that this entrance was no longer open. Adults continued to squeeze around the calendar with their children because they knew that it was the entrance when they were children. Once the calendar was removed, old style building blocks and toy soldiers were added to give it the original look.

1994 *Flying the Skycoaster*

In 1994, The Skycoaster debuted at Kennywood. While many additions to the park took years of planning, this one did not. Harry Henninger, Jr., president of the park, decided to buy the ride in November, and it was installed in Kennywood the following May. Henninger became intrigued with the ride after seeing photographs of it at the International Association of Amusement Parks and Attractions (IAAPA) trade show. The company that built the ride, Sky Fun 1 Inc. of Boulder, Colorado, had not been able to place one in any amusement park yet, but the ride was in several tourist locations. Henninger and Jim Bouy, who was then Kennywood's general manager, went to Ft. Lauderdale where there was one operating "to fly it," as the manufacturer described the experience. Several other staff members, Rich Henry, Jeff Checcio, and Mark Gallagher, were sent to test the new attraction, and everyone raved about it. Although it was not Kennywood's practice to buy prototypes, the purchase was made. Carl Hughes had one stipulation, "we [Kennywood] would not advertise it because the ride could not be included in the one-price admission." (Prices were $24.95 for a single flyer; $19.95 each for two; $14.95 each for three.) Hughes' concern was the prices would be perceived as outrageous - something Kennywood had always avoided. "How wrong can you be," Hughes commented. "It was an immediate hit."

Kennywood needed a new ride to help offset the publicity of new coasters being added at neighboring parks. The original intent was to buy the ride, operate it at Kennywood Park for one or two seasons, and then transfer it to Sandcastle, but the $300,000 attraction proved to be so popular it became a permanent addition to Kennywood's skyline.

Again, as with all major additions to the park, the question was where to put it. In a stroke of genius (well, perhaps not genius, but good luck since the ride was not going to be "permanent,") Harry Henninger decided to showcase the ride by putting it in the very heart of the park where people would fly over the stage and Lagoon. It was a spectacular location with only one drawback; the park lost the use of the Island Stage, but it gained a great

The 180-foot Skycoaster.
(Photograph by Charles J. Jacques, Jr.)

Released from the launch tower.
(Photograph by Charles J. Jacques, Jr.)

Flying.
(Photograph by Charles J. Jacques, Jr.)

attraction. Putting the 180-foot Skycoaster in place was not an easy task because it required a 450-ton crane to erect the three steel towers that were arranged in an A-frame pattern.

"Think of it as a big, VERY BIG, yard swing. Riders swing back and forth in a pendulum motion," Rex Rutkoski of the *North Hills News Record* commented. The adventurous donned full-body flight harnesses at a loading platform on the Lagoon stage. They were then pulled aloft to a launch tower 180 feet above the ground, where by pulling a rip cord, fliers fell face down from the launch tower and swung along an arc-shaped trajectory across the Lagoon at speeds approaching 60 miles per hour. They plunge to within nine feet of the Lagoon stage floor at the end of two stainless-steel cables, each capable of supporting 9,000 pounds, before climbing skyward toward the Racer roller coaster. The Flyers swooped back and forth several times before they were lassoed in and pulled to a stop by the ride's operators.

Perhaps Peter Passell best described the ride in the July 23, 1995, issue of *The New York Times Magazine*:

> The view of the western Pennsylvania hills and rusting mills lining the Monongahela River could hardly be better. But the perch leaves some thing to be desired. I'm dangling from a steel cable, 200 feet above the pavement.
>
> The idea of the Skycoaster, the hottest ride at Kennywood, just east of Pittsburgh, is to simulate bungee jumping. And I've just remembered that bungee jumping was pretty far down my to-do list, just behind swimming the Bosporus.
>
> But it's too late to back out now. On the count of three, I pull the rip cord

Souvenir shop window.
(PHOTOGRAPH BY CHARLES J. JACQUES, JR.)

The Skycoaster is often sold out.
(PHOTOGRAPH BY CHARLES J. JACQUES, JR.)

and plummet toward the crowd below. Fractions of a second before a hard landing, the cable miraculously wins the battle with gravity, hurling me in an arc like the weight on a great pendulum. Brain-numbing fear instantly gives way to euphoria: I'm flying!

Skycoaster was the closet thing yet to actual skydiving, and according to Carl Hughes, "the publicity was fantastic for the new ride." Major events that first season included a wedding on Skycoaster, and a great-grandmother, Catherine Kudley, flying with two of her grandchildren. The park was taken completely by surprise at the positive reaction the ride generated. Not only was it a great ride, but it was the type of ride that people who rode it could brag about to their friends. And it was also a terrific spectator ride. The Skycoaster provided a free thrill show every ten minutes - all day long.

Unfortunately, the new attraction could handle only six flights per hour. It had not occurred to Kennywood's staff that capacity would be a problem, presuming that the price would keep riders low. But the cashier booth was swamped immediately with even a queue-line to the cashier needed. Reservations

The 85-foot Wonder Wheel's gondolas can hold six passengers.
(PHOTOGRAPHS BY CHARLES J. JACQUES, JR.)

became necessary, on a first come - first serve basis. Flight times were assigned with the ticket sale, and usually a couple hours after the gates opened the Skycoaster was sold out for the day - right up to 11 p.m. closing.

A canceled flight!

Because of rain, Peter McAneny, a vice president and general manager of the park, closed the park one night before all the reservations could be fulfilled. Refunds, as always, were made. But one lady vehemently complained to McAneny that she did not want a refund but a ride. She had come a long way to ride. And since airlines paid motel bills when flights were canceled, she felt she should get a free motel room. She received a refund.

Kennywood shuffled many of its other rides in 1994. The Bayern Kurve bobsled returned after a long absence. The Enterprise also returned to a spot behind the park office and displaced the Wipeout, which was moved to the site formerly occupied by the Wave Swinger. The Wave Swinger was removed from the park for one year so it could be renovated and then returned as one of the rides in Lost Kennywood. The Fountain site at the entrance to Raging Rapids was remodeled.

Eating a corn dog.
(PHOTOGRAPH BY
CHARLES J. JACQUES, JR.)

Uncle Sam greets visitors at the Grand Victorian Festival.
(PHOTOGRAPH BY
CHARLES J. JACQUES, JR.)

High school teacher Ed Henke supervises Physics Day.
(PHOTOGRAPH BY
CHARLES J. JACQUES, JR.)

Joe, the lovable old cowboy statue, returned to a park bench in that area.

Kennywood held its first Physics Day in the park in 1988. Nineteen hundred students from 36 area high schools participated by taking a field trip to the park. The day was planned by Ed Henke, a physics teacher from the Pittsburgh School District. By 1994, the event drew more than 9,000 students from 180 high schools in the tri-state area.

Kennywood's first annual Grand Victorian Festival was held in 1994. The event attracted thirty-three booths with artisans from seven different states. The booths in a "Marketplace" were set up around the Lagoon. Throughout the week, visitors viewed turn-of-the-century entertainment, including early circus acts, jugglers, magicians, spoofs, and skits.

UNLEASH YOUR MIND!
PHYSICS
ARCHITECTURE
COMMUNICATION

LET IT RUN WILD AT THE BIGGEST EDUCATIONAL EVENT OF THE YEAR!

POP QUIZ: PHYSICS 101
How high does the end of Noah's Ark rise above its level position?

DID YOU KNOW?
Noah's Ark, perhaps the most famous symbol of Kennywood, celebrates its 60th birthday in 1996. Ironically, construction of the Ark was delayed by the legendary St. Patrick's Day Flood of 1936 that saw Pittsburgh's rivers crest at 46 feet before receding. There are two other Arks in existence, both in the UK: one at Frontierland, the other at Blackpool Pleasure Beach on the Irish Sea. All three Arks are being refurbished this year.

Publicity Director Mary Lou Rosemeyer.
(Photograph by Charles J. Jacques, Jr.)

The Popcorn Wagon.
(Photograph by Charles J. Jacques, Jr.)

Fun on the Kiddie Swing.
(Photograph by Charles J. Jacques, Jr.)

In his article, "The Business of Kennywood," published in 1994, Joe Compagni compared Kennywood to "a local restaurant with everything on the menu from pancakes to lobster - something for everyone, and the kind of place you might bring an out-of-town guest. On one hand it's a thrill ride park...[and on the other hand] America's finest traditional amusement park, a community park where generations of families have come to picnic, relax and see their neighbors."

"We're different from the major theme parks," Quinn, community affairs director, told Compagni. "Most of our business is based on group sales. School groups, churches, businesses, ethnic groups and community groups make up 65 percent of Kennywood's business each year." Quinn added, "Our biggest single day is Italian Day [in July], when we'll have about 21,000 people."

After thirty years as public relations director, Ann Hughes, wife of Carl O. Hughes, retired. Her daughter, Mary Lou Rosemeyer, who had worked for the park for seven years, was named to fill the position. Rosemeyer was the third member of her family to hold the job, following in the footsteps of her parents, Ann and Carl Hughes. Rosemeyer commented on the park, "It's simply the best of the old and the new. I think we continue to be successful because we give people what they want. We hear their suggestions and try to accommodate them."

Kennywood Park received another prestigious award in 1994, the National Preservation Honor Award from the National Trust for Historic Preservation. The award recognizes exceptional

The Gift Shop was Kennywood's first walk-in souvenir stand.
(PHOTOGRAPH BY CHARLES J. JACQUES, JR.)

Aerial view of the Lagoon area.
(PHOTOGRAPH BY CHARLES J. JACQUES, JR.)

accomplishment in preservation, rehabilitation, and interpretation of our architectural and cultural heritage. Unlike most previous award-winners, Kennywood had the rare distinction of being commended for not having to undertake a massive rescue effort. Also the National Amusement Park Historical Association, a group made up of persons interested in preserving and documenting the history of amusement parks, presented its Life Membership Award to park officials. Marlowe McClasky Futrell, NAPHA public relations coordinator, lauded Kennywood for maintaining and preserving its collection of historic rides. Members of the organization also voted Kennywood their favorite traditional amusement park for the eighth consecutive year.

CHAPTER 10

1995 Lost Kennywood

Stepping back in time

On May 25, 1905, Luna Park, a giant new "electric park," opened in the Oakland section of Pittsburgh (or as it was spelled then Pittsburg) at the intersection of Baum Boulevard and Craig Street. The amusement park, built by Frederick Ingersoll, featured a beautiful entrance gate topped by a crescent image of the moon, ornate buildings, a central lagoon, and at the far end of the basin, a giant Shoot the Chutes. The "Chutes" was a water ride where boats were pulled to the top of a tower and then released to splash down into a lagoon. At night, all of the structures were illuminated with electric lights. Here is how the *Pittsburgh Index* described it in June 1905:

> The park at night presents a truly dazzling appearance, illuminated with 38,000 incandescent lights, 120 arc lights, and a powerful, search light mounted on the Chutes Tower, and the illumination can be seen for miles around.
>
> The grounds are well arranged and have wide promenades in front of all the buildings, making a sort of circular pike upon which all

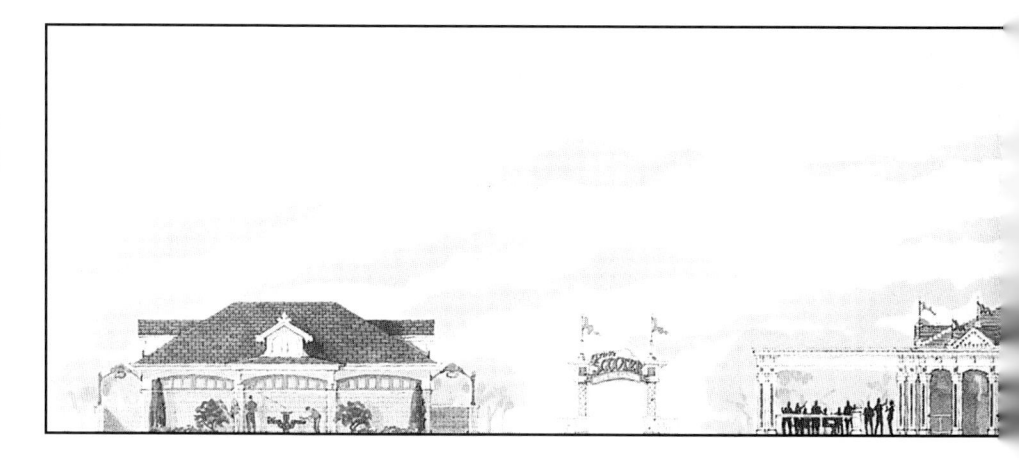

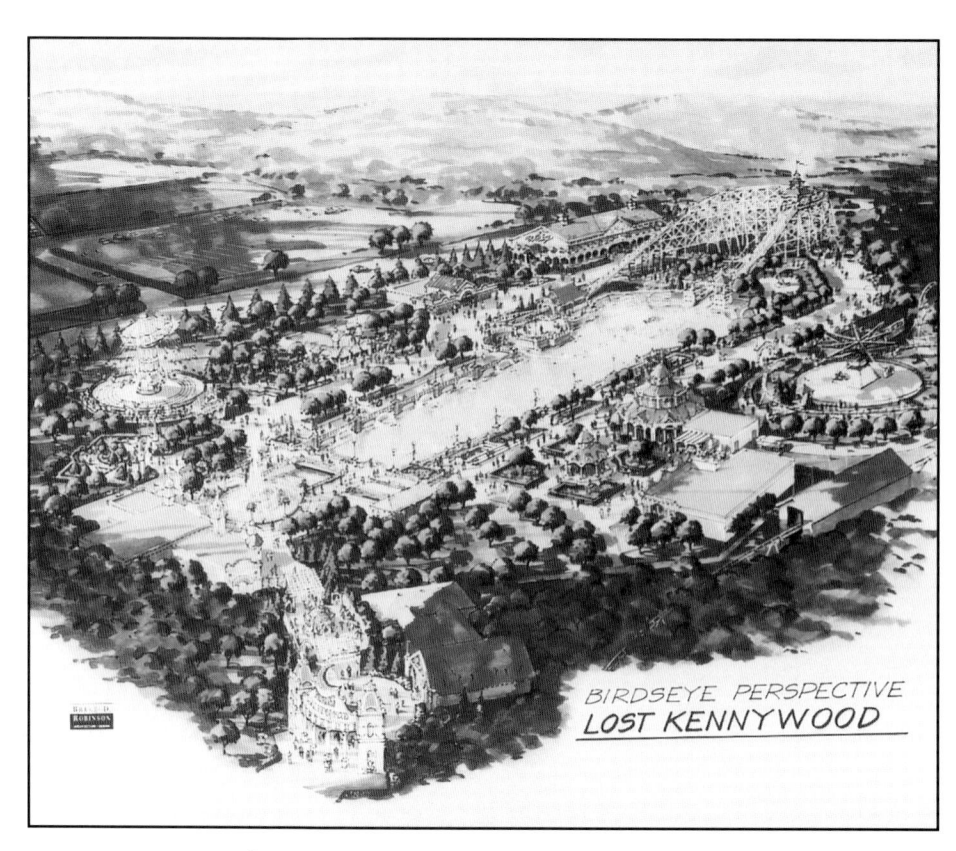

BIRDSEYE PERSPECTIVE LOST KENNYWOOD

A refreshment stand that resembles West View Park's Carousel Pavilion was built in Lost Kennywood.
(Photograph by Charles J. Jacques, Jr.)

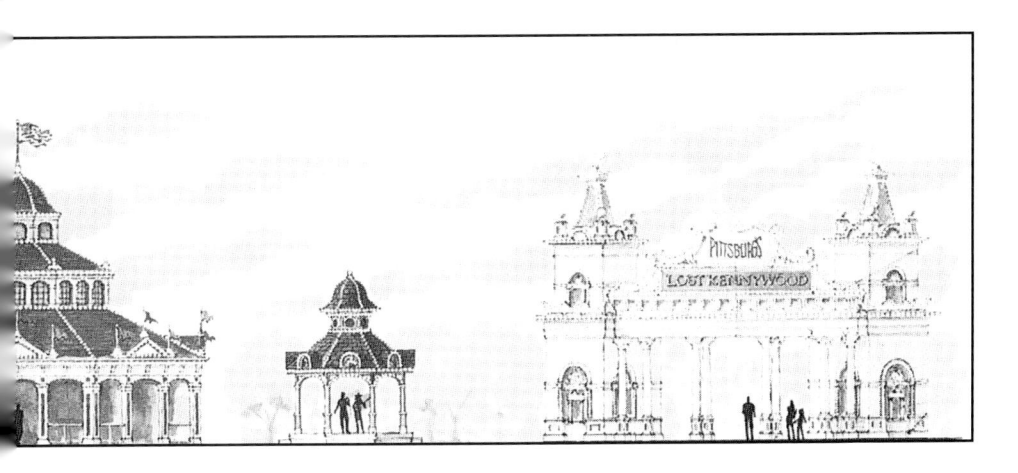

The Steel Phantom is adjacent to and overlooks Lost Kennywood.
(Photograph by Charles J. Jacques, Jr.)

amusements front, with the beautiful lagoon as the central figure. Comfortable benches for resting are placed throughout the park. The beautiful arch entrance has been the admiration of thousands and will continue to be throughout the season. It is surmounted by a crescent and flanked by tall towers bearing gilded globes. The whole is a mass of incandescent lights and presents a gorgeous appearance at night.

The Pittsburgh Railways Company, which owned Kennywood, looked with mixed emotion on the new park, since its opening meant more business for its street cars, but at the same time the competition hurt its own parks - Kennywood, Southern, and Calhoun. Day after day stories appeared in all the Pittsburg newspapers about Luna Park's grand opening. The *Pittsburg Bulletin* reported there was nothing of the fake or catchpenny about the new park. Kennywood employees were afraid this new park might put them out of a job. They wished Kennywood had more electric lights, a spectacular entrance, and most of all, a Shoot the Chutes.

The following season (1906), the

MEMORIES by Design!

Lost Kennywood was designed by Bruce D. Robinson.
(Bruce D. Robinson Architecture-Design, Inc.)

Pittsburgh Railways Company leased Kennywood to Andrew S. McSwigan and Frederick W. Henninger. McSwigan and Henninger fought the big new urban Luna Park by adding new attractions and offering the best concert bands and vaudeville acts available, but the employees of Kennywood would have to wait until 1995 (90 years later) until the Henninger and McSwigan families would spend nearly seven million dollars developing a new theme section called Lost Kennywood whose primary attraction was a Shoot the Chutes.

There is an old saying "if you wait long enough nearly everything will come back into fashion," and the Shoot the Chutes is proof of that saying. At the turn of the century the Chutes were the most thrilling rides an amusement park could offer. When the most exciting figure-eight coasters or scenic railways were only 30 feet high with dips of ten feet, sliding down a 200 foot ramp from a height of 50 feet and splashing into a lagoon was much more exciting. However, within a few years, much higher and faster roller coasters were built, and the Chutes, which cost a lot to maintain, were removed and all but disappeared. With the increased interest in water rides in the late 1980's, a new version of the old shoot-the-chutes ride with high-speed water pumps, fiberglass boats, and computer controls, was developed. However, while a turn-of-the-century Chutes would not get its passengers wet, the new Chutes were specifically designed to throw water. The earlier version was controlled by a boatman with an oar who directed the boat, which would merely bounce on the surface of the water like a skipping rock. He would then direct the boat over to the side of the lagoon. The 1990's version was computer-controlled with each boat climbing a lift hill and then being held in a controlled channel during the splash and the return to the loading pavilion.

The souvenir and games building under construction.
(Photograph by Charles J. Jacques, Jr.)

Andy Quinn, the director of community relations, in the Guest Services Office.
(Photograph by Charles J. Jacques, Jr.)

Bruce D. Robinson with a model of Lost Kennywood.
(Photograph by Charles J. Jacques, Jr.)

The new Whip Building under construction in Lost Kennywood.
(Photograph by Charles J. Jacques, Jr.)

The Pittsburg Plunge and fountain under construction.
(Photograph by Charles J. Jacques, Jr.)

The "lost" electric park

In the early years of the century, there were two distinct types of amusement parks. One, the trolley or resort park, was located in the countryside at the end of a train, trolley, or steamship line. These parks developed slowly. Their owners did not have a master plan but would add rides, food stands, dance pavilions, and other attractions in a random manner when they could afford them.

The second type, the urban "electric park," copied the Columbian Exposition of 1893 and other world's fairs of that era. This architectural style featured elaborate buildings, usually painted white, constructed around a reflecting lagoon that provided the basin for a shoot-the-chutes ride. Electric parks got their name from the use of thousands of electric light bulbs used to showcase the buildings and rides at night. These parks were planned by architects and engineers who designed elaborate buildings and grand vistas. They were laid out and built all at once in cities. Once built, these parks tended to change less than the trolley and resort parks.

Frederick Ingersoll, a native Pittsburgher and a great pioneer in the amusement park business, not only built Luna Park in Pittsburg, but along with his brothers, built a number of other electric parks around the country - including Luna Park in Cleveland and Electric Park in Kansas City. Ingersoll designed Pittsburg's Luna Park around a large reflecting pool surrounded by a group of buildings with decorative fronts and towers, and a Shoot the Chutes at the far end. Luna Park lasted only five years, closing during the summer of 1909. It was not managed well and was poorly capitalized. However, the biggest reason that it failed was that after its grand opening, people grew tired of the same old rides and attractions the park offered. Commenting on the electric park at a National Association of Amusement Parks, Pools and Beach convention in Chicago in 1958, Brady McSwigan, president of Kennywood, said:

> In the 1900's there was a boom of park building brought on by the expanding use of electricity. Simultaneously at least eight fantastic "Luna Parks" were built, not counting many a "Dream City," "Dreamland," "White City" etc. etc. Those glittering "night parks," while enjoying immense popularity for a brief time, missed the boat for

Sue Fontanese, director of Guest Relations.
(Photograph by Charles J. Jacques, Jr.)

Landscaping Lost Kennywood.
(Photograph by Charles J. Jacques, Jr.)

The Pittsburg Plunge under construction.
(Photograph by Charles J. Jacques, Jr.)

several simple reasons. The Luna parks were all sparse of trees and grass. More important, all outdoor recreational parks cannot survive on transient business alone - promotional activity (primarily picnics) to keep people coming is vital.

While resort and trolley parks were often modest and less elaborate than their electric park "cousins," more of them survived because they expanded and changed over the years. These rustic parks made the most of their trees, gardens, lakes, and green spaces. Most electric parks closed within a few years of their creation. Even the greatest electric parks, Chicago's White City and Coney Island's Luna Park, closed by the 1940's. The electric park in America died out and was lost.

While Luna Park and the other electric parks declined, Kennywood's owners became experts at blending the new with the old, preserving what was important from the past while changing when change was needed. In the good years, more money was spent, and in the bad years, they became masters at seeming to offer something new, even if it was just a new facade on the fun house or a few

The entrance to Lost Kennywood runs under the Steel Phantom.
(Photograph by Charles J. Jacques, Jr.)

Painting the Whip building.
(Photograph by Charles J. Jacques, Jr.)

new stunts for its dark rides.

It seems only fitting that Kennywood, "America's Most Historic Amusement Park," should revive the historic style of the lost electric park. In 1992, Kennywood's board of directors debated what to do with its old pay parking area. It was the last large tract in the park, containing more than five acres. Some wanted to develop it in stages - one or two rides at a time, while others wanted one large development. The board finally decided to have Harry W. Henninger, Jr. president of the park, and Carl O. Hughes, chairman of the board, come up with a master plan for the area, leaving the decision whether to do it all at once or in stages until later.

A park within a park

Hughes and Henninger selected the firm of Bruce D. Robinson Architecture - Design, Inc., an amusement park architect and design firm from Cincinnati, Ohio, to do the master plan. Bruce D. Robinson, the founder of the firm, had worked on a number of other amusement park projects including ones for Kings Island, Kings Dominion, and Dollywood. After preliminary discussions, Hughes, Henninger, and Robinson agreed that one large project was probably best. Slowly the idea of a historic, turn-of-the-century theme area was formulated. Robinson was then given the task of creating the new section, which became Lost Kennywood, but first he studied Kennywood closely and how it developed over the years. Although Robinson had worked for a number of other parks, he knew that there was no place like Kennywood - it wasn't a cookie-cutter park - it was one of a kind. Developing Lost Kennywood required a master plan from the ground up including water, sewage, and electricity for the new area.

Robinson had one very special advantage - he had lived in the Pittsburgh area for a few years and still remembered going to Kennywood for his sixth grade picnic. "There is nothing like a school picnic at Kennywood," Robinson said. "There is no other amusement park in the world that emphasized school picnics to the same extent as Kennywood." Lost Kennywood would be both a historic and educational experience. Hughes and Henninger both liked the historical concept and accepted Robinson's design, but they all agreed the new section should not become a museum. The new section would blend right in with the park's traditional role as a leader in the school picnic business. The final design was produced by Robinson with input from Hughes and Henninger. Robinson pushed Kennywood to spend more money on theming than they had originally intended in order to make his design a reality. Carl Hughes confessed, "In the past we often cut things off because of money concerns, but this time we put in everything that Robinson designed."

"At the time we built Lost Kennywood, I didn't know of any other amusement park that was using a historic theme, but it seemed a natural choice for us," Carl Hughes observed. "Everybody seemed to be going with the futuristic stuff, with the virtual reality type rides," Hughes said. Robinson's Lost Kennywood design was attractive, efficient, and economical. He designed an area that worked and would attract people. It was hoped that the area would appeal to adults as well as teenagers.

Lost Kennywood is really a mini-park within a park. Once a patron crosses through the Luna Park gate, all the elements of a park are found: food, games, souvenirs, rides, and rest room facilities.

"There are an awful lot of people who are nostalgic, and they want something that is from their background," Hughes explained. "It is exciting to see the park expand and change with the times but also acknowledge its past."

Robinson knew that the older sections of Kennywood had a mature looking environment with gardens, trees, and landscaping that were fully developed. Since Lost Kennywood was built in a former parking lot area, it had no trees, no environment. Therefore, Lost Kennywood required elements that would blend with

Lost Kennywood after dark.
(PHOTOGRAPH BY CHARLES J. JACQUES, JR.)

The Wipeout was first placed between Noah's Ark and Le Cachot.
(PHOTOGRAPH BY CHARLES J. JACQUES, JR.)

Games building in Lost Kennywood.
(PHOTOGRAPH BY CHARLES J. JACQUES, JR.)

154

the rest of the park. To keep the new section from seeming too hot when the temperature went up, Robinson designed the area with a large reflecting lagoon and a fountain with mist as a major element. Robinson encouraged Bill Henninger, who supervises the park's landscaping, to use the largest trees possible in the new area.

Construction of Lost Kennywood started in 1993. Rich Henry, Kennywood's operations manager, was named to head the new development. Henry admitted, "Kennywood didn't know whether to try and open Lost Kennywood in 1994 or 1995, but literally a large piece of Kennywood's history made the decision for us." When the excavator started to prepare the ground for the reflection pool, he discovered huge hunks of concrete and reinforced steel bars left over from the bottom and foundation of the park's old Swimming Pool. It seems that when the Pool was closed in 1973, bulldozers merely covered the Pool over with dirt. "It was a job breaking it up, and that decided that it [Lost Kennywood] would open in 1995," Henry said.

Lost Kennywood incorporates many of the elements of the electric park style. It has a spectacular entrance gate that is styled after Pittsburg's Luna Park portal, which quickly became a landmark and a central meeting place for people going in or coming out of the new themed area. Although buildings in the original Luna Park were painted white, Kennywood decided to paint its themed buildings turquoise, pink, light purple, and cream. However, Lost Kennywood's buildings, just like the original electric park's structures, are outlined with electric

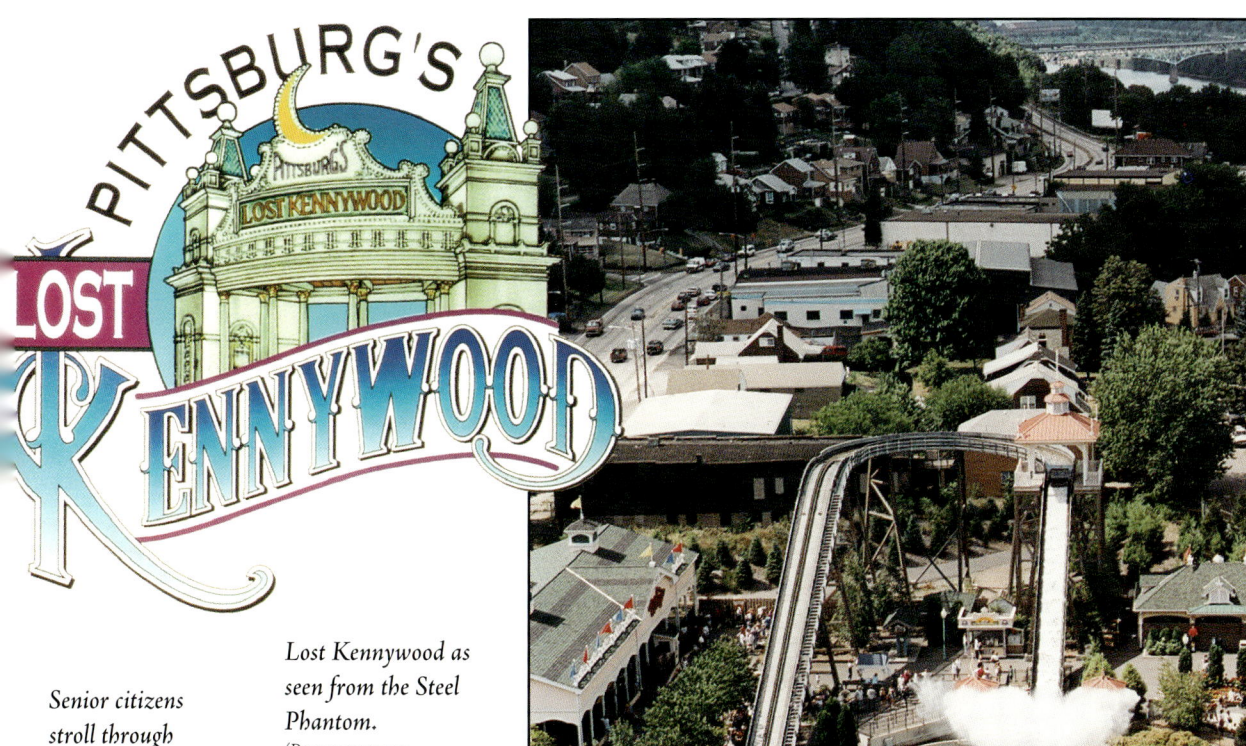

Senior citizens stroll through Lost Kennywood.
(Photograph by Charles J. Jacques, Jr.)

Lost Kennywood as seen from the Steel Phantom.
(Photograph by Charles J. Jacques, Jr.)

An ornate refreshment stand in Lost Kennywood.
(PHOTOGRAPH BY CHARLES J. JACQUES, JR.)

lights. There is a fiber-optic sign with Lost Kennywood on the entrance portal and on exiting through the gate, there is a large red heart with the words "Goodnight." This was the exit sign used for years at Coney Island's famous Luna Park.

Upon crossing through Lost Kennywood's main entrance, one sees a series of showcase boxes that contain historic photographs, posters, and postcards of "lost" (defunct) amusement parks from western Pennsylvania, eastern Ohio, and northern West Virginia compiled by Jim Futrell. Futrell, an amusement park historian for the National Amusement Park Historical Association, wrote the captions for postcards and pictures for the display, which includes West View, Rainbow Gardens, Burke's Glen, Aliquippa, Alameda, White Swan, and many other parks.

Taking the plunge

Beyond the gate, the ground rises to a fountain, which is similar in design to the electric fountain that operated for many years in Kennywood's Swimming Pool. Then comes the centerpiece of the new themed section - a reflection basin with fountains and a Shoot the Chutes at the far end. Kennywood's new Chutes, named the Pittsburg Plunge, is built from wood just like the turn-of-the-century Chutes and was patterned after the Chutes in Riverview, a defunct Chicago park. It towers over the other rides and buildings in Lost Kennywood, and the cupola at the top of the Plunge's main

Hands held high on the way down the Pittsburg Plunge.
(PHOTOGRAPH BY CHARLES J. JACQUES, JR.)

Taking the Plunge!
(Photograph by Charles J. Jacques, Jr.)

tower is clearly visible from Kennywood Boulevard. The reflecting basin is surrounded by a formal railing and paved walkways. There is a bridge at the far end of the lagoon and steps leading back up to the electric fountain and the exit. Unlike its forerunner, the Pittsburg Plunge is controlled by a computer, and modern day riders will get soaked. Not only does the Plunge get its passengers drenched, but it soaks any bystanders who stand in the splash area of the boat. Occasionally an unsuspecting adult will wander by to get a better view of the ride, only to be soaked when the Plunge's boat hits the water. The Pittsburg Plunge was built by O. D. Hopkins Associates, Inc. of Contoocook, New Hampshire. The ride is 275 feet long by 110 feet wide with a lift height of 50 feet. It has two 20-passenger boats that give the ride a capacity of 1,000 passengers per hour.

In addition to the Plunge, there are sites for four other rides in Lost Kennywood, but unlike the original electric parks, all of these ride spots are interchangeable and "new" old rides can be moved or substituted. The first rides chosen for Lost Kennywood all had an important nostalgic or historic connection with the park. The oldest ride, the Whip, was moved out of its corrugated metal

You will get wet on the Plunge.
(Photograph by Charles J. Jacques, Jr.)

A new Roll-O-Plane is one of the rides in Lost Kennywood.
(Photograph by Charles J. Jacques, Jr.)

building located near the Log Jammer into a newly constructed turn-of-the-century styled building with two cupolas and a row of colored pennants. It is Kennywood's oldest "flat ride," dating from the 1920's, but has been superbly maintained and even rebuilt several times.

The Phantom Phlyer (an earlier version was called the Dipsy Doodle) is a ride with metal swings and rudders allowing the Phlyer's cars to change direction. The "new" one used in Kennywood was rebuilt by Conklin so it was turned by tires against a metal rim, rather than the old gear system, which was constantly breaking down. The 39-foot ride was placed within the track of the Steel Phantom. The Phantom Phlyer had previously run at West View Park, another Pittsburgh park. When West View closed in 1977, the ride was purchased by Idora Park, Youngstown, Ohio, and then when Idora Park closed in 1984, it was bought by Kennywood.

Another ride, this one from the 1950's, was a Roll-O-Plane or salt and pepper shaker. Kennywood operated the bullet-shaped four-car (two at each end of a main column) ride from the 1950's until 1985. The ride turned its passengers every which way, but not completely upside down. The new model for Lost

158

The Wave Swinger was moved to Lost Kennywood.
(PHOTOGRAPH BY CHARLES J. JACQUES, JR.)

Phantom Phlyer (Flying Scooter) was removed after two seasons and replaced by the Pitt Fall.
(PHOTOGRAPH BY CHARLES J. JACQUES, JR.)

Cooling off by the Plunge.
(PHOTOGRAPH BY CHARLES J. JACQUES, JR.)

Kennywood was the first Roll-O-Plane built in many years, and Kennywood had to talk ORI of Salem, Oregon, into building it for them.

The Wave Swinger, one of the most popular rides of the 1980's, and one of the featured rides in *Kennywood Memories*, returned after several years' absence. This German-built ride was completely rebuilt and restored before it was placed back in operation in Lost Kennywood. The ride, which hydraulically lifts the riders off the ground, features an oscillating movement along with its circular movement.

Kennywood paid homage to West View Park by naming one of the refreshment stands in Lost Kennywood the West View Pizza Pavilion. The stand resembles West View's old merry-go-round pavilion, which was demolished in 1980. In a tribute to White Swan, a small amusement park located near the Greater Pittsburgh Airport, a white swan was placed on the facade of the souvenir and arcade building located near the fountain.

The gift shop is a replica of the front entrance gate at Wonderland at Revere Beach, Massachusetts, and the games building is copied from the photographic studio at Idora Park in Youngstown, Ohio. An arcade next to the gift shop was patterned after the "Electric Theater," an early motion picture theater in Luna Park, Pittsburg.

The floral calendar, another piece from the park's past, was relocated to Lost Kennywood. The letters and numerals are changed each day to keep the calendar current. Finally, to carry out the electric park theme, Kennywood presents a nighttime "Luna Phantastic" light show in the new area. At 10 p.m. daily, the reflecting pool comes to life with dancing fountains, water explosions, fire, fog, and colored laser lights. Carl Hughes told the *Pittsburgh Tribune-Review* it was a dream come true. "I'm ecstatic about it," he said. "It is far in excess of what we expected or dreamed of."

The Ladder Climb is one of the games in Lost Kennywood.
(Photograph by Charles J. Jacques, Jr.)

Noah's Ark with the whale's red mouth.
(Photograph by Charles J. Jacques, Jr.)

Riding the tiger on the Dentzel Carousel.
(Photograph by Charles J. Jacques, Jr.)

As good as Kennywood is at preserving history (and it is good), it is even better at recreating it. Trying to preserve things exactly as they were sometimes can be costly and counterproductive. Kennywood, perhaps taking a cue from Williamsburg's "air-conditioned" colonial buildings, has rebuilt and even redesigned where necessary, while trying to keep the historic feeling alive. Lost Kennywood is a perfect example of honoring the past of amusement parks without creating a museum, which might have to be subsidized. Because it is so distinctive Lost Kennywood is fast becoming an important part of the park's history.

First Annual Alumni Day

Kennywood held its first "Kennywood Alumni Day" for former employees on Sunday, June 18, 1995. It was somewhat akin to a high school reunion with hundreds of people gathered under a picnic pavilion to see faces from

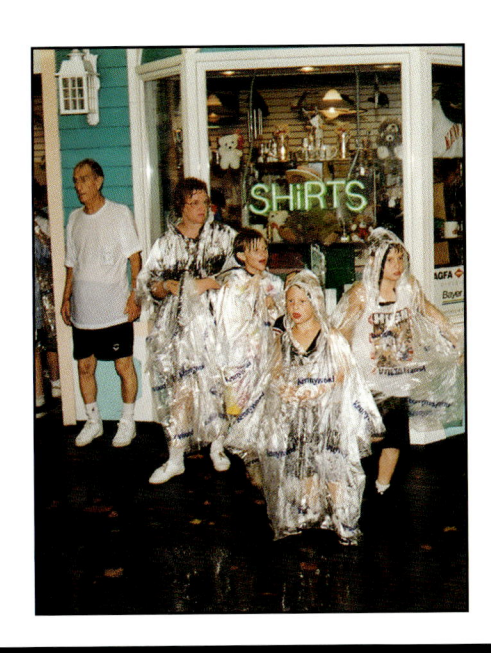

A family decked out in plastic rain gear.
(Photograph by Charles J. Jacques, Jr.)

Lost Kennywood's heart-shaped exit sign.
(Photograph by Betty Jacques)

The "Kennywood" souvenir shop and arcade.
(Photograph by Charles J. Jacques, Jr.)

161

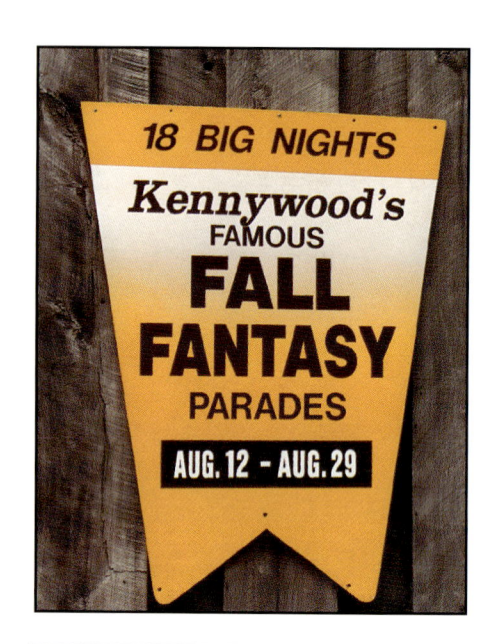

Stringing lights in early August for the Fall Fantasy Parade.
(Photograph by Charles J. Jacques, Jr.)

the past. Jeff Vavro, a former employee himself and feature editor of *The McKeesport Daily News*, commented that "people who have never worked at an amusement park are destined never to understand it." The long hours become more than just a summer job. The ability to get along with fellow employees was crucial to survive the l-o-n-g summers.

Alumni told their most memorable stories. Tina Napolitano Borgony remembered when a local radio station promoted a Jello Jump. Guests got to jump into a large container of gelatin on the Lagoon Stage to try to win a car. Later that day, Tina went to the employees' cafeteria, the Sunshine Inn, to eat and the special dessert was Jello -- all you could eat for free. Helen Olasz Sobocinski's fondest memory was a practical joke. Her supervisor asked her to sweep inside the '76 Fountain next to Kiddieland. The water was temporarily shut off. Just as she stepped into the center to start cleaning, the water was turned back on soaking her from head to toe.

Fall Fantasy Parades become a tradition

When the Fall Fantasy was begun in 1950, it was only one week or six nights long since the park was closed on Mondays. By 1995, the event had grown to 18 nights (covering almost three weeks). Stringing the lights along the parade route now begins in late July. One hundred thirty different high school bands from four states take part, and there is a waiting list of bands that would like to participate. Mary Lou Rosemeyer, the park's publicity director, said "high school bands have traveled to Kennywood from as far east as State College, as far west as the Canton area, south from central West

Mary Ann Spanagel has designed the Fall Fantasy's floats for many years.
(Photograph by Charles J. Jacques, Jr.)

A dragon was in the parade in 1987.
(Mary Ann Spanagel collection)

162

Rich Henry, who is facilities director, also oversees the Fall Fantasy Parades.
(Photograph by Charles J. Jacques, Jr.)

Detail from the Teddy Bear Picnic float designed by Mary Ann Spanagel in 1993.
(Mary Ann Spanagel collection)

Virginia, and some from Maryland. The farthest one to the north is Bradford." Rosemeyer added, "It takes them longer to get here than anyone because there aren't any good roads. They leave after the parade and don't get home until 3 in the morning." Kennywood employees, who take part in the parade, do it on a volunteer basis. Nightly they don costumes chosen to complement the parade's theme, bringing their characters to life. Some ride, while others walk the parade route. Young children carry signs announcing the floats. Rosemeyer still fondly remembers the time when she carried one of the parade signs.

Andy Quinn, director of community relations, often says "there are two days in the life of a child - there's Christmas and there's Kennywood." The park, just to make sure it has all of its bases covered, annually has Santa Claus ride the last float in its Fall Fantasy parade.

High school band directors are given a few simple instructions:

FORWARD MOTION ONLY -- NO DRILLING; PLAY MUSIC THROUGHOUT THE PARK -- NO DRUMMING; ASSEMBLE AT BUSES AT ABOUT 7:45 P.M. FOR REHEARSAL -- PARADE BEGINS PROMPTLY AT 8:30 P.M.

Uniformed band members and band directors are given a pay-one-price bracelet. For seventeen years, Rich Henry has given the signal that starts the parade. Weather is a factor, but remarkably few parades have been rained out or even delayed.

Although the parade started with a Chicago company providing the floats, Frank Ross, an art instructor at Langley High School in Pittsburgh and later a member of the Indiana University of Pennsylvania faculty, took over designing and building the floats in 1962. His protégé, Mary Ann Spanagel, Indiana, Pennsylvania, assumed the role in 1979.

Tracy Simmen working on a float.
(Mary Ann Spanagel collection)

Park employees don costumes for the parade.
(Photograph by Charles J. Jacques, Jr.)

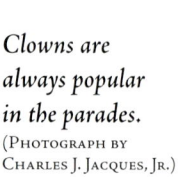

Clowns are always popular in the parades.
(Photograph by Charles J. Jacques, Jr.)

Fred Weber, director of maintenance, oversees the floats in the parades.
(Photograph by Charles J. Jacques, Jr.)

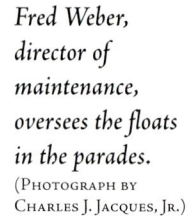

The Time Machine float from the 1997 parade.
(Photograph by Charles J. Jacques, Jr.)

Spanagel admits that the majority of her training for such a unique calling comes on-the-job. When Ross, her art teacher, and a handful of high school students that included Spanagel started, "we didn't know how to build floats," she told *The McKeesport Daily News* in 1990. "We just refined it as the years went along."

Long before the park opens in the spring, a theme is chosen for the parade by Kennywood's staff, and Spanagel submits between 12 and 15 designs that are in keeping with the theme. Rich Henry generally chooses the designs he likes best. By July, the floats are under construction. Spanagel has several rules in making her floats. She believes in keeping it simple; a float goes by in a hurry so she uses traditional images that are easy to recognize. She also likes papier-mache as her basic material and light, clean colors. Of all the designs she creates, Spanagel says, "the human figures are always the most challenging."

Spanagel, a commercial artist in Indiana, Pennsylvania, spends her summers in the Pittsburgh area. She stays with her sister Tracy Simmen, who has helped her with the floats since 1984. Kennywood provides the materials and the wagons, which are 16 to 20 feet long and 8 feet wide. The actual building takes place in a warehouse not far from the park, and a few days before the parade the floats are brought to Kennywood.

West Mifflin's residents who live near the park are accustomed to seeing Santa's Rocket Ship or a large Blue Dog or a Dragon being transported down the highway toward the park in mid-August. There the floats are stored in a large pavilion behind the Old Mill until the evening of the first parade. Kennywood's mechanical and electrical departments install generators and check out the park's

A Park employee dressed as a Cheshire cat.
(PHOTOGRAPH BY CHARLES J. JACQUES, JR.)

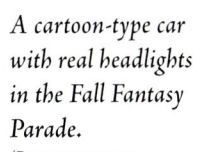

A cartoon-type car with real headlights in the Fall Fantasy Parade.
(PHOTOGRAPH BY CHARLES J. JACQUES, JR.)

eight used Suzukis (at one time old Jeeps were used, but they became undependable over time.) Park security and designated park employees patrol the parade route providing crowd control. Spanagel and her sister remain available during the whole Fall Fantasy to make minor repairs to the floats. One year real lollipops were used on the Candy Land float and they were stolen, so Tracy Simmen quickly made new lollipops out of foam, painted them, applied glitter, and glued them on the float. The liberal use of glitter is another Spanagel trademark, and anyone who gets too close to the floats is likely to acquire tracks of glitter.

In 1995, the Fall Fantasy Parade, as it wound its way through the park, passed by Lost Kennywood for the first time. It was the blending again of an old tradition with a new one. The Friday evening before Labor Day is always a sentimental time because it is the last day for the parade. As soon as the parade is over, Spanagel dismantles her creations and removes materials she thinks she may be able to use next year.

The McKeesport High School Marching Band.
(PHOTOGRAPH BY CHARLES J. JACQUES, JR.)

Candy Land float in the 1997 parade.
(PHOTOGRAPH BY CHARLES J. JACQUES, JR.)

Chapter 11

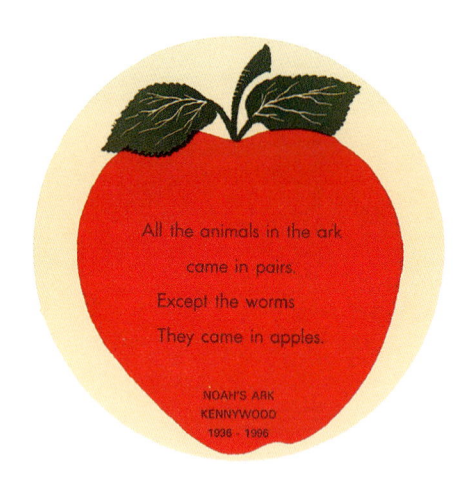

1996-1997
Noah's Ark and the Pitt Fall

All the animals in the ark came in pairs. Except the worms They came in apples.
NOAH'S ARK
KENNYWOOD
1936 - 1996

Something old and something new

For the 1996 season, Kennywood decided to renovate Noah's Ark, which had been built 60 years earlier. Over the years, the ark had been upgraded, with the last major reconditioning occurring 27 years earlier in 1969. There had been some thought of building a new fun house in the Lost Kennywood section, "but once we saw the condition of the ark, we decided that needed attention," stated Carl Hughes, chairman of the board of Kennywood Entertainment Corp. He was quick to add that the attraction was safe. A sprinkler system, smoke alarms, and new fire exits had been added in 1969, but the ark was worn out in several places and generally needed sprucing up.

In the 1920's and early 1930's, the Noah's Ark Co. which was owned by William Dentzel, who built Kennywood's current Merry-Go-Round, specialized in rocking-boat-style fun houses. The company built a number of arks in many amusement parks in the United States and abroad. Hughes told Jeff Vavro of *The McKeesport Daily News*, "It used to be an off-the-shelf item for amusement parks. You just automatically ordered a merry-go-round and a Noah's Ark for your park." However, over the years, most

Kennywood's Noah's Ark was rebuilt in 1996.
(PHOTOGRAPH BY CHARLES J. JACQUES, JR.)

166

Noah's Ark's original "ground floor" was preserved.
(Photograph by Charles J. Jacques, Jr.)

Bill Henninger is vice president of Kennywood Entertainment Company and head of the refreshment company.
(Kennywood)

of these unique walk-through attractions had been removed or destroyed in fires, and by 1996, only three arks remained. Kennywood's Noah's Ark was the only one in America. (The other two were located in England at Blackpool Pleasure Beach and Frontierland.) Key to the ride was a large eccentric gear with a long arm that "rocked" the boat gently back and forth. Another part of the ballyhoo was an ominous fog horn warning people to be careful when entering the attraction. The 1969 renovation included a new entrance in the shape of a whale's mouth with a soft spongy tongue, and a rock-like mountain addition built on the side of the ark. For the 1996 renovation, it was decided to remove the old whale entrance and relocate the queue-line to the rear of the ship because of congestion. Most of the rest of the ark would be retained including the mountain addition.

Kennywood's Noah's Ark has a very strange meteorological history. The year the ark was built, Pittsburgh experienced its worst flood ever on St. Patrick's Day 1936. The flood was of such magnitude that, although Kennywood Park was not directly affected because of its location high above the Mon, some of the park's row boats were needed to rescue people who were stranded by high water in Homestead. Jeff Vavro, who knew about the attraction's history, concluded his 1995 *Daily News* article with these prophetic words, "If the area starts experiencing constant rain over the next 40 days and nights, we'll at least know who to blame." Ironically, the spring of 1996 was one of the wettest on record, and the unpredictable Allegheny and Monongahela Rivers overflowed their banks submerging many homes and businesses. This time, although Kennywood again escaped, its sister parks, Sandcastle and Idlewild, were not so lucky. Both of these parks were inundated by the third worst flood ever in western Pennsylvania.

Carl Hughes was asked in August 1995, "How much of a challenge is it to renovate the boat?" Hughes replied, "Not much when one weighs it against last year's work. Compared to Lost Kennywood, the ark will be a snap," he said. Plans called for lifting the ark from its base with a huge crane so that the bottom could be renovated. According to Mary Lou Rosemeyer, publicity director, "the event would've been a perfect photo opportunity, but the ship's condition would not permit that to happen." When the ark was last renovated in 1969, most of the base had been replaced and several rooms added to one side, but the ship had

Dave Moll, superintendent of Kennywood's carpenters, rebuilt the ark.
(Photograph by Charles J. Jacques, Jr.)

Snakes await people who make a misstep in the ark.
(Photograph by Charles J. Jacques, Jr.)

not been moved. When the park's carpenters looked closely at the boat, they found it would be impossible to lift the ark without it completely breaking up. So the old boat was razed and replaced with a "new" one. David Moll, superintendent of the park's carpenters, painstakingly rebuilt the ark from notes he made before the original was demolished. Part of the attraction, the frame that the boat sat on, the mechanism that rocked it, and fortunately, even the fog horn, were saved. The maze-like passageways that created a feeling of being lost under the boat were saved. The movable floors (one that shook side to side and one that bounced up and down) were rebuilt. Once the project was started, the park decided to buy more high-tech elements which required adding more rooms to the attraction. Harry Henninger, Kennywood Entertainment Corp. president, had seen some interesting stunts in a fun house at Liseberg Park in Sweden, and he felt they could be copied and used in the rebuilt Noah's Ark.

Renovating the ark nearly got the best of Carl Hughes. The new attraction, which was supposed to accept its first passengers in June, did not open until August 12, 1996. A job that was to cost a few hundred thousand dollars ended up costing close to two million. All summer long Hughes had to answer the questions, "What happened to Noah's Ark and when will it reopen?" He had a sign erected at the ark with Noah looking at a blueprint and a sign saying "Not only did it snow for forty days and forty nights... It was a renovation with many surprises! Thanks for your patience. Noah." What seemed like a simple job of adding a few new stunts turned into practically rebuilding the attraction from the ground up. The high-tech stunts took longer to build and install. More time was required until the maintenance department had them working properly. But the wait was

Father Noah looks at his blueprints.
(Photograph by Charles J. Jacques, Jr.)

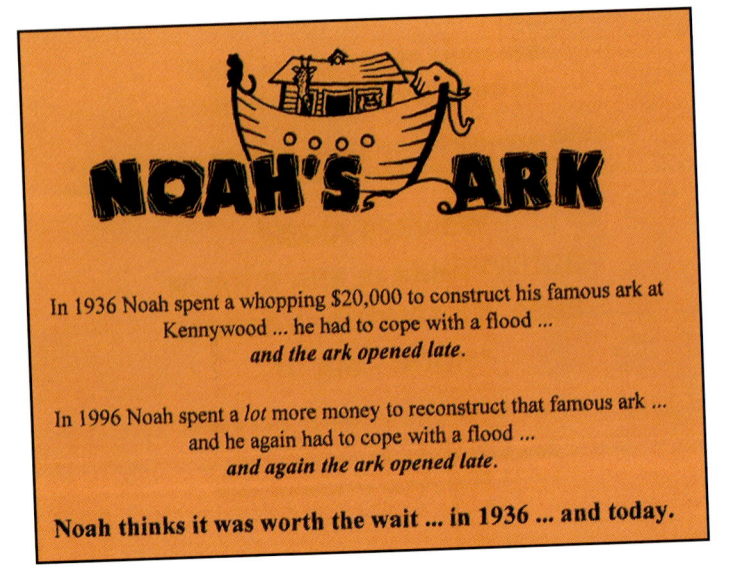

NOAH'S ARK

In 1936 Noah spent a whopping $20,000 to construct his famous ark at Kennywood ... he had to cope with a flood ...
and the ark opened late.

In 1996 Noah spent a *lot* more money to reconstruct that famous ark ... and he again had to cope with a flood ...
and again the ark opened late.

Noah thinks it was worth the wait ... in 1936 ... and today.

168

An employee is available to help people who are terrified by the ark's stunts.
(Photograph by Charles J. Jacques, Jr.)

Just watching can be fun.
(Photograph by Charles J. Jacques, Jr.)

Noah's Ark's new front and its Elevator of Doom.
(Photograph by Charles J. Jacques, Jr.)

A pelican was added to the ark.
(Photograph by Charles J. Jacques, Jr.)

worth-while, because the wonderful ship was saved for another generation of park goers.

The park's media invitation, for August 12, 1996, acknowledged that rebuilding the ark was not easy:

In 1936 Noah spent a whopping $20,000 to construct his famous ark at Kennywood...he had to cope with a flood... and the ark opened late.

In 1996 Noah spent a lot more money to reconstruct that famous ark...and he again had to cope with a flood...and again the ark opened late.

Noah thinks it was worth the wait...in 1936...and today.

(Kennywood management states, "There is little truth to the rumor that if Noah didn't finish before Labor Day, he and his ark would lose their lease."

When Noah's Ark was built in the mid-1930's, there was little fear of law suits for slight injuries. In the early years of the century, fun houses offered stunts like dropping floors, revolving barrels, and collapsing stairs. Since the 1930's, Kennywood had modified Noah's Ark, along with its other fun houses, and dark rides, always searching for safer alternatives. Noah's Ark's latest renovation continued this trend.

The changes made to the ark were designed by Bruce D. Robinson Architecture - Design, Inc., of Cincinnati, Ohio,

The new stage area in front of the ark was called Kennyville High School.
(Photograph by Charles J. Jacques, Jr.)

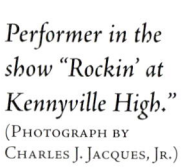

Performer in the show "Rockin' at Kennyville High."
(Photograph by Charles J. Jacques, Jr.)

the designer of Lost Kennywood. Most of the high-tech additions in the ark were created by Techni-Flex, a California firm that designed the Phantastic Laser Show in Lost Kennywood. Computers rather than tape units control the sound for each of the new attractions. The entrance is now made through the menacing Elevator of Doom, which creates the sensation of a rise and sudden drop into a dusty archaeological site packed with skeletons, spiders, pots of gold, and blood. People must cross a chasm on round steps over a hole (a modern version of the barrel tops) to exit the stunt.

At one point, visitors go over a concrete bridge while the hull of the ark seems to spin around them, creating the illusion they are moving and not the ark. A trip through the renovated ark takes longer with each major section requiring an introduction before a short adventure takes place. The voyage ends with the High Seas Storm and a final stop in a chamber that floods and tends to get visitors a little wet. The ark is now larger and can accommodate more passengers at one time - 800 per hour, as opposed to 450 for the old one.

Carried over from the old ark are scenes with Noah and his wife surrounded by animals (although more

Riders face each other in the Wipeout.
(Photograph by Charles J. Jacques, Jr.)

The new ark and the Steel Phantom as seen from the Pitt Fall.
(Photograph by Charles J. Jacques, Jr.)

animation is used with these figures). Another high-tech addition, which was developed by Carnegie Mellon University professor Ihor Lys and robotics engineer George Mueller, is a computer that produces fast-moving light images.

A back-to-the-'50's entertainment area was added just opposite the ark's exit, in the space formerly occupied by the Wipeout. A new song and dance show, "Rockin' at Kennyville High," was performed there three times a day. Public Relations Director Mary Lou Rosemeyer told Candy Williams of the *Tribune-Review* in 1995 that "'Kennyville High'

Running lights on the Thunderbolt.
(Photograph by Charles J. Jacques, Jr.)

Hitting the lift chain on the Thunderbolt.
(Photograph by Charles J. Jacques, Jr.)

came about as a solution to a bottleneck situation. With the addition of Lost Kennywood, the corner became congested. To alleviate the problem, we brainstormed and came up with an idea that will provide more table seating and another venue for entertainment." A false front with the name Kennyville High was built at the back of the refreshment division's offices and employee cafeteria. In 1997, the area's name was changed to Kennywood Resort Hotel when the show was rethemed to take place in a resort.

As the park grew over the years, more parking space was required. The park opened a third-level parking lot in 1994 and provided a shuttle to and from the front gate. To provide a faster and more exciting way of getting to the gate, midway through the 1996 season, Kennywood constructed a ski lift, called Kenny's Parkway, between the third-level parking lot and the entrance to the park. The lift solved two problems, distance to the gate and change of elevation, at the same time. The ride, which is similar to ski lifts used in resort areas to carry people up the slopes, can carry as many as 396 people at one time in its 99 seats. The difference between Kenny's Parkway and most ski lifts is that it carries most of its passengers in both directions. The lift, which travels at 3 m.p.h., is 1,550 feet one way or 3,100 feet round trip. The ride was built by Salt Lake City-based Garaventa CTEC Inc. Dale Freeman, who worked on erecting the Steel Phantom, served as chief engineer on the ski lift project.

Also in 1996, the Wipeout was moved and became part of a new second entrance into Lost Kennywood, which ended near the Pirate. The other new ride was a junior-size steel coaster called the Lil' Phantom purchased from Molina & Sons of Miami, Florida. It was substantial enough that parents could ride with their children.

Kennywood Park, which had reorganized itself into the Kennywood Entertainment Co., became equity managing partners of another amusement park, Lake Compounce, in Bristol,

Only the brave hold their hands up on the Thunderbolt.
(Photograph by Charles J. Jacques, Jr.)

Kenny's Parkway is the name of the ski lift in the parking lot.
(Photograph by Charles J. Jacques, Jr.)

Sharing a foot vibrator.
(PHOTOGRAPH BY CHARLES J. JACQUES, JR.)

Taking a break by the Racer.
(PHOTOGRAPH BY CHARLES J. JACQUES, JR.)

Lil' Phantom brought thrills to children and adults in 1996.
(PHOTOGRAPH BY CHARLES J. JACQUES, JR.)

Connecticut, in 1996. This park is the oldest continuously operating amusement park in the United States, opening in 1846. Keith Hood, former general manager of Idlewild, was named manager of Lake Compounce. The park has a classic carousel and a wooden roller coaster, the Wildcat, which was built by the Philadelphia Toboggan Company, but that is another story for another time.

1997 Nervous going up, laughing coming down

When Kennywood decided to build the world's tallest and fastest free-fall ride in 1997, it chose a wonderful name for the new attraction - the Pitt Fall. According to Rich Henry, director of facilities, choosing the colors was just as easy. "Black and gold is the Steelers, it's the Pirates, and it's the Penguins. It's Pittsburgh and everything the city and our region stand for." The giant tower, which is about 20 feet taller than any previous free fall, replaced the Phantom Phlyer in Lost Kennywood. (The Phlyer was sent to Lake Compounce.) For a park, which prior to 1980 had no skyline, the Pitt Fall added yet another piece to one of the most imposing skylines of any amusement park in America. The 251-foot tower is so tall, FAA regulations mandated it be equipped with flashing lights; however the park did not mind because they added ballyhoo to the attraction.

The Pitt Fall is completely surrounded by the track of the Steel Phantom, which flashes past ever few minutes. Some might question replacing a historic ride like the Phantom Phlyer with a hot new high-tech one like the Pitt Fall, but too many parks have failed because they

Carl O. Hughes, chairman of the board.
(Photograph by Charles J. Jacques, Jr.)

The Pitt Fall replaced the Phantom Phlyer in Lost Kennywood in 1997.
(Photograph by Charles J. Jacques, Jr.)

The 251-foot-tall Pitt Fall under construction in the spring of 1997.
(Photograph by Jim Futrell)

were not willing to change. The site is perfect for the new ride, which is highly visible, and draws more people to the furthest corner of Lost Kennywood, especially after dark.

The new free fall transports riders to the top of the tower at speeds up to 16 feet per second...then drops them to the ground at a free fall rate of nearly 100 feet per second or 65 mph. The thrill seekers are in open air seats with their arms and legs hanging freely. The ride does have a shoulder harness to hold on to. The Pitt Fall carries 16 people per trip in rows of four that form a square around the cylindrical center tower. The view from the top of the tower to the river below is breathtaking. It is a great spot to photograph the Steel Phantom, Thunderbolt, and the rest of the park.

Writing for the *Pittsburgh Post-Gazette*, Beth E. Trapani describes her fall:

> There is a moment at the top when you think you'll be OK. You've secured your grip around the harness - maybe held your breath so as not to lose it on the way down.
>
> You've resigned yourself to the ride as you hear the clanging of machinery behind and above you, positioning

The Phlyer lifts 16 passengers at a time in four-abreast seats.
(Photograph by Charles J. Jacques, Jr.)

you for the plunge.

It's a quiet moment - the Monongahela River is soft and lazy from 250 feet above.

And the familiar skyline rising gently in front of you is strangely comforting.

But as you dangle there on the edge of anxiety, legs hanging free and heart waiting for a place to go, the next few seconds tick off like a bomb.

You know it's coming, but you don't know when. And the waiting feels a lot longer than you imagined it would be.

Watching the Pitt Fall drop.
(Photograph by Charles J. Jacques, Jr.)

Then with no warning, no coaster track in front of you leading the way, no back of heads to follow, no grinding of cogs to tip you off - you drop.

The Pitt Fall was designed and manufactured by Intamin AG of Zurich, Switzerland, which also manufactured both the Laser Loop and Raging Rapids. Construction began in July of 1996. Rich Henry, who supervised the construction, said since many of the measurements for the ride are so exact, with tolerances of 1 mm, the park used laser beams to properly align the rails on the ride's metal tower base structure. Because of the sun's ability to distort the metal, the construction workers erected the rails after dark. Braking the ride is done using fail-safe magnetic brakes called LSMs, or linear synchronous motors. Electric engineer Bjorn Castrischer, an employee of Intamin, adjusted the brakes and said that no electricity is needed for braking. "It always works," he explained. The ride works on a system of pulleys and magnets that form an extremely strong magnetic field to smoothly stop the ride about 70-feet above the ground. The magnetic field is created by two rows of magnets (one positive, one negative) that run parallel in the tower. Nothing rubs or ever touches

The Pitt Fall was manufactured by Intamin AG of Switzerland.
(Photograph by Charles J. Jacques, Jr.)

Pete McAneny is vice president and general manager of the park.
(Photograph by Charles J. Jacques, Jr.)

The Pitt Fall has become another addition to Kennywood's growing skyline.
(Photograph by Charles J. Jacques, Jr.)

against the ride to stop it, which saves on wear and tear. The system works best with a total of 920 pounds in each four-row car, and employees attempt to balance each group.

Although earlier versions of free falls have been around since the 1980's this version debuted in the United States at Kentucky Kingdom, Louisville, Kentucky, in late 1995. Harry Henninger had wanted to buy a free fall in the 1980's, but he waited until the technology was perfected. Kennywood's was the seventh new high-tech, free-fall ride built by Intamin in the United States and Canada.

Other additions to Kennywood in 1997 included a virtual reality display in the Penny Arcade. A dart game (similar to a dart game at a bar) was added with the winner receiving a large stuffed animal. A small stage was erected near the building that formerly housed The Whip, which had been turned into a large picnic pavilion for use by groups during ethnic days and for radio promotion days. The facade of the main office building was given a refurbishing. Several new stunts were added to Noah's Ark.

Food additions included such new treats as bear claws in the cafeteria, chocolate fudge cake, chicken strip pita pocket sandwiches, and Kennywood

Crunch ice cream, which was made exclusively for the park. Hetzel's Pretzels were introduced in a variety of flavors and toppings. The pretzel stand was located near the Log Jammer where visitors could watch workers hand twist the pretzels and then put them in an oven.

Kennywood's most popular food stand, the Potato Patch, got a little brother, "Small Fries," in Lost Kennywood. More than 450,000 pounds of Idaho potatoes are served by the Patch each year. The secret (if there is a secret) is that they are served fresh and hot. Then come the cholesterol-toppings of brown gravy, creamy cheddar, traditional ketchup or the somewhat less fattening spicy seasoned salt and vinegar.

Another favorite at Kennywood is cotton candy, which is one hundred percent sugar heated and spun at the same time. Coloring and flavoring are added. Kennywood's candy store, located in the double decker building near the exit, offers, among other things, homemade fudge and Clark candy bars.

Kennywood's school picnic business continues to grow. When West View Park closed in 1977, the park got the schools that had formerly gone there. Now virtually every school district in southwestern Pennsylvania has a Kennywood picnic day. Larger school districts like Penn Hills, Gateway, Plum, and Woodland Hills have the park to themselves on picnic day. Smaller school districts are combined on other dates to reach a similar number.

Picnics remain the bread and butter of Kennywood's business. Although the park has continued to add picnic pavilions over the years, the new ones, along with

The Pitt Fall offers a new view of Le Cachot.
(PHOTOGRAPH BY CHARLES J. JACQUES, JR.)

Through the years the park has been made more accessible to the handicapped.
(PHOTOGRAPH BY CHARLES J. JACQUES, JR.)

Kennywood uses large numerals on the side of Le Cachot.
(PHOTOGRAPH BY CHARLES J. JACQUES, JR.)

the old, are booked solid from the beginning of July to the park closing on Labor Day. Kennywood is still the only major park in the United States that permits people to bring lunch baskets into the park.

The park hosts nineteen community day picnics each year from late June until late August. There are now ten nationality days that help keep alive the traditions of the Old World. The groups include Carpatho-Russian, Serbian, Italian, Slovak, Greek, Byzantine, Slovene, Polish, Hungarian, and Croatian. Italian Day is the largest. The Serbian picnic may be the oldest, celebrating their 80th picnic at the park in 1997, although the Croatian may be as old, if not a little older.

Kennywood in the 1990's has continued to thrive without easy interstate access. (Management would like to see the Mon Valley Express Way built.) The park, which was built overlooking steel mills and surrounded by mill towns, is accessible only via meandering main streets punctuated with stop signs and stoplights. In addition to conventional directions, most people are told - "to follow the yellow signs, and if you get lost, stop and ask - everyone knows where Kennywood is."

Kennywood has become a local icon along with Heinz 57, Iron City Beer, and the Steelers. The historic amusement facility is part of the fabric of Pittsburgh and the surrounding area, and if anything would happen to it, the park would be sorely missed. Kennywood is strong and prosperous and is a welcome exception in a business where the rule has been parks failing rather than succeeding. Kennywood is a survivor, almost an anachronism, a successful urban amusement park in the 1990's.

Lost Kennywood at night.
(Photograph by Charles J. Jacques, Jr.)

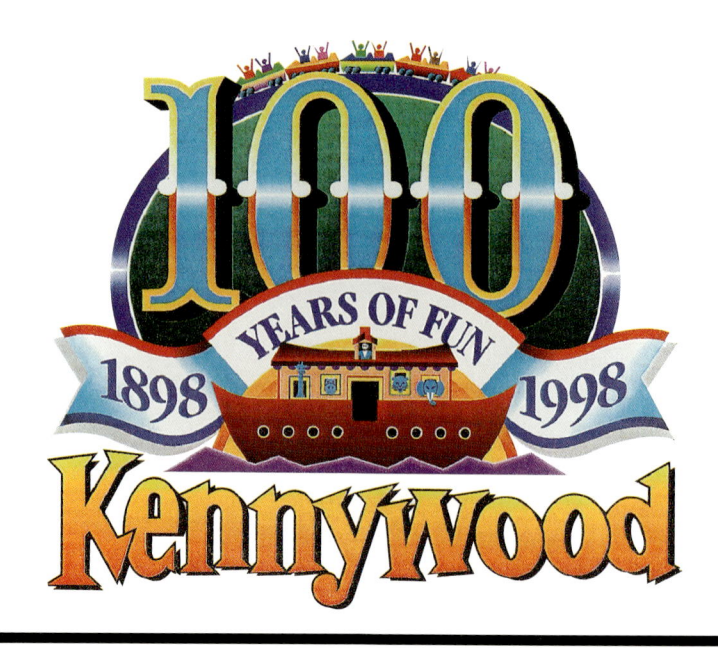

Postscript

More than anything, Kennywood is shared memories - of open air trolleys, dance bands, and the Jack Rabbit's famous double dip.

There are the sounds of the park's wheezy band organ, Noah's Ark's fog horn, and the Windmill creaking as it turns. There are the screams from inside Le Cachot, the smell of cotton candy, and that special feeling of being tossed about on the Turtle.

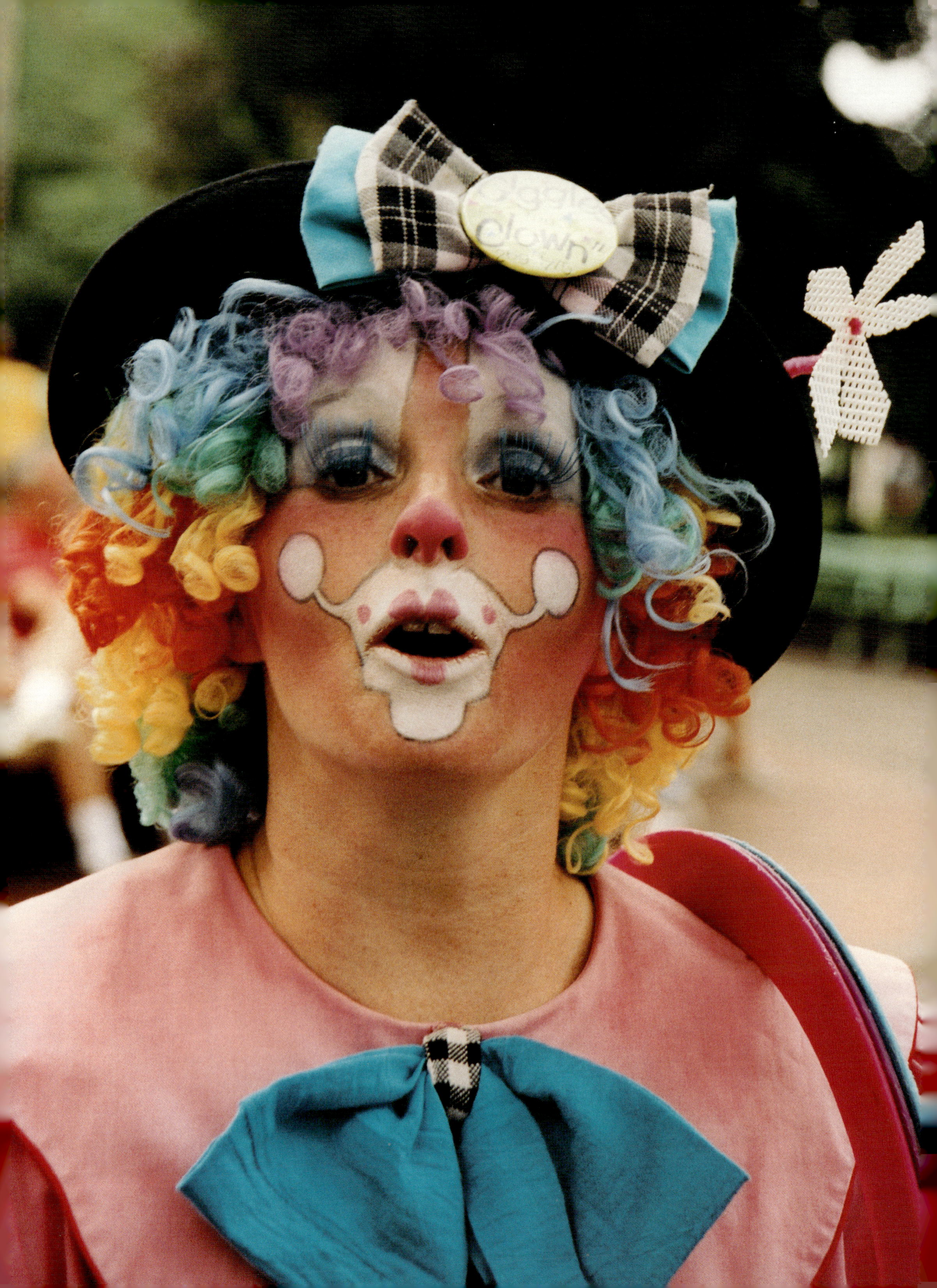
clown"

Memories linger of bumps given and taken on the Gran Prix, of the taste of french fries and corn dogs, and of the shared wetness of a trip down the Pittsburg Plunge.

As darkness falls, there are the visions of an earlier century in Lost Kennywood, stark fear on the Steel Phantom as it plunges into a darkened ravine, and the letters R-A-C-E-R being repeated over and over again.

182

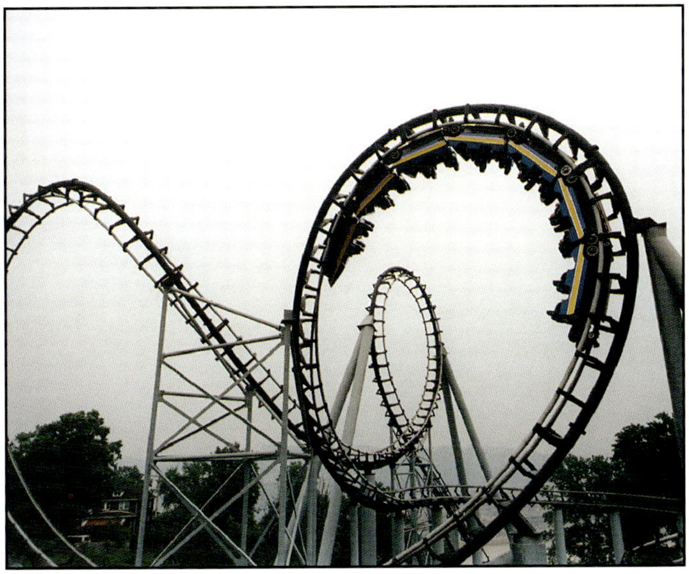

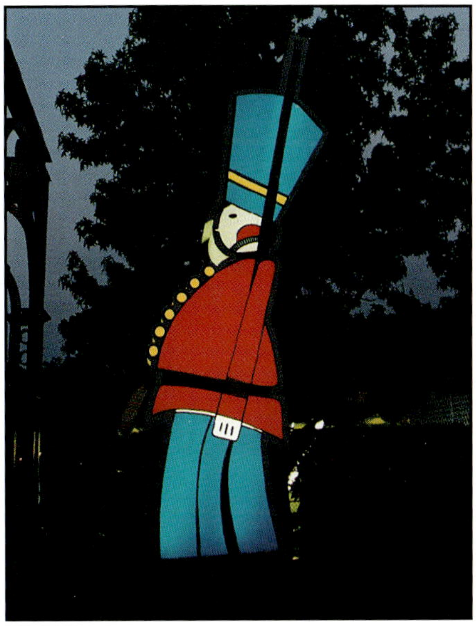

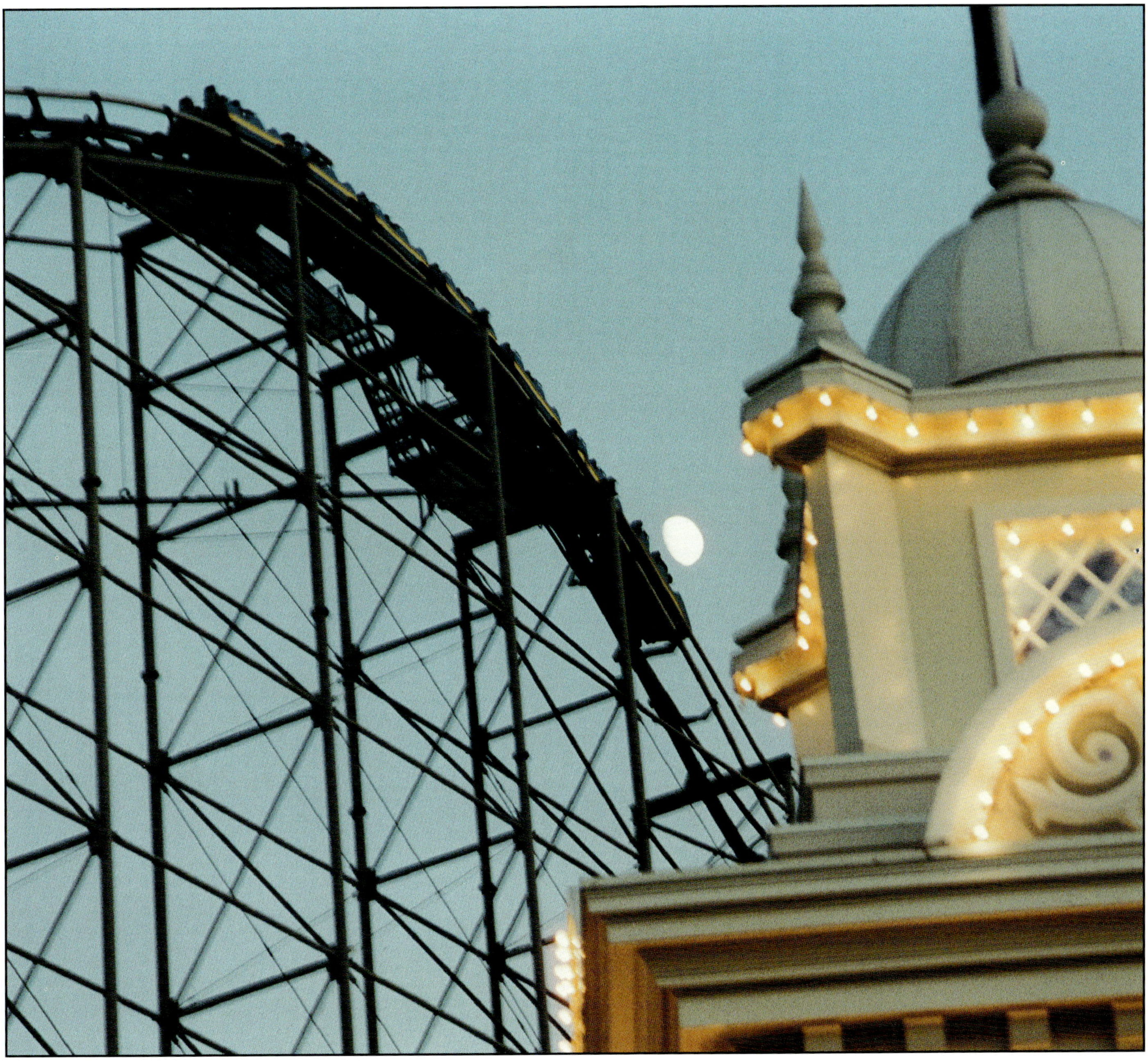

The carousel slows and stops. Lights shimmer on the surface of the Lagoon as the crowd hurries toward the exit, and soon all that remains are memories.

(All of the photographs in the Postscript were taken by Charles J. Jacques, Jr. with the exception of the large photograph at the bottom of page 183 and the toy soldier also on page 183 that were taken by Betty Jacques.)

A Kennywood Tradition

Kennywood sending Christmas cards is a tradition that dates back to 1929. (At least 1929 is the earliest card in the park's collection). The card is annually sent to thousands of summer patrons, including school board directors, politicians, and members of picnic committees. During the Great Depression of the 1930's, the park did not always send cards, but starting in 1939 the park has sent a card or some other item (two times records, posters, and in 1997 a Christmas ornament) every year. For a number of years Brady McSwigan, with the help of Albert Kennedy (Rosey) Rowswell, created the card. Following Rowswell death in the early 1950's, Carl O. Hughes, who was then assistant manager of the park, worked with Brady McSwigan. Since 1964, Hughes has been primarily in charge of designing the card. For years the cards were all addressed in long hand and mailed about December 15.

Christmas 1953

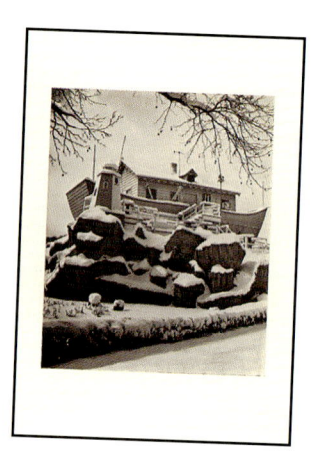

Christmas 1956

Christmas 1973

Christmas 1976

Christmas 1979

Christmas 1991

Christmas 1992

Christmas 1994

Christmas 1995

Christmas 1996

Appendix

What's new at Kennywood this year?

1898

MONONGAHELA STREET RAILWAY COMPANY leased 141 acres from Anthony Kenny. On the grounds was a picnic grove called Kenny's Grove, which had been an outdoor meeting place since the Civil War. The street railway company built the amusement park. The name Kennywood was chosen by Andrew W. Mellon, who was one of the officers of the street railway company.

KENNYWOOD PARK was laid out by George S. Davidson, chief engineer of the Monongahela Street Railway Company, who became its first manager. Construction was supervised by Wilkins & Davidson Engineers.

1899

OPENING DATE: Tuesday, May 30

BAND ORGAN provided music for the Merry-Go-Round.
BOWLING ALLEY was one of the original attractions.
CASINO was a large open-air restaurant that cost $10,000. The building measured 115 feet by 175 feet, stood two stories high, and was encircled by a spacious verandah. The front facade, facing the Lagoon, had seven bays, with the three center ones projecting out.
DANCE PAVILION was a large open-air structure. It was built in the Queen Ann style and cost $8,000. The dance floor measured 120 feet by 70 feet with a promenade 15 feet wide that encircled the entire structure and was separated from the dance floor by a small railing.
ELECTRIC LIGHTS placed all around the new park permitted it to remain open in the evening. All of the buildings had electric lights.
LADIES COTTAGE or comfort station was the ladies' rest room and cost $1,000.
LAGOON was a small artificial lake or pond approximately three feet deep that contained several little islands. A rustic bridge crossed it. The Lagoon was sometimes called Lake Kennywood. There were several other small ponds around the grounds.
MERRY-GO-ROUND was a three-row stationary machine purchased from G. A. Dentzel of Philadelphia, PA. It was a menagerie machine, meaning besides horses it also had other animals such as a lion and a tiger. The Merry-Go-Round, which had winged chariots and a brass ring machine, cost $2,500.
MERRY-GO-ROUND PAVILION cost approximately $2,500. The structure was large enough so that people could sit or stand around the machine.

OCTAGON BUILDING was originally used as a bandstand. Later it became a refreshment stand. It was located on the current site of the Pagoda Refreshment Stand.
ROW BOATS made of wood were available for rent on the Lagoon.
SHOOTING GALLERY, located in a covered building, was one of the original attractions.
TENNIS AND CROQUET COURTS were original attractions in the park.

1900

OPENING DATE: Friday, April 27

BANDSTAND - A new bandstand was built at a cost of $15,000 on the current Raging Rapids site. The structure was designed by J. F. Kuntz. The bandstand had a stage measuring 40 feet by 40 feet and a proscenium arch 30 feet high. The bandstand had a white canvas curtain for Biograph pictures. On stage was seating for 200 musicians. There were six dressing rooms - three on each side of the stage. The bandstand was covered with more than 500 incandescent lights. The bandstand was not finished in time for opening day, but M. S. Rocereto's 40-piece band played from the unfinished structure before a crowd estimated to be 7,000.
BASEBALL GROUND, also called ATHLETIC FIELD, was 400 feet by 400 feet. It had a grandstand that could seat 600 and two sets of bleachers, each capable of seating 700. The space under the grandstand held dressing rooms for the players, a refreshment stand, and a storage room. The baseball grounds were on the site now occupied by Lost Kennywood.
DINING PAVILIONS and KITCHENS - The park's first picnic shelters were built.
RUSTIC REFRESHMENT STAND was added.

1901

OPENING DATE: Not available

OLD MILL was built. It was powered by an old fashioned mill wheel. A current carried boats "through dark caverns and deep caves brightened here and there by flashes of light showing grotesque and fantastic novel and realistic forms of entertainment." One scene depicted St. Nick. All the boats had cushioned seats. The ride was advertised as "cool and comfortable" and "lasting six minutes." The Old Mill ride ended with a shoot the chutes where the boats were lifted up and then sent down a small slide.

1902

OPENING DATE: Not available

MONONGAHELA STREET RAILWAY COMPANY was merged into the Pittsburgh Railway Company.

DEW DROP slide was located in back of the Wonderland Building.
FERRIS WHEEL was installed in the park.
FIGURE EIGHT TOBOGGAN, also called a THREE-WAY FIGURE EIGHT TOBOGGAN, was the first chain lift roller coaster built in the park. This figure-eight style coaster, built by Fred and Bob Ingersoll of Pittsburg, PA, was 85 feet wide and 225 feet long. It had ten little two-seat coaster cars that ran on a hard maple track. The incline that carried the cars was 70 feet long, but the coaster was less than 40 feet high. This coaster was built on the current Turnpike site.
LAUGHING GALLERY was an early fun house located near the Old Mill. "No two people laugh alike." It was imported directly from the Paris Exposition and the only one in the United States. The fun house was installed by the Amusement Construction Co., Fred Ingersoll, President, Pittsburg, PA. The attraction consisted of glass mirrors arranged to give the most amusing and grotesque distortions. Each mirror was 4 feet by 7 feet. "Visit the Laughing Gallery and hear everybody laugh."
PHOTOGRAPHIC GALLERY was installed in the park.
FRANKLIN WENTZEL became manager of Kennywood's restaurant in the Casino. He and his brother Washington would head the refreshment company until 1946.
WONDERLAND BUILDING was a fun house from Germany with distortion mirrors, a "Slippery Slide," and "Earthquake Floor."

1903

OPENING DATE: Sunday, May 10
(A band concert was delayed one week to Saturday, May 16)

PITTSBURGH RAILWAY COMPANY subleased Kennywood to the Pittsburg Steeplechase (Steeple-Chase) & Amusement Company headed by W. S. Dodge of Boston. The company was to build a theater on the grounds.

CAMELS with Arab attendants offered rides.
ELECTRIC LAUNCH ran on the Lagoon.
HOUSE OF TROUBLE with its many mazes adjoined the Great Steeplechase Arena.
PONY TRACK with both ponies and buggies was located near the current park office.
SIOUX INDIAN TRIBE camped at the park.
STEEPLECHASE RIDE was a gravity-type ride copied from Steeplechase Park in Coney Island on which patrons rode small horses around an undulating half mile track. "Even babies can ride the horses with safety," and "Everybody rides the horses."

1904

OPENING DATE: Saturday, May 14

PITTSBURG AND STEEPLECHASE AMUSEMENT COMPANY was taken over by the Moorhead family of Sharpsburg, PA. W. S. Dodge was ousted.

BANDSTAND'S arch was repainted.
CINEMATOGRAPH VIEWS, early motion pictures, were shown on Sunday afternoons and evenings.
DEW DROP giant slide, also called the DOWN AND OUT, was located at the back of the Steeplechase (a.k.a. Wonderland) Building.
INDIAN VILLAGE was set up in the park.

LANDSCAPING with more shade trees and new flower beds was improved.
MINIATURE RAILWAY - Two steam powered trains carried people through the "Wabash Tunnel" and visited the "World's Fair." It was located on the current site of the park's office.
STEEPLECHASE RIDE was removed from the park at the end of the season.
VAUDEVILLE THEATER was built inside the Steeplechase Building. This little theater could seat 600 and had a stage measuring 40 feet by 60 feet. The stage had "lots of fine scenery."

1905

OPENING DATE: Monday, May 15

CIRCLE SWING or airship ride was introduced and was located behind the Wonderland Building.
MOTION PICTURE — *The Great Train Robbery* was shown the entire season.
ROLLER SKATING was offered.
SCENIC RAILWAY ROLLER COASTER, "one of the largest in the world," was located near the Steeplechase Building with its entrance through the building. The loading station was elevated and the scenic railway featured mild dips. It was built near the current site of the entrance to Lost Kennywood and ran out toward Braddock Road (Kennywood Boulevard).

1906

OPENING DATE: Sunday, May 6

PITTSBURGH RAILWAY COMPANY resumed management under the direction of Andrew S. McSwigan, manager of amusements for the railway company.

CIRCLE SWING was moved from the Wonderland area into the park.
ELECTRIC LIGHTS were doubled.
FIGURE EIGHT was renamed the Whirly-Whirl.
"GREAT WESTERN TRAIN HOLD-UP" was a train holdup spectacular with real cowboys, cowgirls, and Sioux Indians. An old locomotive and several coaches from the Southern Pacific Railroad were brought up to the park from the Pennsylvania railroad tracks below. The show featured lasso experts, bucking broncos, and thrilling scenes. Thousands of feet of canvas were attached to the Scenic Railway coaster and were painted to look like the prairie with the Nevada Mountains in the background.
GROTTO OF VISIONS was installed at the park.
HOUSE OF TROUBLE and DOWN AND OUT had free admission that season.
IRISH VILLAGE was added.
OLD MILL was renamed the FAIRYLAND FLOATS.

1907

OPENING DATE: Saturday, May 4

KENNYWOOD was leased to Andrew S. McSwigan, A. F. Megahan, and Fred W. Henninger. McSwigan had run the Pittsburgh Railways Company amusement enterprises. Megahan had previously managed both West View and Kennywood parks. Henninger was one of the organizers of West View Park and held a number of concessions in amusement parks throughout the country including large holdings at Conneaut Lake.

ELECTRIC LAUNCH was purchased for use on the Lagoon.
KEMP SISTERS' WILD WEST SPECTACULAR AND AMERICAN HIPPODROME included a train holdup and wild west show.
LANDSCAPING was added to the park.
PONY DRIVE - A new pony track was developed.
ROLLER SKATING RINK adjoined the Wonderland Building and was said to be the largest and best-equipped rink in the Monongahela Valley. The rink had 1,000 of the latest model ball-bearing skates to accommodate the skaters.

1908

OPENING DATE: Not available

1909

OPENING DATE: Sunday, May 2

BABY SHOW was held at Kennywood with decorated carriages. Over 1,000 babies entered.
"THE ROUNDUP," a western thriller featuring Jim Wright, Texas Cowboys, and live horses, played in an arena at Kennywood.

1910

OPENING DATE: Sunday, April 24

RACING ROLLER COASTER built by the Ingersoll Brothers of Pittsburgh, PA. Also called the "Aerial Racer," "Mountain Joy Ride," or "Aerial Joy Ride," this ride was finally called The Racer. Kennywood said this ride cost $50,000. It was a side-friction coaster whose cars were held on the track by side rails rather than wheels and so could tolerate only gentle hills and dips. It was designed by John A. Miller. This coaster was built on the current Kiddieland site.

1911

OPENING DATE: Sunday, April 16

AMERICAN POCKET BALL game was purchased.
BOXING EXHIBIT at the park, Crouse vs. Berger, September 4, 1911.
CANE RACK game was added.
ELECTRIC AMERICAN FLAG was placed in the Dance Pavilion and later moved to the Bandstand.
FIGURE EIGHT ROLLER COASTER was renamed Gee Whiz Dip the Dip.
MECHANICAL SWINGS were purchased.
PENNY ARCADE BUILDING was destroyed by a fire believed to have been set by burglars. Located in the building were the Shooting Gallery and Nickelodeon. The loss did not exceed $10,000.
SPEED-O-PLANE, a side-friction coaster, was built to replace the Scenic Railway. Park officials said the coaster cost $30,000. The location was the current site of the Steel Phantom's first drop.

1912

OPENING DATE: Sunday, April 21

DAFFY DILLA, located in the old Wonderland Building, became a fun house or a fun factory that had a Human Roulette Wheel and "57 other varieties of amusements."
DOLL RACK game was added.
PENNY ARCADE AND THEATER BUILDING - A new building was constructed to hold the Penny Arcade and Vaudeville Theater. The theater could seat over 500 persons. It was built on the current site of the Arcade.
POOL ROOM was located next to the Daffy Dilla.

1913

OPENING DATE: Sunday, April 20

BAND ORGAN was purchased from Berni Organ Company, New York, NY.
CAROUSEL - A new jumping horse carousel was purchased from T. M. Harton (trading as the T. M. Harton Company), Pittsburgh, PA, to replace the park's original Dentzel Carousel. The new three-row machine cost $7,500. Kennywood gave Harton a five-year lease with two one-year renewals. The park had the right to purchase the carousel. Some of the horses on the carousel were probably carved by the Mullers. Harton took the old Dentzel Carousel for trade and gave the park a $2,000 credit. The carousel was to be either the one Harton ran at the Pittsburgh Exposition on the Point in 1912 or one similar to it. Kennywood advertised that this was a $10,000 Carousel.
CAROUSEL PAVILION was remodeled to make room for the Harton Carousel. As part of the lease T. M. Harton was required to move the inside posts of the Carousel Building outwardly three feet.
DUCKS game was added where players tried to ring live ducks (later wooden ducks). This game was created and run by A. B. McSwigan, who was a college student at Carnegie Tech at the time.
SILK HAT HARRY game was added where players threw balls to try to knock a hat off of a person.
WATER WELLS - Five new wells were drilled on the property.

1914

OPENING DATE: Sunday, April 26

BOWLING ALLEYS were removed and sold for $200.
CHINA KITCHEN game was added where players attempted to break dishes. The prize was a cigar.
OLD MILL - The Panama Canal was again named the Old Mill.

1915

OPENING DATE: Sunday, April 25

HILARITY HALL - A new front and new stunts were added to the fun house in the old Wonderland Building. The name Hilarity Hall was given to the renovated attraction. The fun house, which measured 60 feet by 80 feet, was remodeled by Zarro Amusement Device Company, Inc., Beaver Falls, PA. The following devices were installed: Joy Wheel, Bull Moose Glide, Shaker Stairs, Earthquake Stairs, Electric Slide, Revolving Divan,

Ring the Bell, Tango Hustle, Bumping Twister, Jumble Board, Rocker Walk, Turkey Trot, Sliding Stairs, Alternating Floor, X-Ray, Electric Grip, Lung Tester, Perfume Machine, Hot Foot Walk, Rolling Wave, Virginia Shuffle, Undulating Walk, Wire Maze, Crash & Bumper, Dog House, and Maple Slide.
RAPIDS GORGE - The Old Mill was renamed the Rapids Gorge. Its channel was deepened, and the ride was given new scenic effects. Pumps were used instead of a wheel. The Zarro Amusement Device Company created the following scenes: Venetian Scene (Mechanical), Scene Portraying New York Harbor, Spring Scene with May Pole and eight figures (Mechanical), and Marine Scene with moving waves, battle ships, boats, and a light house with a revolving light.
RED DEVIL BALL GAME was added.
TILT HOUSE was built by the Zarro Amusement Device Company. It was a small room that tilted on a swinging axis to give the illusion that people were moving. It could hold up to 16 people at a time.
TUMBLE INN, "the latest laughter-provoking creation with its trick floors, wobbling steps and innumerable contrivances which are sure to surprise," was installed for $10,000.

1916

OPENING DATE: Sunday, April 23

KENNYWOOD PARK CORPORATION was incorporated to replace the limited partnership.

FLORAL CALENDAR was added to the park.
WURLITZER BAND ORGAN was purchased for the Merry-Go-Round.

1917

OPENING DATE: Sunday, April 29

BARBER SHOP - A barber shop was located in the Service Building for a few years. Kennywood also had its own post office.
FROLIC RIDE, a spin ride with cars suspended on a central axle, was purchased from R. S. Uzzell, New York, NY, and 20th Century Amusement Company, New Brighton, PA.
OLD MILL was rebuilt and renamed Fairyland Floats.
SHOOTING GALLERY - A new Shooting Gallery was installed for $10,000 on the midway between the back of the Casino and the Circle Swing.
SKEE BALL ALLEYS were purchased from National Skee Ball Company, Inc., Coney Island, NY.

1918

OPENING DATE: Sunday, May 5

1919

OPENING DATE: Sunday, April 20

FIRE destroyed the main arcade building, the motion picture theater, and a number of smaller buildings with the loss estimated between $50,000 and $100,000.
WHIP, a 12-car model, was purchased from W. F. Mangels Carousell Works, West Eighth Street, Coney Island, NY. The attraction featured a speeded-up whip-like action as the cars negotiated the two ends of the ride.
WATER WELLS - Five new wells were drilled on the property.

1920

OPENING DATE: Sunday, April 18

BAND ORGAN was placed in the Old Mill.
CIRCLE SWING cars were replaced with new ones that resembled airplanes.
FIGURE EIGHT received new larger cars.
JACK RABBIT - A $50,000 roller coaster was built by Miller and Baker, New York, NY. It was designed by John A. Miller with an 84-foot double dip. The Jack Rabbit used the natural ravine in the park and was 2,132 feet long. There was a tunnel after the first drop. More than 140,000 board feet of lumber were used in construction the coaster. The chain that pulled the coaster to the top of the coaster had 1,020 links.

1921

OPENING DATE: Sunday, April 17

OLD MILL - New boats were purchased from the Philadelphia Toboggan Company, Germantown, Philadelphia, PA.
RACER was remodeled. According to the park it was "faster and more exciting, practically rebuilt."
SPEED-O-PLANE was remodeled.
TUMBLE INN - The park's fun factory was remodeled with new devices installed.

1922

OPENING DATE: Sunday, April 16

BRIDGE - A new arched bridge with electric lights replaced the old flat bridge that crossed the Lagoon at the entrance to the Dance Pavilion.
DANCE PAVILION was remodeled.
DODGEM PAVILION, measuring 42 feet by 80 feet, was designed by Miller and Baker, Bridgeport, Connecticut, and was built on the site of the Figure Eight.
DODGEM RIDE - A Dodgem ride with 20 cars was purchased from Stoehrer & Pratt Dodgem Corporation, Lawrence, Massachusetts. The ride cost $8,400.
OBSERVATION BALLOON was operated as a concession at the park.
OLD MILL - New scenes were painted in the Old Mill by Edward Vandermark, 352 Sheridan Ave., Pittsburgh.
PARK BUILDINGS - Exteriors of the park buildings were painted "celestial yellow."

1923

OPENING DATE: Sunday, April 15

ANDREW S. MCSWIGAN, president of the park, died unexpectedly on January 12, 1923. ANDREW BRADY MCSWIGAN succeeded his father, A. S. McSwigan, as president of the park.

AUTOMOBILE RAFFLE was held on Labor Day.
BAND ORGAN, a rebuilt Organ #1700, was purchased from the Rudolph Wurlitzer Company of Pennsylvania, 615 Liberty Avenue, Pittsburgh, PA.
CATERPILLAR ride was purchased from Traver Engineering Company, Beaver Falls, PA, for $7,000.
KIDDIE AUTO RIDE was purchased from W. F. Mangels Carousell Works, Coney Island, NY.
KIDDIE CAROUSEL was purchased from W. F. Mangels Carousell Works, Coney Island, NY. It cost $1,400.
SPEED-O-PLANE was removed from the park after the 1923 season.
TUNNEL was built underneath the street car tracks to a free parking lot and to streets cars headed toward Duquesne.

1924

OPENING DATE: Sunday, April 13

AUTOMOBILE PARKING LOT was enlarged.
CAT'S MEOW BALL GAME was designed by McTighe and built by Charles Mach of Kennywood. The game was licensed to Dayton Fun House & Riding Device Mfg. Co., Dayton, OH.
ENTRANCE - A new entrance to the park was constructed.
KIDDIELAND consisting of four kiddie rides (Whip, Ferris Wheel, Swan Swing, and a 2-row carousel) was established across from the Jack Rabbit.
PIPPIN roller coaster was designed by John A. Miller, Homewood, IL. Miller called the coaster a Deep Dip Coaster, but the name was changed to Pippin before it opened. Hardware for the coaster cars was furnished by Dayton Fun House & Riding Device Mfg. Co., Dayton, OH. This $60,000 ravine coaster was built at the opposite end of the park from the Jack Rabbit. Its double dip was different than the Jack Rabbit's in that the first dip was short and the second dip was long.

1925

OPENING DATE: Sunday, April 12

ATHLETIC FIELD, a.k.a. Baseball Field, was moved across the road to make room for the new swimming pool.
BABY BAND ORGAN was purchased from W. F. Mangels Carousell Works, Coney Island, NY.
CIRCLE SWING - A new Circle Swing was purchased from Traver Engineering Company, Beaver Falls, PA. The ride had a 25 h.p. motor and six seaplanes, each with a 1 1/2 h.p. motor to turn the propeller. The previous circle swing, which was owned by the Pennsylvania Amusement Company, New York, NY, was purchased by Traver and dismantled.
GRANDSTAND, with a seating capacity of 2,500, was built in the free parking area across the road.
MECHANICAL SEE SAW was purchased from Pinto Bros., Coney Island, NY.
MINIATURE RAILWAY, electrical third rail, was manufactured by Dayton Fun House & Riding Device Mfg. Co., Dayton, OH. The $3,500 attraction had 1,000 feet of track, one 5-h.p. locomotive, and four cars. It was equipped with an electric headlight, warning signal, bell, sand box, pilot's and operator's upholstered seat. The locomotive was 55 inches long and 27 inches wide; the height above the rail was 35 inches. Driving wheels were 4-10 inch wheels. Later in the season a second locomotive with a 7 1/2 h.p. motor and four, six-passenger cars with three seats each were purchased from Dayton Fun House & Riding Device Mfg. Co. for $2,400. The railway was built on the Pony Track site (current main office site).
MINIATURE WHIP for Kiddieland was purchased from W. F. Mangels Carousell Works, Coney Island, NY, for $1,750.

PONY RIDE was moved to the current Auto Ride site.
SWIMMING POOL, designed by Lynch Brothers, New Haven, Connecticut, was 350 feet by 180 feet. The $150,000 pool held 2,250,000 gallons of water. It had a colonial-style pavilion with a 2,500-seat grandstand built over the dressing room. A 25-foot wide sand beach containing 20 railroad carloads of white sand surrounded the pool on three sides.
YELLOW SIGNS with the word Kennywood on them were adopted. These directional signs were generally placed on trolley poles near important intersections.

1926

OPENING DATE: Sunday, April 11

BUG HOUSE was converted into Tut's Tomb for two seasons.
DODGEM JUNIOR CARS (smaller and faster cars) were purchased from Dodgem Corporation, Salisbury Beach, Massachusetts. Cars cost $300 each for a total cost of $16,000.
MINATURE RAILROAD track was relocated.
OLD MILL was rebuilt and enlarged by the park under the supervision of Charles Mach, Kennywood's maintenance supervisor. The front structure work was done by the Blaw-Knox Company, Blawnox, PA.
RACER - The original Racer closed after the 1926 season.
SEAPLANES for the circle swing were purchased from Traver Engineering Co., Beaver Falls, PA.
TROLLEY STATION - A new trolley shed for passengers was built on the current Gran Prix site.
WHIP, a 16-car park model, was purchased from W. F. Mangels Carousell Works, Coney Island, NY, for $5,500. The building for the Whip was constructed by the Blaw-Knox Company, Blawnox, PA.

1927

OPENING DATE: Sunday, April 10

ALPHABET BLOCK FRONT - Kiddieland received a new entrance made to resemble large alphabet blocks stacked on each other. The idea was copied from Riverview Park, Chicago.
AUTO PARKING was enlarged to accommodate 4500 cars.
BUG HOUSE - Thirty-nine new devices were purchased from Dayton Fun House & Riding Device Mfg. Co., Dayton, OH. The front of the building was repainted.
CAROUSEL PAVILION - To house the new Dentzel Carousel, a new steel structure in the shape of a dome was erected. The steel building was manufactured by Pittsburgh-Des Moines Steel Company.
CIRCUS ACTS - Free Circus Acts were performed on a newly erected stage on a small island in the lagoon. Performers had to be taken to the island by boat.
DENTZEL CAROUSEL, which was to be a "show piece" for the Philadelphia Exposition of 1926 (a.k.a. the Sesquicentennial) was bought by Kennywood. It was still in the Dentzel factory when the exposition closed, so Kennywood made a deal to purchase it for $25,000 from William H. Dentzel Carrousells and Organs, Philadelphia, PA. William Dentzel, the owner of the company, personally supervised the installation. Traditional laughing jester heads and angelic faces decorate the rounding boards and interior of the machine. There are 72 animals hand-carved from bass wood arranged in four rows, one with 20 stationary animals and three with 50 jumpers. There are also four chariots, one lion, and one tiger (a Dentzel trademark). The carousel is illuminated by 1,400 50-watt Mazda lamps. It was originally advertised as "the largest and most elaborate carousel ever built."

FERRIS WHEEL was purchased from C. W. Parker Amusement Co. Leavenworth, Kansas, for $5,000. The new attraction was a Superior Park Model Parker Wheel with 10 coaches, a light star, and a 10 h.p. electric motor.
ISLAND STAGE was constructed on an island in the Lagoon.
KIDDIELAND was relocated from a spot in front of the Jack Rabbit to a new site formerly occupied by the old Racer. There were now eight or nine kiddie rides.
KIDDIE MERRY-GO-ROUND was purchased from R. S. Uzzell, New York, NY, for $2,000. The ride was manufactured by W. F. Mangels, 8th Street, Coney Island, NY. It was a three-row miniature galloping horse carousel powered by a 1 1/2 h.p. motor. Kennywood traded in a two-abreast Mangels Miniature Carousel and was given an $800 credit.
KIDDIE SWAN SWING was purchased from R. S. Uzzell, New York, NY. The ride was manufactured by W. F. Mangels, Coney Island, NY.
LANDSCAPING - Several hundred trees were planted.
LOCOMOTIVES - Two locomotives were rebuilt by the Dayton Fun House & Riding Device Mfg. Co., Dayton, OH
MCSWIGAN MEMORIAL, a large boulder with a bronze tablet, was dedicated in honor of Andrew S. McSwigan, first President of the National Association of Amusement Parks. The monument was purchased from Eckles Granite & Marble for $450.
MECHANICAL SEESAW was purchased from Pinto Bros., Coney Island, NY.
MINIATURE MOTOR BOATS were purchased from W. F. Mangels Co., Coney Island, NY, for $750.
MINIATURE WHIP - A new Miniature Whip with a 16 foot by 32 foot platform and 8 little whip cars was purchased from by W. F. Mangels, Coney Island, NY.
RACER - A completely new $75,000 racing coaster replaced the old racing coaster that had been built in 1910. The new Racer was 72 1/2 feet tall and 2,250 feet long; it was built along the southernmost edge of the Lagoon. The new Racer was one continuous track with banked curves and curved dips; two sets of coaster cars "raced" on parallel tracks and the coaster that started on the left side of the loading area would finish on the right and vice versa. The new Racer was designed by John A. Miller, for the John A. Miller Company, Homewood, IL. Charles Mach of Kennywood along with A. M. Browne of the Miller Company supervised the construction. Miller also designed the station front and station trusses. Twelve four-seat cars were purchased from Dayton Fun House & Riding Device Mfg. Co., Dayton, OH at $700 per car. The old racing coaster was demolished.
RESTAURANT AND KITCHEN - A new concrete block foundation was added by John Eichleay Jr. Company. (The Casino was raised for a new foundation and the kitchen was added to the back of the building.)
ROW BOATS - Ten boats were purchased from Frank B. Reiman, Conneaut Lake, PA.
SODA FOUNTAIN was placed in the old Merry-Go-Round building.
TUMBLE BUG was purchased from Traver Engineering Co., Beaver Falls, PA. Five cars seating eight persons each were built to resemble bugs. The cars traveled over a laminated metal track.
UZZELL BABY SWING by R. S. Uzzell, New York, NY, was purchased for $750.
WHIP, new 16-car stationary or park model, was purchased from W. F. Mangels, Coney Island, NY.

1928

OPENING DATE: Sunday, April 29
(The scheduled opening date of April 22 was postponed due to snow.) Brady McSwigan commented to Charles F. Danver of the *Pittsburgh Post-Gazette* in 1959 "The last time the opening was postponed because of snow was April 22, 1928. It was so wintry that day . . . they had to put blankets on the merry-go-round horses."

AIRPLANE was raffled on Labor Day. This WACO Airplane was manufactured by Advance Aircraft Company, Troy, OH, and purchased from the distributor, Clifford Ball, Bettis Field, McKeesport, PA.
BABY BAND ORGAN for the kiddie carousel was repaired and repainted by J. S. Gebhardt Organ Company, Tacony, Philadelphia, PA, for $230.
ELECTRIC PENNY GAME - Two boards were purchased from Kerstetter & Junker, Buffalo, NY, at $150 a board.
ISLAND STAGE was enlarged to 50 feet by 35 feet.
LITTLE BROWNIE COASTER had a 22 foot by 55 foot oval track elevated about 2 1/2 feet with two curves and four dips. The kiddie coaster had five cars in its train with each car able to seat two children. It cost $2,000. Two life-like mechanical figures representing the little brownies of the fairy tales seemed to provide the motive power for the cars.
REST ROOM - A rest room comfort station, the park's third, was built behind the Racer.
SKEE BALL ALLEYS - Twelve used skee ball alleys were purchased from Chester Park, Cincinnati, OH, through John A. Miller Company for $600 each. The alleys were 4 feet wide and 36 feet deep with a net frame 9 feet high and a 10 foot playing space in front. They had been manufactured by Skee-Ball Company, Coney Island, NY.
TILT-A-WHIRL 7-car model was purchased from Sellner Manufacturing Company, Faribault, Minnesota, for $6,650. It was located next to the Racer.
WINDMILL - An ornamental windmill was built by the park on an island in the Lagoon. Construction was supervised by Charles Mach. It was built on the current Garden Stage site.

1929

OPENING DATE: Sunday, April 14

CHRISTMAS CARD: Tower Stand in black and white with the caption: "The Voice of Kennywood."

DODGEM - New cars were purchased from the Dodgem Corporation, Lawrence, Massachusetts. This was the last season for the ride.
ISLAND STAGE BRIDGE was built by Pittsburgh Iron Works.
MARY QUITE CONTRARY GARDEN opened next to the main office. This garden and the name were copied from Rye Playland, Rye, NY.
OLD MILL got new scenes.
TOWER REFRESHMENT STAND was built by the park with "Masonite, Celotex, and a little wood paneling." All lighting on the building was indirect. A refreshment stand occupied the first floor, and the Voice of Kennywood and the amplification tower occupied the second and third floors.
"VOICE OF KENNYWOOD," an internal public address (called an internal radio station) began daily operation on May 16 with Izzy Cervone's band. Ed Sprague was in charge of the station, and Jim Page became the announcer. (Page also served as announcer in the ballroom.) The studio was located on the second floor of the Tower Refreshment Stand.

1930

OPENING DATE: Sunday, April 13

AUTO RACE electric car ride was purchased from Traver Engineering, Beaver Falls, PA. This attraction was later called the Auto Ride.
FRONT for Auto Race and Miniature Railroad was designed by Raymond Marlier.
GOLF DRIVING RANGE was built across the highway in the free parking lot. It lasted only one season.

KIDDIE AUTO RIDE was purchased from W. F. Mangels Company, Coney Island NY.
KIDDIE MENAGERIE CIRCUS was a small attraction made up of a number of domestic animals such as geese, swans, and rabbits in small circus cages under a big top (tent).
LAFF-IN-THE-DARK was a $5,800 dark ride purchased from Traver Engineering, Beaver Falls, PA. The old Dodgem building was completely enclosed. The ride had ten cars and 825 feet of track. Traver also supplied ten stunts. At times this ride was called Laugh-In-The-Dark.
LUCKY STAND was built. It was located on the midway in the midst of the Bug House, Pippin, Whip, and Sea Planes. The building was done in a "modernistic style, with subdued lighting effects." No one at Kennywood remembers how the stand got the name "lucky."
MINIATURE RAILROAD was moved to a site next to the Auto Race.
MONKEY CAGE was built in front of the Bug House.
PONY TRACK was enlarged and relocated to a spot next to the Racer.
TOM THUMB miniature golf course was built on the old pony track site near the original Merry-Go-Round Pavilion.
VOICE OF KENNYWOOD, a four-page park newsletter edited by A. K. "Rosey" Rowswell, began publication. It was first mailed to friends of the park.

1931

OPENING DATE: Sunday, April 12

BAND ORGAN was repaired with parts from Rudolph Wurlitzer Mfg. Company, North Tonawanda, NY. Two new music rolls were also purchased.
BEACH PLAYGROUND with children's playground equipment was developed close to the Swimming Pool.
BIRTHDAY CAKE was introduced. The plaster cake was five feet high and twelve feet in diameter. It was created to celebrate the park's birthdays; the first year it had 33 candles with one more added every year.
CHAIR-O-PLANE was purchased as a used ride.
COMPTON-HUGHES GREAT WILD WEST RODEO SHOW performed at Kennywood during July and August in a specially constructed arena in the free parking lot.
FLIGHT TUTOR, an airplane training ride, was operated as a concession by Aircraft Appliance Sales Corporation, Springfield, OH. It provided "the thrills and sensation of a real airplane flight, with 100% safety assured."
FLORAL BASKET AND FLORAL ELEPHANT were introduced.
KIDDIE TICKLER was built by W. F. Mangels Company, Coney Island, NY. It was the only miniature Tickler Mangels ever built. Versions of this ride are also called Virginia Reel.
MARY MARY QUITE CONTRARY'S GARDEN (later shortened to MARY'S GARDEN) was developed next to the office. Copied from Mary Mary Quite Contrary's Garden at Rye Playland, Rye, NY.
MUSIC TOWER was built on the Island Stage and used as part of the park's public address system. It was also used to announce acts on the stage. The tower was designed by Raymond Marlier.

1932

OPENING DATE: Sunday, April 17

DANCE PAVILION was remodeled.
DAUGHTERS OF THE AMERICAN REVOLUTION unveiled an inscription commemorating George Washington's crossing of the Monongahela River at the park site.
LAFF-IN-THE-DARK - New stunts (barrels, piers, and floors) were purchased from Traver Engineering.

1933

OPENING DATE: Sunday, May 7

MOUSE CITY that contained 300 white mice was built.
OLD MILL changed its stunts.

1934

OPENING DATE: Sunday, April 29
    Billboard reported "Favorable weather has moved up opening of Kennywood Park from May 6 to April 29."

FDR DAY was celebrated.
FUN ON THE FARM, a carnival-type walk-through with a canvas top, was purchased from Spillman Engineering Corp., North Tonawanda, NY.
ROLLER SKATING was offered in the Dance Pavilion during the winter.

1935

OPENING DATE: Sunday, April 21

CAROUSEL was repainted by the Philadelphia Toboggan Company for $750. The job included coats of primer, paint, and varnish on all the horses, animals, and chariots.
CUDDLE UP was purchased from Berks Engineering Company, Reading, PA. This attraction was placed on the current site of the Pirate ride.
SKOOTER replaced Bug House in the old Wonderland/Steeplechase building. Raymond Marlier did the engineering drawings, and the Skooter cars and ride were purchased from Lusse Brothers, Philadelphia, PA.
TEDDY BEAR roller coaster, a junior coaster, was built. Designed by Herbert Schmeck of the Philadelphia Toboggan Company, Philadelphia, PA, the coaster was about 20 feet high and 600 feet long. The coaster was similar to one built the same year at Coney Island, Cincinnati, OH. Three bear cub cars with two seats per car were also purchased from PTC. The coaster was given the number PTC 95. PTC was paid $2,950.

1936

OPENING DATE: Sunday, April 19

DANCE PAVILION was remodeled and redecorated in art deco style.
LOOP-O-PLANE was purchased from Eyerly Aircraft Corporation, Salem, OR.
MOTION PICTURE-VAUDEVILLE THEATER was removed from the Penny Arcade so that the arcade could be expanded.
NOAH'S ARK fun house, was a walk-through themed as a boat that was perched atop a miniature Mount Ararat. It rocked back and forth imitating the motion of a boat on the water and contained a moving floor and other disconcerting features. It also had a high pitched ship's whistle and rope handrails. It cost approximately $20,000 with the engineering done by the Philadelphia Toboggan Company, Philadelphia, PA. PTC also furnished the stunts.
RUDY VALLEE and his "Connecticut Yankees" appeared at Kennywood on July 15, 1936. He played from 9 p.m. to midnight. Vallee was paid $750 when he signed the contract and $750 at 11 p.m. on the night of the engagement.

1937

OPENING DATE: Saturday, April 17

BANDSTAND was redecorated.
DOUBLE DECKER PICNIC PAVILION was built in the grove next to the Jack Rabbit.
FIRE FIGHTER tiny-tot fire truck was added to Kiddieland. It was purchased from Spillman Engineering Company, North Tonawanda, NY, for $1,580.
FOUNTAIN was built in the Swimming Pool by D. F. Nellis & Sons Company, East Liverpool, OH, for $5,729.00. It was located 90 feet from the east end of the pool and was lighted.
GAMES BUILDING was erected next to 13 Spook Street to hold the Electro Ball and Auto Game.
KIDDIE OLD MILL, a.k.a. Kiddie Dutch Mill, was designed by the Philadelphia Toboggan Company. It was copied from a similar miniature mill at Coney Island, Cincinnati, OH. The ride included six kiddie two-seat swan boats that were 8 1/2 feet long and 34 1/2 inches wide across the beam. PTC was paid $2,100.
PENNY ARCADE was enlarged to occupy the entire building. More than a hundred new amusement machines were added, including athletic devices, Skee Roll, and Radio Markmanship. A new front, which featured a large penny, was designed by Raymond Marlier.
PONY CART-GO-ROUND was added to Kiddieland. The ride was purchased from Pinto Brothers, Coney Island, NY, for $800. The ride was 25 feet in diameter and had 16 metal horses and eight carts that were covered with striped canopies,
SERVICE BUILDING was remodeled with a new front by Raymond Marlier.
SPORTLAND, a modernistic-styled building, housed three games.
13 SPOOK STREET (a.k.a. OLD HAUNTED CASTLE) was an electro-mechanical walk-through built between the Jack Rabbit and Racer. This fun house was featured at the Great Lakes Exposition. Stunts, including a magic carpet, were provided by the Philadelphia Toboggan Co., Philadelphia, PA. W. F. Larkin designed the fun house, which he called "The spookiest place on earth." Larkin furnished eight scenes for which he and his agent Fred Fansher were paid $3,175. The park built a new structure 32 feet wide by 50 feet deep to house the attraction.
UTILITIES - An underground power line was installed and the sewer system was improved.

1938

OPENING DATE: Sunday, April 17

ADMINISTRATION BUILDING - A new office building was built for $35,000. Raymond Marlier, architect, Empire Building, Pittsburgh, PA, designed it.
AUTO SKOOTER CARS - 30 new front-wheel drive models were purchased from Lusse Brothers, Inc. Philadelphia, PA, for $7,700. The little cars were a "good peppy red, trimmed with aluminum touched with yellow stripe."
ISLAND STAGE in the lagoon was enlarged.
MONKEY GAME was purchased from National Amusement Device Company, Dayton, OH, for $1,350.00.
RIDEE-O, was purchased from Spillman, North Tonawanda, NY, for $9,800.
STRATOSHIP, a rocket ship on a pylon ride, was purchased from R. E. Chambers Company, Inc., Beaver Falls, PA.

1939

OPENING DATE: Sunday, April 16

CHRISTMAS CARD: Small characters, each in color, formed a parade: Band (health), Horse & Elephant (good cheer), Elephant (wealth), Clown (joy), Dog drawing cart (friendship), Horse with toe dancer (success), and Calliope (happiness). "Kennywood Park - Hopes you will enjoy this parade of good things."

CEMENT SIDEWALKS replaced many of the old gravel sidewalks around the park.
LAFF-IN-THE-DARK was remodeled and received a new facade. New stunts were purchased from Leo Kathe, Cleveland, OH, for $330.
NOAH'S ARK - New stunts were purchased from Leo Kathe, Cleveland, OH, for $750. These stunts included Hissing Snake, Mice in Cheese, Running Rat, Dummy in Floor, and Skeleton.
13 SPOOK STREET purchased new stunts including a magic carpet exit from the Philadelphia Toboggan Company, Philadelphia, PA. Other stunts (Falling Boxes and Trick Doors) were purchased from Leo Kathe, Cleveland, OH, for $425. The walk-through was originally developed by W. F. Larkin at Luna Park, Coney Island, NY, in 1933.

1940

OPENING DATE: Sunday, April 14
(The weather was cold and it snowed.)

CHRISTMAS CARD: The Wind Mill (black and white).

CIRCLE SWING was moved to the island in the Lagoon. New rocket ships, which replaced the Seaplanes, were purchased from R. E. Chambers, Company, Inc., Beaver Falls, PA. A platform was erected on the island and a bridge built. The Rocket Ship was designed by Leo Kathe, Cleveland, OH. The circle swing was erected by Pittsburgh-Des Moines Steel Company.
DIPSY DOODLE (generic name: Flying Scooter) was purchased from Bisch-Rocco Amusement Company, IL. The ride was named after Rosey Rowswell's famous strike out call.
LAUGHING SAM, a mechanical laughing man was purchased from the Philadelphia Toboggan Company, Germantown, Philadelphia, PA. This mechanical person was placed as part of the Noah's Ark's front.

1941

OPENING DATE: Sunday, April 13
(The weather was an ideal 80 degrees!)

CHRISTMAS CARD: A small Christmas tree before the fireplace with a caption "Is there a Santa Claus?"

AUTO RAFFLE - On Labor Day the park held its last auto raffle until the end of the war.
BANDSTAND was redesigned in modern decor by Leo Kathe, who used snow-white stucco embellished with chromium trimming in a style of severe simplicity. Neon and indirect lighting were used extensively. A new seating area in front of the music stage was expanded to accommodate 5,000 people giving the bandstand the largest seating capacity in the area except for Pitt Stadium and Forbes Field. The total renovation cost was approximately $50,000.

CALLIOPE was installed on a General Motors truck and used by the promotion department.
DAFFY KLUB walk-through fun house replaced 13 Spook Street. New stunts were purchased from the Philadelphia Toboggan Company, Philadelphia, PA, for $2,314. James L. Martz from PTC supervised the remodeling. Included were plans and details for a tilted room and four welded pipe rails, ramps, passages, and a new front. Stunts included Pinocchio and Geppetto Figures, and Jack-in-the-Box.
LAFFING SAL, with an amplifier and record-playing device, was added to the front of Laff-in-the-Dark, and four animated profile panels approximately 54" by 60" at $95.00 each were purchased from the Philadelphia Toboggan Company, Philadelphia, PA, for $380.00.
NOAH'S ARK added an additional walkway at the entrance.
PENNY ARCADE added a new wing to accommodate six skee ball alleys. New machines were also purchased from Exhibit Supply Company and International Mutoscope.
ROTO WHIP, a kiddie ride, was purchased from W. F. Mangels, Coney Island, NY.
SKY ROCKET KIDDIE RIDE was purchased from Pinto Brothers, Coney Island, NY, for $1,350.
SNAPPER was purchased from the Philadelphia Toboggan Company, which manufactured it and had operated it at the New York World's Fair of 1939-40. The ride cost $6,500 and included the Snapper sign. The generic name of the ride was the Cuddle Up.

1942

OPENING DATE: Sunday, April 26
(Postponed from the scheduled opening date of Sunday, April 19.)

CHRISTMAS CARD: Little booklet with a small color photo of the Three Wise Men on camels.

CAROUSEL was repainted by Tom Moran from Philadelphia, PA.
NOAK'S ARK got new stunts from the Philadelphia Toboggan Company, Philadelphia, PA.

1943

OPENING DATE: Sunday, April 18

CHRISTMAS CARD: Christmas cards were not sent in 1943. Voice of Kennywood took the place of the card and was mailed to names on "Voice list" and to Kennywood boys in the service.

KIDDIE FERRIS WHEEL, a used Mangels machine, was purchased through R. S. Uzzell of New York, NY.

1944

OPENING DATE: Saturday, April 22
(A dance was held Saturday night, April 22; the rest of the park opened on Sunday, April 23.)

CHRISTMAS CARD: Noah's Ark in black and white showing people going up the steps.

DANCE PAVILION was restyled.

FERRIS WHEEL, a Number 12 Big Eli Wheel, was purchased from Doolan. It was a used 12-seat model that had been manufactured in 1936 by Eli Bridge, Jacksonville, IL.

1945

OPENING DATE: Sunday, April 22

CHRISTMAS CARD: Little Choo Choo in black and white.

CAROUSEL was repainted by Tom Moran, of Germantown, PA. It cost $650, which included the labor, paint, and one coat of varnish.
LITTLE CHOO CHOO - Two 5-ton, 35 inch gauge gasoline locomotives and six 24-passenger cars were purchased from Lillian J. Cagney, Leonardo, NJ, for $7,000. The Cagney Brothers had operated the attraction, called a "Trip Around the World," at the New York World's Fair of 1939-40. The ride was similar to a conventional gravity scenic railway except that the dips were quite mild and the trains traversing the ride were powered by gasoline locomotives. Trains were larger than the ordinary miniature train and could haul 70 adults or 90 children. At the World's Fair, the trains had been sponsored by Gimbel's Department Store. The miniature railroad's track extended to nearly a half mile overlooking the Monongahela River. There were three engines in all. The ride was called the Little Choo Choo after a juvenile book *Little Choo Choo*, written by Helen Sterling and illustrated by Denison Budd.

1946

OPENING DATE: Sunday, April 21
(The weather was fair, temperature 70 degrees; receipts were good.)

CHRISTMAS CARD: Two small girls in Kiddie Whip Car (taken from a glossy black and white photograph).

ADMINISTRATION BUILDING and SERVICE BUILDING were expanded adding rest rooms and quarters for park employees.
BUBBLE BOUNCE was purchased from the Custer Specialty Company, Inc. of Dayton, OH, for $12,500.
EMPLOYEE CAFETERIA behind the restaurant was enclosed. It had formerly been open-air.
RACER FACADE was redesigned with "ultra-modern" architecture featuring lofty pylons and sheltering marquees done in a "World's Fair" style. It was designed by Warren L. Hindenach, a registered engineer from Philadelphia, PA.

1947

KENNYWOOD PARK CELEBRATED ITS 50TH ANNIVERSARY

OPENING DATE: Sunday, April 20
(The weather was fair with a shower at 8 p.m.; temperature 76 degrees. Receipts were fair.)

CHRISTMAS CARD: Entrance to Kiddieland (blocks) in black and white with the word KIDDIELAND in red ink.

KENNYWOOD celebrated its golden anniversary because several years earlier it had been decided to call 1898 instead of 1899 the park's first season.

LAKE ERIE RAILROAD'S last year of operating picnic trains to the park.
LOOPER was purchased from Allan Herschell Company, Inc., North Tonawanda, NY, for $13,357.00. It had a frontage of 53 feet. "We so underestimated its appeal that a reorder of tickets was necessary in midseason," said park president A. B. McSwigan in an ad in *Billboard* Feb. 7, 1948. The Looper was designed by Norman Bartlett.
TEDDY BEAR junior roller coaster was removed from the park at the end of the season to make room for the new midway.

1948

OPENING DATE: Sunday, April 18
(Weather was cloudy and cool, temperature 68 degrees; receipts fair.)

CHRISTMAS CARD: Silver Lining booklet.

AUTO RIDE (formerly the Auto Race) got new streamlined cars. The hills were removed from the track.
DAFFY KLUB added new stunts purchased from Traver Enterprises, Inc, for $1,150.
JET KIDDIE RIDE for Kiddieland was purchased from Bisch-Rocco Amusement Company, Chicago, IL, for $1,980.00. The ride, which was nine feet high, had five cars and occupied a 24 foot diameter space.
LAFF-IN-THE-DARK - 10 cars were rebuilt (not including the motors on the rear wheels) by Chambers, Beaver Falls, PA, for $6,418. New stunts from Traver Enterprises, Inc., including a Witch, Hoot Owl, Rats On Wall, Gorilla, Frog on Mushroom, and Andy Gump, were also added to the attraction.
LITTLE DIPPER, a junior roller coaster, was designed by Andy Vettel, Kennywood's chief engineer.
LUCAS KIDDIE BOAT RIDE (sailboats) with a steel tank was purchased from Traver Enterprises, Inc., Painesville, OH, for $3475.00.
MALL was formed with Auto Ride, Little Choo Choo Train, and the Little Dipper on one side and the Sportland Building, skee ball alleys, and a shooting gallery on the other. There was a green strip in the middle with a fountain surrounded by park benches. The Mall was designed by Leo Kathe.
NOAH'S ARK added new stunts from Traver Enterprises, Inc.
SHOOTING GALLERY, a No. 60, was purchased from W. F. Mangels, Coney Island, NY, for $3,350.00. It was 24 feet wide by 12 feet high and had a three horsepower motor.
SKEE BALL ALLEYS - 12 alleys were purchased from the Philadelphia Toboggan Company, Germantown, Philadelphia, PA, and placed in the Sportland Building.
SPORTLAND BUILDING was moved to make room for the new Mall. Neon lighting was added.
TILT-A-WHIRL was purchased from Sellner Manufacturing Co., Inc., Faribault, Minnesota, for $10,500.00.
TUMBLE BUG ride got a new set of cars fashioned to resemble turtles from R. E. Chambers, Beaver Falls, PA.

1949

OPENING DATE: Sunday, April 17
(Weather was cool with showers, temperature 54 degrees; receipts were bad.)

CHRISTMAS CARD: Boy and girl eating cotton candy in Kiddieland Swan boat with Santa (in color).

CAROUSEL was repainted by Tom Moran of Germantown, PA. The $750 cost covered labor, paint, and one coat of varnish.
DIPSY DOODLE (generic name Flying Scooter), received 10 new metal planes from Bisch-Rocco Amusement Company, Chicago, IL, at a cost of $3,350.00.
HURRICANE was purchased from Allan Herschell Company, Inc., North Tonawanda, NY, for $29,500.00. Designed by Norman Bartlett, it was placed on the Mall replacing the Looper, which was relocated between the Ponies and Racer.
MERRY-GO-ROUND REFRESHMENT PAVILION was remodeled with translucent glass and stainless steel and partitioned into three stands that sold taffy, popcorn, and drinks. Leo Kathe redesigned the building adding pylons and neon to the outside.
PENNY ARCADE got 50 new machines.
PIPPIN FACADE was redesigned by Leo Kathe.
POST OFFICE at Kennywood was discontinued on March 31, 1949.
RACER'S "home stretch" dip was redesigned by Andy Vettel.
RESTAURANT'S delivery service area was rebuilt.
RIDEE-O was rebuilt at the Allen Herschell factory in North Tonawanda, NY.
TILT-A-WHIRL returned after a 15-year absence.
TUMBLE BUG'S (Turtle) front was redesigned.
WATER LILY DISPLAY was added to the fountain in the Midway Mall.

1950

OPENING DATE: Sunday, April 16
(Weather was fair and cool, temperature 60 degrees; receipts were fair.)

1st FALL FANTASY PARADE: Alice in Wonderland Floats by McDonald Art Studios of Chicago
CHRISTMAS CARD: Glossy black and white photograph of people walking on the Mall outside of Kiddieland.

FREDERICK W. HENNINGER dies on September 18, 1950. He was secretary-treasurer of the park from 1906 until his death.

JUNIOR TURTLES (Baby Bug Amusement Ride) in Kiddieland were purchased from R. E. Chambers Company, Inc. of Beaver Falls, PA, for $3,500.
LITTLE DIPPER was redesigned by Andy Vettel, and 440 feet of track were added. This was done to give the coaster more speed and much deeper dips and to make it a more "grown-up" ride.
LOOP-O-PLANE was removed from the park.
ROLL-O-PLANE, 3-phase, was purchased from Eyerly Aircraft Company, Salem, OR. It replaced the Loop-O-Plane near the miniature golf course.
SKY FIGHTER ride was purchased for Kiddieland.
STRING GAME was added to the Penny Arcade.

1951

OPENING DATE: Saturday, April 21

2nd FALL FANTASY PARADE: Storybook Land on Parade
CHRISTMAS CARD: Fat, laughing Santa in red looking into a trick mirror reflected as a skinny Santa.

AUTO SKOOTERS added new cars.
DAFFY KLUB - New stunts and distortion mirrors were purchased. This was the first time the mirrors had been used in the park in 19 years. The original mirrors were hand-made in Germany, brought to Kennywood in

1902, and installed in Wonderland.
JACK RABBIT - New trains were purchased from the Philadelphia Toboggan Company, Germantown, Philadelphia, PA.
KIDDIE SKY FIGHTER was added to Kiddieland.
MINIATURE MERRY-GO-ROUND was added in Kiddieland.
OLD MILL - New stunts were purchased.
ROCKETS - New rocket ships were purchased for the Rocket ride in the Lagoon.

1952

OPENING DATE: Sunday, April 27

CHRISTMAS CARD: A Day at Kennywood - with sketches by Nat Youngblood (like Kennywood's old letterhead sketches).
3rd FALL FANTASY PARADE: Kandy Kapers on Parade

BULGEY THE WHALE was purchased from Eyerly Aircraft Company, Salem, OR.
LITTLE CHOO CHOO railroad added new stainless-steel shells on the old cars. The railroad was said to be a real sight-seeing tour along the rim of the Monongahela Valley.
MINIATURE GOLF COURSE, Golfland, a completely new layout, was designed by Holmes Cook Company.
OCTOPUS (serial no. 2627) was purchased from Eyerly Aircraft Company, Salem, OR, for $8,592.00. The attraction had eight arms with two cars at the end of each arm; it was placed on the Dipsy Doodle site.
OLD MILL - The area inside the loading platform was rebuilt and painted.

1953

OPENING DATE: Sunday, April 26

4th FALL FANTASY PARADE: Circus on Parade
CHRISTMAS CARD: Two kids in front of Wishing Well.

ANTIQUE WISHING WELL with an old oaken bucket was added on the site where Kennywood for many years exhibited its birthday cake.
DANCE PAVILION was closed.
FLORAL CLOCK was planted with 8,000 plants as part of the new Mall.
HAND-CAR RAILWAY was constructed with a 300-foot track.
KIDDIELAND received a new front with giant toy soldiers.
MOTHER GOOSE TINY TOT COMFORT STATION, a children's rest room, was installed in a circular building topped by a huge Mother Goose and decorated with characters from nursery rhymes. It was designed and built by Modern Art Studios in Chicago, IL, which produced the first Fall Fantasy and 10 subsequent parades. The Mother Goose figure was later moved to Storybook Forest in Idlewild Park.
RODEO, a merry-go-round type ride for cowboys and cowgirls of all ages was purchased from Allan Herschell Company, Inc., North Tonawanda, NY. The attraction was large enough that adults also could ride it. Each rider was given a pistol with an electronic beam to shoot at bandits in the center of the ride. When a bandit was hit, a bell rang and a light flashed.
SNAPPER (generic name: Cuddle Up) manufactured by the Philadelphia Toboggan Company, was removed at the end of the season. At the end of the 1955 season the ride was sold to Seaside Heights Casino, Seaside Heights, NJ, for $3,000.
SPEEDBOAT RIDE was installed in Kiddieland.
SWIMMING POOL was closed during the season.
U-DRIVE-'EM MOTORBOATS were placed in Kennywood's swimming pool as a concession from B. A. Schiff of Miami, Florida.

1954

OPENING DATE: Sunday, April 18

5TH FALL FANTASY PARADE: Gay Nineties on Parade (Tuesday, August 24, had no parade due to a storm.)
CHRISTMAS CARDS: Three Christmas Balls (one green and two red above the words "Greetings of the Season."

DIPSY DOODLE, A Flying Scooter, was reinstalled after being absent for two years.
ENCHANTED FOREST - The park's ballroom was converted into an Alice-in-Wonderland type children's walk-through designed by Modern Arts Studios of Chicago, IL, with new stunts that cost $5,000.
FASCINATION, a game, was operated as a concession by John T. Gibbs.
ZOOMERANG, a pretzel dark ride, occupied the Snapper site. It was a jungle themed dark ride with animated cannibal figures from Animated Display Company of Minneapolis, Minnesota. The ride's name was chosen in a television contest.

1955

OPENING DATE: Sunday, April 24

"Well, the grind is on for another season, incidentally my thirty-third (plus some others in teen years). The first day of the 1955 season on the books. The weather wasn't exactly in accord with a good start because it rained cats and dogs all Sunday morning, clearing about eleven, then sunshine off and on until around five o'clock when it darkened up and showers were back again with us at six-thirty for about an hour. Then some light rain around nine. So you see the day's weather could not be considered conducive to good business. However, we did have a nice crowd in the clear portion of the day and they rode, munched, and quenched throats; surprisingly we got about 89% of last year's take.

"The Rotor, while not ready until 7 PM got off to a good start. I do not have figures (I am in City Office) but know it did a satisfactory business in the four hours of last night. The device seems like it will go right well in good old Kennywood." (Brady McSwigan to George A. Schmidt, April 15, 1955)

"Kennywood has traditionally opened weekends (Saturdays and Sundays) before our daily operational season began. This helped us get the bugs out and helped us organize before our daily opening. Off hand I would say the weather is risky but we have found if the weather is nice in early season the receipts are better than later in the summer." (Brady McSwigan to George A. Schmidt, September 15, 1955)

6th FALL FANTASY PARADE: Frontier Days on Parade
CHRISTMAS CARD: Christmas Reflection - very small photo of two people in a chair before a small fireplace.

DAFFY CLUB was removed and replaced by Fascination.
DIPPER ROLLER COASTER was lengthened by 440 feet ("Phase number one"). Construction was designed and supervised by Andy Vettel. New coaster cars were purchased from the Philadelphia Toboggan Company.
LITTLE TURNPIKE RIDE (generic name Kiddie Kaddys) was purchased from B. A. Schiff. It had 600 feet of track and a tunnel. The ride was often called caddy cars at Kennywood.
PICNIC PAVILION - A 100 feet by 60 feet steel building with a smooth concrete floor was constructed; it could also be used for dancing.
ROTOR was leased from Anglo Rotor Corporation, Ltd., London, England. The ride was 60 feet wide, 40 feet deep, and 20 feet in diameter and could carry up to 30 people at a time. The Rotor also had a gallery for spectators that could hold 300. The first one was built in Germany in 1949 by Ernest Hoffmeister, who received a 10 percent royalty from the ride. The Rotor was a centrifugal ride where the floor "drops" and riders are left

clinging to the walls. It was the first imported ride in Kennywood.
STAR REFRESHMENT STAND was designed by Jack Ray of Belmont Park, Mission Beach, CA. The modern-style stand was located near the pony track and was called the "Star Stand" because a Ferris Wheel with a star in lights used to be near the site.
VOICE OF KENNYWOOD ceased publication in February 1955 following the death of its editor A. K. "Rosey" Rowswell. The last issue was Vol. 25, No. 4.

1956

OPENING DATE: Sunday, April 22

7th FALL FANTASY PARADE: Wild West Days on Parade
CHRISTMAS CARD: Front view of Noah's Ark in gray tint with snow.

FOUNTAIN REFRESHMENT STAND got a new front designed by Leo Kathe.
PENNY ARCADE - The exterior was remodeled, and a new front was given a futurist designed by Jack Ray, Mission Beach, CA.
ROCK-'N-ROLL (generic name: Rock-O-Plane) was purchased from Eyerly Aircraft Company, Salem, OR. An enclosed car, which held two riders, was suspended on a huge upright wheel like the face of a clock with the cars in place of numbers. Passengers had the option of making each car operate separately, turning a complete flip-flop while rocking and rolling.
SWIMMING POOL reopened. The park reported, "Pool had been closed after the 1952 season because extensive repairs were needed." The pool was 357 feet long and 180 feet wide and could hold as many as 8,000 bathers at one time.
THREE-IN-LINE game was enlarged to 24 tables. It was purchased from David Simon, Inc.

1957

OPENING DATE: Easter Sunday, April 21

8th FALL FANTASY PARADE: Mardi Gras on Parade
CHRISTMAS CARD: Large card with a boy and girl on a Merry-Go-Round horse (in color).

DRINKING FOUNTAINS - Two refrigerated fountains were added.
ENCHANTED FOREST walk-through added a television camera so everyone could "become a TV star." The following season the TV system switched to Dumont Industrial Television rental for $225 per month.
LONE RANGER appeared in the Bandstand before 8,000 people.
NOVELTY STORE and REFRESHMENT STAND were built near the Auto Ride.
OLD MILL added scenes depicting a "Trip Around the World" with mechanized and life-sized characters. It cost $5,000 for scenes such as a bull fight for Spain, a hula dance for Hawaii, a tiger for India, a dragon for China, and a harem for Arabia.
SATELLITE (generic name: Round-Up) was purchased from Frank Hrubetz & Co., Salem, OR. The 30 foot model holding 30 passengers cost $19,500. It whirled its riders in a circle and then tilted them almost vertically.
SWIMMING POOL got new white sand and an additional grassy sunbathing area.
ZOOMERANG, a dark ride, added new stunts.

1958

OPENING DATE: Sunday, April 20

9th FALL FANTASY PARADE: Arabian Nights on Parade
CHRISTMAS CARD: Little Choo Choo with Mother Goose and a wee bit of Kiddieland in the background (in color).

COMMANDO MACHINE GUN shooting gallery had ten Commando guns in two galleries of five guns each at right angles. The price at first was 25 cents but was later reduced to 10 cents.
DIPPER - New trains were purchased from the Philadelphia Toboggan Company, Philadelphia, PA.
DRINKING FOUNTAINS - Six more refrigerated fountains were added.
MERRY-GO-ROUND had its horses repainted by Frank Moran of Philadelphia, PA, one of the few old-time merry-go-round painters. John Allen of the Philadelphia Toboggan Company recommended him.
MINIATURE GOLF COURSE was revamped and a patio installed for golfers awaiting their turn. The changes were based on a design from Coney Island, Cincinnati, OH.
PENNSYLVANIA RAILROAD ceased all short excursion business, and 22 groups that regularly traveled to the park by train were cut off. The only group that still came by train was the Connellsville School, which came on the Baltimore and Ohio Railroad to Braddock and then by bus to the park.
PIPPIN - Three trains of new streamlined coaster cars with rotating headlights in front were purchased from National Amusement Device Company, Dayton, OH, and a new front was designed for the loading station.
PONIES were changed from counter-clockwise to clockwise after 50 years so that the kids could get on from the left without crossing in front of the animals.
ROTOR moved to a site near Music Plaza. At the end of the season the Rotor was removed from the park.
STREET CAR NO. 68 operated by the Pittsburgh Railway ended service at the end of the season and was converted to a No. 68 bus.
SWIMMING POOL had to be drained during the season and repaired because water was leaking out. This closed the pool for two months.
WHIRLYBIRD (generic name: Helicopter) with small cars shaped like helicopters was purchased from Allan Herschell Company Inc., North Tonawanda, NY. The Helicopter ride was designed by David Bradley of Beverly Kiddieland, Los Angeles, CA. Each car had individual controls for lifting riders. The ride was placed behind The Whip.
WILD MOUSE, a single-car roller coaster from B. A. Schiff and Associates, Inc., Miami, Florida, was located opposite the Lagoon stage. The ride was developed first in Germany and originally called "Wilde Maus." B. A. Schiff operated the ride as a concession.

1959

OPENING DATE: Sunday, April 26

10th FALL FANTASY PARADE: Neptune's Kingdom on Parade
CHRISTMAS CARD: Mary's Garden with Noah's Ark and the Office Building and Service Building in background (in color).

No. 16 BIG ELI WHEELS - Two Aristocrat Wheels were purchased from the Eli Bridge Company, Jacksonville, IL, for $14,612 per wheel. These Ferris wheels were erected at the end of the Mall side by side in honor of George Washington Gales Ferris, a Pittsburgh native who built the original Ferris Wheel at Chicago's Columbian Exposition of 1893. Joe Spradlin, erection foreman for Eli Bridge Company, supervised the erection of the wheels.
CRAZY ORBIT (generic name: Scrambler) was purchased from the Eli Bridge Company, Jacksonville, IL.

PARATROOPER, serial number 511, was purchased from Frank Hrubetz, Salem, OR.
RIDEE-O was removed from the park at the end of the season.
SWIMMING POOL was patched up for another season at a cost of $12,000.00.
TROLLEY RAILS were removed from Kennywood Boulevard along the amusement park's frontage.

1960

OPENING DATE: Easter Sunday, April 17

11th FALL FANTASY PARADE: Holiday on Parade
(Saturday, August 27, had no parade due to rain.)
CHRISTMAS CARD: William Libby lithograph of three merry-go-round horses in brown.

BOUNCER was fitted with new clown-faced cars designed by Allan Hawes, El Segundo, CA.
COWBOY NAMED JOE, a life-sized plastic cowboy, was purchased through Eric Wedemeyer, Inc., New York, NY. The sculpture was placed on a park bench.
ENCHANTED FOREST received a new entrance through a medieval castle front.
GAMES BUILDING was constructed opposite the Arcade.
KIDDIE CAROUSEL was imported from Germany through Morgan Hughes of Hot Rods, Inc., New York, NY. The ride had motorcycles, racing cars, a fire engine, and even a streetcar.
LAFF-IN-THE-DARK received a new futuristic front.
OLD MILL added a relaxing nature scene complete with waterfall and exotic plants to the boat trip that featured "Around the World" in Eight Scenes.
PATTY'S POODLE PITCH was a game from J. W. Conklin, Brantford, Ontario, Canada. The game gave away a few (11) live poodles and stuffed ones.
PIPPIN - An air brake system was added by Rutledge Equipment.
RACER received a new front, which was designed by Liff, Justh & Chetlin.
WILD MOUSE coaster from B. A. Schiff was removed at the end of the season.

1961

OPENING DATE: Sunday, April 23

12th FALL FANTASY PARADE: Winter Wonderland on Parade (This 1961 parade was the last one produced by McDonald Art Studios. The parade was expanded from eight to ten nights.)
CHRISTMAS CARD: William Libby Merry-Go-Round lithograph in black and white.

BRIDGE over the Lagoon in the center of park was redesigned by John C. Ray of Mission Beach, CA.
CALYPSO, a ride manufactured in Hamburg, Germany, was purchased through Morgan Hughes of Hot Rods Inc. of New York, NY. It had 5,208 lights and was run as a concession by John T. Gibbs, LTD, Beverly Hills, CA. The park's percentage in the original agreement was 30 percent, later increased to 32 1/2 percent, and still later to 35 percent.
HOWDY DOODY height-measuring signs were first used in the park.
MUSIC PLAZA, a bandstand that opened in 1900, burned to the ground on opening day, April 23, 1961. Hours before the fire a final concert was performed by Eddie Pupa, leader of the Kennywood Park band. Fifty-five hundred seats in front of the band shell were not damaged.
OCTOPUS, serial no. 2627, was rebuilt by Eyerly Aircraft, Salem, OR.

This 1950 model with eight-car arms was modified, and eight additional cars and cross arms were added along with modernization of the cage and controls.
OLD MILL - New redwood and oak boats were built by the McKeesport Lumber Company.
RIVER QUEEN RIDE, a kiddie ride with eight passenger boats, was purchased from the Chance Manufacturing Company, Wichita, Kansas, through McFadden Amusement Company, Clarence, NY, for $3,850.00.
RIVER THAT REMEMBERED, a 16 mm sound motion picture, was produced by William G. Beal and narrated by Ed Schaughency. The 21 minute documentary begins with George Washington as a young officer in 1753 and ends with Kennywood over 200 years later.
ROLL-O-PLANE ride was purchased from Eyerly Aircraft Company, Salem, OR.
SAFARI, formerly the Zoomerang ride, was created by adding a new front and new stunts (menacing gorillas, cannibals, weird birds, and serpents) to the old dark ride. The decorated facade included a Zulu man 15 feet tall and a cannibal pot. The remodeling by Modern Art Studios, Inc., Chicago, IL, cost $5,400. Safari was a Saturday morning program on KDKA-TV, Channel 2 with Bwana Don Riggs. On the special "Safari Day" at Kennywood all youngsters who were members of the "Safari" TV show club (they could receive club cards by mail request) were admitted to the Safari ride free of charge.
SUNLITE POOL was the new name of the swimming pool. It received a new entrance with a gate and refreshment stands.

1962

OPENING DATE: Easter Sunday, April 22

13th FALL FANTASY PARADE: Toyland on Parade
CHRISTMAS CARD: Boats with shed in Kiddieland in gray.

ALLEZ OOP (generic name: Flying Cages) was a ride that permitted people to go over the top. Twelve cages were purchased from B. A. Schiff and Associates, Inc., Miami, Florida. A set of four cages cost $6,000.00. Six Schiff cages were 36+ feet long, 21 feet deep, and 20+ feet high. The ride replaced the Dipsy Doodle.
DIPSY DOODLE (generic name: Flying Scooter) was removed from the park because the transmission broke down.
FERRIS WHEELS - Eight-pointed stars were put on Kennywood's two No. 16 Eli Wheels. They were purchased from Eli Bridge Company, Inc., Jacksonville, IL, for $680.45 each.
FLYING SAUCERS kiddie ride was purchased from S. A. Roller Works, San Antonio, Texas, for $4,475.00. The ride was 27 feet in diameter and weighed 3,830 pounds. It was made of steel except for the saucers, which were aluminum.
KANGAROO (generic name: Flying Coaster) was purchased from Aeroaffiliates, Inc., Ft. Worth, Texas for $30,381.00. The ride, designed by Norman Bartlett with a layout by E. McNabb and Jack Reel, had a 50-foot diameter.
KENNYWOOD BRIDGE over a deep ravine linked the City of Duquesne and West Mifflin Borough. It was dedicated by Pennsylvania Governor David L. Lawrence, who rode over the new $760,000 bridge in the park's Wells Fargo Pony Express wagon.
STARVUE PLAZA, a new bandstand, was a diamond-shaped concrete and steel structure that balanced a sweeping roof at two points of contact with the stage. Opening acts were Al Morgan and Baron Elliott and his "Stardust Melodies."
WELLS FARGO PONY EXPRESS was a 5/8th size Concord Stage Coach with a red body and yellow undercarriage, which was purchased from Carriage Crafts, Winnetka, IL, through McFadden Amusement Company, Clarence, NY, for $1,150.00.

1963

OPENING DATE: Easter Sunday, April 14
"The earliest opening in a couple of decades. Easter 'bunnies'—girls in costumes—greeted visitors. The winter here has been the severest since 1936. When spring comes, the populace, penned up indoors so long, will be hungry to get out into the open auguring well, we think, for Kennywood." (Brady McSwigan to John T. Gibbs, April 15, 1963)

14th FALL FANTASY PARADE: Space Age on Parade
CHRISTMAS CARD: Clock with Ferris wheels in background (grayish with a red tassel).

HODGE HAND CARS - 12 new hand cars were purchased from Hodge Amusement & Mfg. Company, Indianapolis, Indiana, for $250 each.
KENNYWOOD BOULEVARD, Route 837, was widened at a cost of $1.7 million.
PEDESTRIAN TUNNEL under Kennywood Boulevard was lengthened.
REFRESHMENT PATIO at Sunlite Pool was remodeled.
SANTA'S WORKSHOP was added as a scene in the Old Mill.
SUNLITE POOL added a children's white sand play area. Also there was less sand and more grass in most of the area surrounding the pool.
TILT-A-WHIRL, the 1948 model, was sold.
TORNADO, a dark ride with antique cars, was purchased from Freedomland, Bronx, NY. The ride, manufactured by Arrow Development Corp., Mountain View, CA, was put in the old Dance Pavilion replacing the Enchanted Forest. The front, which resembled a turn-of-the-century Midwest town, and much of the interior was designed by Jack Ray of Mission Beach, CA. This ride was a trip through a Kansas twister that simulated the opening scene from *The Wizard of Oz*. Two new cars costing $2,300 each were manufactured for Kennywood by Arrow Development Company and arrived in August. Kennywood purchased two large rubber cow heads from Conklin Shows, Brantford, Ontario, Canada, for $1,000. Stunts purchased from Funni-Frite Industries, Lancaster OH, included six falling milk cans, falling brick wall, whinnying horse, flying chickens, man in bath tub, spinning outhouse, spinning auto, bat, building with flapping door, flying cow, water tower and power lines, razed home, couple in bed, man in rowboat, falling hay bales, rocking chair spider, big blower, and a revolving barrel.

1964

OPENING DATE: Sunday, April 19

15th FALL FANTASY PARADE: Old West on Parade
CHRISTMAS CARD: Record of favorite Christmas Carols.

ANDREW BRADY MCSWIGAN, 70, president of Kennywood for 41 years, died October 31, 1964. He was twice president of the International Association of Amusement Parks.

BRADDOCK'S CROSSING HISTORIC PLAQUE was dedicated on September 7, 1964, by West Mifflin Mayor George Lynn and State Senator Leonard C. Staisey. "Colonial Frontiersman" Steve Tomasic of Smithton, PA, and his "Indian" daughter, Stephanie, assisted in the dedication.
DABSTRACT PAINTING GALLERY was added.
FASCINATION, which had been operated as a concession, was purchased from John T. Gibbs, Beverly Hills, CA.
GUNSMOKE shooting gallery was purchased from MacGlashan Guns, Inc., Stanton, CA. The gallery had 12 rifles and used tubes to load rounds. The attraction had a western motif front designed by Liff & Justh and was placed on the maintenance shop site between the Jack Rabbit and Racer.
LEO THE LION, electric trash collector, was purchased from Harry J. Batt Associates, Pontchartrain Beach, New Orleans, Louisiana. Trash was vacuumed into the machine. There was a recorded message which repeated, "I'm a paper-eating lion, not the children-eating sort."
MAINTENANCE SHOP was moved.
MON RIVER RAILROAD was the new name for the miniature railroad. A small town station was built and a new tunnel put on the right-of-way.
ROUND-UP, Model 30, was purchased from Frank Hrubetz & Company, Inc., Salem, OR, for $22,000. The old 1957 model was traded in for a credit of $9,000.
SKY DIVER (generic name: Paratrooper), serial No. 814, was purchased from Frank Hrubetz and Co., Inc. Salem, OR. It was the new hydraulic park model that cost $28,000. The park received $7,500 as a trade-in allowance.
SKEE BALL ALLEYS were purchased from the Philadelphia Toboggan Company, Philadelphia, PA. The old alleys were sold to West Point, Holland, PA. Kennywood now had both 5 cent and 10 cent alleys.
SPACE SHIP kiddie ride was added.

1965

OPENING DATE: Easter Sunday, April 18

16th FALL FANTASY PARADE: Circus on Parade
CHRISTMAS CARD: Black and white drawing of a little girl on a merry-go-round horse.

ALLEZ OOP flying cages ride was sold at the end of the season.
ENTRANCE to the pay parking lot was framed by new columns made from Belgian Block, old Pittsburgh street cobblestones also called Gray Ligonier Block along with shrubs and trees planted along the new four lane highway.
FLYER, a new and improved version of the Dipsy Doodle or Flying Scooter, with new cars painted with the word "Flyer" was purchased from Rocco Amusement Company, Argo, IL.
HOSTS AND HOSTESSES BOOKLET was published by the park. Advice included: be polite and courteous (Smile!), be neat and clean (Wear your Kennywood shirt), and treat guests as you would expect to be treated. Employees were given three Kennywood shirts. They had to wear one every day they reported. The shirts were to be kept laundered — which was why they were given three. An employee badge was to be worn at all times while on duty and was the "ticket" to the Employees' Cafeteria and to discounted employee food prices.
KENNYWOOD BOULEVARD, the new four lane highway, was dedicated May 2nd.
KIOSK ticket booth was purchased.
OCTOPUS ride was sold by the park at the end of the season.
ROTOR, the centrifugal ride where the floor "dropped" and riders were left sticking to the walls, was added to the park. This was the second Rotor in the park's history.
RUNNING LIGHTS for the Racer were purchased from the Philadelphia Toboggan Company, Germantown, Philadelphia, PA, and installed by Kennywood.
TINY VILLAGE was added to the new train tunnel. It consisted of ninety-four different life-like houses, a town square, a hotel, cathedral, and two fountains made from clay and then baked by Frank Ross of Rosslyn Farms and Everett Sturgeon of Oakdale. The length of the town was 22 feet.

1966

OPENING DATE: Easter Sunday, April 24

17th FALL FANTASY PARADE: Mother Goose Parade
CHRISTMAS CARD: Santa with an elephant at the Pennsylvania Dutch Grove (in color).

ANTIQUE CAR kiddie ride was purchased from San Antonio Roller Works, San Antonio, Texas, for $6,100.
MARY'S GARDEN was removed at the end of the season.
MINIATURE RAILROAD ALTERATIONS were done by Liff, Justh & Chetlin.
TRABANT was purchased from Chance Manufacturing Company, Inc., Wichita, Kansas.
TURNPIKE ride - Twenty-two little gasoline-driven cars were purchased from Arrow Development Co., Mountain View, CA, for $1,750. each. A Kennywood Turnpike Corporation was created to help finance the project, which cost about $100,000. It was Carl Hughes' idea to have the ride visible from the highway. The Turnpike's loading and unloading zone started on a stretch that paralleled the side of the Old Mill. The original gasoline station on the ride was copied from Lagoon Park, Salt Lake City, Utah, and was designed by Liff, Justh & Chetlin. The first sponsor was Gulf Oil Company.

1967

OPENING DATE: Sunday, April 23

18th FALL FANTASY PARADE: Americana on Parade
CHRISTMAS CARD: Santa on the Turnpike in a car with packages (in color).

BRADDOCK'S DEFEAT CAMEO created along the miniature railroad. It included life-sized figures of the French and Indians firing from behind trees and bushes at the trapped British and Colonials. Also in the scene were wagons and other implements, and the field was strewn with the wounded and dying. The sounds of muskets and smoke and fire from British cannons were part of the audio-visual display. It was designed by William J. Rodgers.
GHOST SHIP dark ride replaced the Tornado in the former Dance Pavilion. Theming, stunts, and a new front were done by Amusement Display Associates, owned by Bill Tracy, Cape May, NJ.
ORIENTAL GARDEN with a fountain was installed on Mary's Garden site.
PIPPIN closed at the end of the season.
POP OVER (generic name Skydiver) was purchased from Chance Manufacturing Co., Wichita, Kansas. The ride was 75 feet high by 32 feet wide, and cost approximately $60,000. The thrill ride looked like a Ferris wheel, but as the wheel moved, it "slowly" turned riders upside down.

1968

OPENING DATE: Easter Sunday, April 14

19th FALL FANTASY PARADE: Holidays on Parade
CHRISTMAS CARD: Wishing Well with flowers (photograph).

BAYERN KURVE ride manufactured in West Germany was purchased by the park for approximately $75,000.
ROAD RUNNER (generic name Cuddle Up: formerly called the Snapper) was purchased from the Philadelphia Toboggan Company, Germantown, Philadelphia, PA.
SKOOTER CARS - 30 cars were purchased from Lusse Bros., Inc., Philadelphia, PA.
THUNDERBOLT roller coaster was built on the site of the Pippin coaster. Part of the Pippin was used. The coaster was designed by Andy Vettel. The Thunderbolt was 2,887 feet long and featured a 90-foot final drop. New coaster cars were purchased from National Amusement Company, Dayton, OH. The loading platform was designed by Liff, Justh & Chetlin.
WHIP RIDE and BUILDING were moved from beside the Pippin to a spot close to the Racer at the opposite side of the park to allow room for the Thunderbolt. Engineering work was done by Liff, Justh & Chetlin.

1969

OPENING DATE: Sunday, April 20

20th FALL FANTASY PARADE: Best of the Past on Parade
CHRISTMAS CARD: A drawing of Santa skating.

CATERPILLAR ride was purchased from the Allan Herschell Company, Tonawanda, NY, and place across from the Arcade. This ride had not been in the park since 1945.
FERRIS WHEELS - One of the dual wheels was sold.
KIDDIE KANGAROO ride was purchased, which was called the pink kangaroo.
LOOP-O-PLANE was purchased from Eyerly Aircraft Company, Salem, OR.
NOAH'S ARK underwent major renovation. New stunts were added and a new whale entrance was built. Mount Ararat was added to the side of the ride nearest the Service Building. Miniature railroad track ran around the base of the Ark with a different animal on each car. The changes were designed by Liff, Justh & Chetlin.
ROLL-O-PLANE was removed after the end of the season.

1970

OPENING DATE: Sunday, April 19

21st FALL FANTASY PARADE: Wizard of Oz on Parade
(On Saturday, August 22, the parade started but a sudden hard downpour ended it.)
CHRISTMAS CARD: Photograph of Santa on Rowland Emett's "Gentleman's Flying Machine."

CRAZY ORBIT (generic name: Scrambler) replaced an older version of the same ride. It was manufactured by Eli Bridge, Jacksonville, IL.
"GENTLEMEN'S FLYING MACHINE," a three dimensional cartoon, by Rowland Emett of Wild Goose Cottage, Ditchling, Sussex, England, was displayed in a building in front of the Thunderbolt. This building would later become the Potato Patch.
MINIATURE BOUNCER was added to Kiddieland.
SATELLITE (generic name: Round-Up) was replaced with a newer version of the same ride, the park's third, from Hrubetz, Salem, OR.
SKOOTER BUILDING was painted in psychedelic colors.
SWIMMING POOL ISLAND was torn out and replaced with concrete block and prestressed slabs.

1971

OPENING DATE: Sunday, April 18

22nd FALL FANTASY PARADE: Storybook Land on Parade
CHRISTMAS CARD: Drawing of a turn-of-century family picnic in front of trolleys.

"AFTERNOON TEA TRAIN" was an exhibit that remained in the park

for the season. It was a three dimensional cartoon with an engine, a passenger car with a very stately passenger, and a caboose. Engine also cooked and served the lady passenger tea and crumpets, and the caboose carried a cow with her own milk to supply the cream for the tea. It was designed by Rowland Emett of Wild Goose Cottage, Ditchling, Sussex, England, famed British cartoonist, who called it a mechanical brain-storm. The display weighed 9,223 pounds and was placed near the Thunderbolt in a building constructed for that purpose. Later the building was used for the Potato Patch.
CADILLAC CAR BODIES, for auto ride in Kiddieland, were purchased from Roberts Fiberglass Products, Miami, Florida for $250 each.
CASINO'S interior was restored with its high pressed-tin ceiling and exposed wooden beams. Slow moving fans were added.
REFRESHMENT STAND, or Tower Stand, was remodeled. The designed was by Liff, Justh & Chetlin.
RIDE-ALL-DAY was initiated with $4.50 for Friday nights in July.
ROLL-O-PLANE was purchased from Eyerly Aircraft Company, Salem, OR. It had light blue and white cars.
SHELTERS for tired adults were built in Kiddieland.
SKOOTER BUILDING received a bright new front designed by Liff, Justh & Chetlin.

1972

KENNYWOOD PARK CELEBRATED ITS 75TH ANNIVERSARY

OPENING DATE: Sunday, April 16
"It looked like the first day of regular season would be rained out, but divine providence intervened at 2:15 p.m., the rain stopped, and sun started shining and the rides started moving. Early crowd was smallish but grew as the weather cleared." Homestead Messenger, April 17, 1972.

23rd FALL FANTASY PARADE: Gay Nineties on Parade
(The parade on Friday, August 18, was delayed 20 minutes due to rain, but it finally went on.)
CHRISTMAS CARD: Drawing of "Joy to You at Christmas" Santa on a 75th birthday cake.

ROBERT F. HENNINGER, 59, a vice president of Kennywood Park Corporation, who was head of the park's food operation from 1946 until his death, died on March 19, 1972.

BAYERN KURVE, manufactured in West Germany, was bought from Conklin Shows, Brantford, Ontario, Canada, for $72,000.
BIRTHDAY CAKE was displayed with 75 candles.
BUBBLE BOUNCE was removed and sold at the end of the season.
LE CACHOT, The Dungeon, (dark ride) was the new name and theme for the Safari. Bill Tracy's Amusement Display Associates, Cape May, NJ, created the displays and front. The facade was 50 feet long and 40 feet high with full round fiberglass towers, walls, and parapets. Eight stunts were animated. The design included two oversized motorcycles with skeletons racing at each other with drawn lances. Inside the structure were 10 animated displays including a 22-foot dragon and a waterfall. New cars were purchased from the Pretzel Company in New Jersey. Bill Tracy's nickname was the "chill man" of America.
HIMALAYA was removed and sold.
MONSTER, built by Eyerly Aircraft, Salem, OR, was put in the park as a concession by Conklin Shows, Brantford, Ontario, Canada. The ride was a much larger variation of the Octopus, also manufactured by Eyerly. The new ride was placed in front of Le Cachot.
"OL' MON RIVER RAILROAD" was the new name for the miniature railroad.

PATIO RESTAURANT was the new name for the Casino. It was remodeled and a porch was added with a yellow and white awning.
PONY RIDING COACH was removed from the Pony Track.
SKEE BALL ALLEYS - Six new alleys were purchased from the Philadelphia Toboggan Company, Philadelphia, PA, for $1,160 each. They had ticket dispensers, winner-lights, and 10 cent coin mechanisms.
TROPICAL STORM AGNES hit the park, and practically closed it for a week.

1973

OPENING DATE: Palm Sunday, April 15

24th FALL FANTASY PARADE: Winter Wonderland on Parade
(The parade on Friday, August 17, started at 9:10 p.m. due to rain from 7:00 p.m. to 8:50 p.m.)
CHRISTMAS CARD: William Libby watercolor of Merry-Go-Round.

BONANZA, an electronic shooting gallery, was purchased. The building to house it was designed by Liff, Justh & Chetlin and was built over the Racer tracks.
BUS STATION was moved out of the park across Kennywood Boulevard.
CHARLIE BROWN was used as a measure of height (52") for certain rides.
DOUBLE DECKER BUILDING, located across from the Old Mill, was constructed. The yellow and white building was originally used as a restaurant on the first floor and a refreshment stand on the second.
GRAN PRIX - Thirty bumper cars and a converter were imported by Daniel I. Glosser from Soli Company, Trieste, Italy. The building was designed by Liff, Justh & Chetlin. The Gran Prix sign was done by McBride Sign.
HENRY was retired as a means for determining whether youngsters were tall enough for certain rides.
HOWDY DOODY was retired as a means for determining whether youngsters were tall enough for certain rides.
MINIATURE GOLF COURSE was re-carpeted before the season. The golf course, Double Decker Restaurant, and #2 rest rooms were to be kept open through October. It cost 75 cents for golf with a refreshment ticket minimum of 50 cents. They were kept open for only two weekends in September and then canceled because of low attendance.
ONE PRICE DAYS were Sundays in May and Fridays in July and August. Adults paid $5.00 and those under 52" paid $4.00.
POTATO PATCH refreshment stand opened.
SNOOPY was used as a measure of height (46") for certain rides.
SUNLITE POOL and BATHHOUSES were closed at the end of the season. The pool, which opened in 1925, was filled in and the bathhouses were torn down.
THUNDERBOLT - Revolving headlights for the front of each coaster train were purchased from the National Amusement Device Company, Dayton, OH, for $200 each.
TURNPIKE received new gasoline-powered cars that were seven inches longer and sportier than the original ones. The cars were designed by Pittsburgh commercial artist Ivozina.

1974

OPENING DATE: Sunday, April 21

25th FALL FANTASY PARADE: Great Events on Parade
CHRISTMAS CARD: Photograph of a girl on a Merry-Go-Round.

ADMISSION FEE of $1.00 to enter the park was charged for the first time.

BOTTLE GAME BUILDING located next to the Arcade was rebuilt.
ROBERT CARTMELL, art history professor and roller coaster historian, rated the Thunderbolt the best roller coaster in the world in the Sunday edition of *The New York Times*, June 9, 1974.
FENCE was built around the park.
GERMAN CAROUSEL was removed.
GIANT GERMAN SWING featuring hand-painted murals was imported from Oktoberfest at Munich. The ride was operated as a concession by Conklin Shows, Brantford, Ontario, Canada.
GRAN PRIX - Lights were put in the letters.
HARDHEADED HAROLD'S HORRENDOUSLY HUMOROUS HAUNTED HIDEAWAY was a new name for the Old Mill. Edward D. Hilbert of Unique Design Company, Baltimore, Maryland, was hired to retheme the attraction. The scenes evoked images of a western ghost town.
HIPPOPOTAMUS WATER FOUNTAINS, voice-activated and made out of fiberglass, were added.
HONDA MOTORCYCLE ride for Kiddieland was purchased from San Antonio Roller Works, San Antonio, Texas, for $12,950. The ride had six sweeps with twelve miniature Honda motorcycles, two abreast on a platform made of aluminum and steel tubing. The platform diameter was 22 feet, and the ride had a 24-foot revolving umbrella.
CARL O. HUGHES served as president of the International Association of Amusement Parks and Attractions.
KENNY KANGAROO, a costume character, was introduced by the park. The suit weighed 20 pounds.
LANDSCAPING was done behind the Double Decker Restaurant by Everett Stugeon. Shrubs from the athletic field were put in front of Kiddieland. Trees and planters made from railroad ties were added to three locations at the end of the lake and nine other locations on the Midway.
MONSTER was removed at the end of the season.
POTATO PATCH - Outdoor tables were added.
SHIRT SHACK was added near the Restaurant next to the Squirt Game.
SPACE ODYSSEY ride, the former Crazy Orbit (Scrambler), was placed under a huge geodesic dome with psychedelic sights and sounds. The dome was 60 feet across and 30 feet high and was made by a local fiberglass firm. Each trip featured five circuits of lights including Christmas twinkle lights and strobes. The lighting effects changed with the music, which was the original movie sound track from *2001-A Space Odyssey*.
TELEPHONE BOOTHS were added to the area near the Old Mill and Restaurant.
ANDY VETTEL JR. became the "Voice of Kennywood" replacing Jim Page.

1975

OPENING DATE: Sunday, April 20

26th FALL FANTASY PARADE: Americana on Parade
CHRISTMAS CARD: "Sounds of Christmas" record.

HARRY W. HENNINGER, SR., president of Kennywood, died on May 13, 1975. He had served as Secretary-Treasurer of the park for over 20 years before being named president.

FIRE on June 19, 1975, destroyed four rides housed in the Dance Pavilion (one of the park's original buildings), causing $450,000 damage. Flames started inside the Ghost Ship dark ride. Also destroyed were the Road Runner, a Mangels Kiddie Whip, Kiddie Carousel, and 17 Skotter Cars. The heat was so intense that it melted part of the superstructure of the Satellite (Round-Up), which had to be replaced. The Calypso was repainted and reupholstered. Also lost was a 5 piece monkey band, kicking mule, and "kangaroo feet." Several youngsters in the Ghost Ship were led to safety by an attendant who then spread the alarm. Kennywood's own fire department was the first to throw water on the fire.
LOG JAMMER, a log flume, was the park's first million dollar ride. The ride was developed by Arrow Development Company of Mountain View, CA, after an old style western log flume. Riders were swept along a water chute in a hollowed-out log-boat. The ride time was approximately 4.5 minutes. The log flume was 1,555 feet long, and had 22 log-boats. It is one of the few log flumes built with a spillway drop, 27 feet deep, about midway through the ride. The ride's final plunge was 53 feet. The Log Jammer was placed in the area formerly occupied by the Pony Track and Riverside Grove. A double station gave the ride a capacity of 1,440 per hour. Pumps move 11,250 gallons of water per minute through the trough to propel the boats. There were 500,000 gallons of water in a holding basin and 90,000 in the channel when operating. The ride cost approximately $1.1 million to install. The lagoon plan and details of the flume ride were done by Liff, Justh & Chetlin.
TELE-COMBAT ride was a concession by Conklin Shows, Brantford, Ontario, Canada, that was imported from Italy. It did poorly and was removed after only one season.

1976

OPENING DATE: Easter Sunday, April 18

27th FALL FANTASY PARADE: Storyland on Parade
CHRISTMAS CARD: "Trolleys," drawing of Kennywood's street car station in 1907.

BLUE MONSTER (Gee Tee) and ORANGE BIRD (Monster Bird) joined Kenny Kangaroo, Colonel Fraudwater, and Bimbo, as costume characters.
BUBBLE BOUNCE was sold to Whalom Park after the 1976 Season.
LE CACHOT received new scenes designed by Henry Pohl Enterprises, Huron, OH, including an octopus and "black light" scenes.
DENTZEL CAROUSEL was restored by Henry Pohl Enterprises, Huron, OH, for $100,000.
FOUNTAIN - The '76 Fountain was built as part of the new entrance to Kiddieland on the site of the former Ghost Ship dark ride. It was designed by Tom Borellis, landscape architect, from the firm of Griswold, Winters, Swain & Mullin. Also included was an arbor of hanging baskets and other flowers.
ISLAND STAGE with dressing rooms was built on the same site as the previous smaller Island Stage. A new bridge was constructed for access.
LAGOON WALL was built from the Jack Rabbit northeast to the area of the Ghost Ship. The work included widening the walkway and the use of "Pittsburgh cobble stones," with old fashioned street lamps, huge flower planters, flowering crab trees and maples, and new surface drainage at a cost of $29,900. Landscaping was done by Tedesco Landscaping Contracting for $17,210. Lagoon Wall and Lagoon modification were designed by GWSM and L. D. Astorias.
MOONSHINE VILLAGE with hillbilly animated characters, animals, and scenery was created for Kennywood's train ride by Henry Pohl Enterprises, Huron, OH. Some of the scenes with the Hatfields and McCoys included: the local bathhouse, a covered wagon, the blacksmith shop, a square dance, and a shot gun wedding. The scenes cost approximately $37,000.
MOTION PICTURE of the park, 21 minutes long, was produced by William G. Beal, Pittsburgh, PA, for $17,500.
NOAH'S ARK received two new scenes, an octopus and monkey, from Henry P. Pohl Enterprises, Huron, OH.
OLD KIDDIELAND ENTRANCE was blocked off and replaced with a floral American Flag measuring 14 feet by 20 feet. A little room was left on either side of the flag and people still used it as an entrance.
OL' MON RIVER RAILROAD was upgraded with railroad cars purchased from Crown Metal Products Company, Wyano, PA. The cars included a gondola and freight car that carried passengers.

PARATROOPER, a hydraulic park model, was purchased from Frank Hrubetz & Co., Inc., Salem, OR, for $47,629.
SUPER ROUND-UP was purchased from Frank Hrubetz & Co., Inc., Salem OR, for $70,380. The paint scheme was similar to the one on the Round-Up at Magic Mountain, CA. The old Round-Up ride was traded in for a $10,000 credit toward the new ride.
TILT-A-WHIRL was purchased from Sellner Manufacturing Company, Faribault, Minnesota, for $27,570.

1977

OPENING DATE: Sunday, April 17
(The weather was beautiful.)

28th FALL FANTASY PARADE: Circus on Parade
CHRISTMAS CARD: Kenny Kangaroo tree ornament.

CINESPHERE DOME, a 29-foot high cloth geodesic dome supported by a network of aluminum bars, was purchased and used as a theater. It was located in front of Noah's Ark and had a capacity of 175. Bill Sandy Company leased to the park a special projector, film, and a 180-degree hemispherical screen, which was 65 feet in diameter. Inside were church pews and visitors could sit or stand. The nine-minute movie had 16 scenes of "first person" camera work.
CUDDLE UP, a 14 car model, was purchased from the Philadelphia Toboggan Company, Lansdale, PA. This was an updated version of the old Cuddle Up, which had been destroyed in the fire. The ride cost $87,500 and was placed under a tent by Helios Tension in the park's new Kenny Lane midway in back of the park's office.
FLORAL CALENDAR was moved to Kiddieland from near the office.
GREEN GABLES, a Duquesne Tavern located across from Kennywood's parking lot, was demolished and replaced by McDonald's and Long John Silver's.
HISTORIC PLAQUE was placed on the Dentzel Carousel by the Pittsburgh History and Landmark Foundation. James Van Trump, vice president and director of research of that organization, represented the foundation at the ceremony. Long-time carousel operator Tony Sacramento was also at the dedication.
KENNY LANE, a new midway with rides and games, was developed in back of the park office.
MATTERHORN ride, which was operated as a concession by Conklin Shows, Brantford, Ontario, Canada, was placed next to Gran Prix in the new Kenny Lane section of the park.
MINIATURE GOLF COURSE was redesigned, switching seven holes to make room for the new Kenny Lane Midway.
MONSTER ride was purchased from Eyerly Aircraft, Salem, OR.
PLAYDIUM ARCADE was opened during the season in a Scandinavian-styled building near the Gran Prix. In the arcade were 20 lanes of skee ball purchased from the Philadelphia Toboggan Company, Lansdale, PA, and 20 other arcade games.
ROLL-O-PLANE was moved to the Kenny Lane Midway.
SERVICE CENTER was opened in a Scandinavian-styled building on the new Kenny Lane Midway.
WAREHOUSE was constructed beside the Racer roller coaster.
WURLITZER BAND ORGAN on the merry-go-round was rebuilt by Gavin McDonough of B.A.B. Organ Company, East Burke, Vermont.

1978

OPENING DATE: Sunday, April 16

29th FALL FANTASY PARADE: Mardi Gras on Parade

CHRISTMAS CARD: Drawing of Kenny Kangaroo with a Santa beard looking in a fun house mirror.

CINEMA 180 replaced CINESPHERE in the dome theater.
ENTERPRISE was purchased from Huss & Co., Bremen, West Germany for $276,788, but with installation expenses the ride cost closer to $350,000. Delivery was delayed for the 1977 season because of a longshoreman's strike. The wheel began in a horizontal position, whipping the riders around, and then shifted until the wheel was vertical and spinning its passengers upside down.
KIDDIE HELICOPTER ride was sold to Bates Brothers Amusement Company.
PARK OFFICE (Administration Building) was enlarged and renovated. A new one-story Guest Relations and Group Sales addition was built.
ROCKETS ended operation at the end of the season.
SERVICE BUILDING, which had been located next to the park office, was removed. The restrooms were rebuilt and a ship's wharf midway was added.
SPORTLAND, a games building, received a new second floor built of steel beams, steel deck, and concrete in such a way that the old games building was left undisturbed underneath. The new second floor was built to house a new dark ride, which did not open until 1981.

1979

OPENING DATE: Saturday, April 21

30th FALL FANTASY PARADE: Mother Goose on Parade
CHRISTMAS CARD: Drawing of Santa on the Laser Loop.

CINEMA 180 received a new film that began with a ride on the Thunderbolt.
FASCINATION - 40 tables were purchased from Taylor Engineering Corp., Beverly Hills, CA, for $46,000.
FAST BALL, which measured the speed of a pitch by radar, replaced the Gunsmoke shooting gallery near the Jack Rabbit.
FOUNTAIN STAND ROOF was renovated.
GARDEN ENTERTAINMENT AREA was built under the Monster ride on the former Rockets site. A portion of the Lagoon was drained for the stage, seating, and garden. A rocky waterfall and a white water stream were part of the garden setting. The design was by GWSM, Inc., a Pittsburgh firm of landscape architects.
GRAN PRIX - 25 new cars were purchased from French Rides Distributing Co., Inc., Pleasantville, NJ.
IBM COMPUTER GAMES were installed.
MERRY-GO-ROUND sprinkler system was installed for $23,600.
MINIATURE TRAIN ENGINES - Two engines were re-powered by Pascoe Equipment at a cost of $7,500. Also, 250 railroad ties were replaced at a cost of $3,000.
MONONGAHELA MONSTER, a Monster ride, was purchased from Eyerly, Salem, OR, for $241,000 and placed on the platform that formerly held the Rockets. Demolition of the Rockets cost $36,300.
PIZZA WAREHOUSE, a restaurant at the new entrance to Kiddieland, which served spaghetti, pizzas, subs, and salads, cost $51,000 to build.
POTATO PATCH was enlarged.
RED BARON, a kiddie airplane ride that used World War I type bi-planes, was purchased from Chance Manufacturing, Wichita, Kansas, for $33,500.
REMOTE BOATS were added in back of Noah's Ark and cost 50 cents or 3 for $1 to operate.
SKEE BALL ALLEYS - Six new lanes were purchased from the Philadelphia Toboggan Company, Lansdale, PA.
SKOOTER BUILDING and the rides it contained ceased operation at the end of the season. The building was demolished on September 13,

1979, to make way for the Laser Loop.
SPORTLAND BUILDING'S first floor was demolished and replaced with a new building that held seven games.
STAR REFRESHMENT STAND received a new walk-in cooler, which cost $3,500, and funnel cake equipment, which cost $5,200.

1980

OPENING DATE: Saturday, April 19

31st FALL FANTASY PARADE: Storyland on Parade
CHRISTMAS CARD: Drawing of Santa at the High Striker.

ENTRANCE - A new entrance from the pay parking lot was made under the loop of the Laser Loop.
FASTBALL, a baseball throw game from Kustom Electronics, was placed in the old Bonanza shooting gallery building next to the Jack Rabbit.
FERRIS WHEEL ended operation at the close of the season.
FRUIT GAZEBO, a new refreshment stand, was built near the new Laser Loop entrance. The stand used part of the old Sunlite Pool refreshment stand.
GENERAL ADMISSION fee was increased from $1.00 to $1.50.
LASER LOOP (generic name: shuttle loop coaster) was manufactured by Anton Schwarzkopf of West Germany and designed by Reinhold Spieldiener, a Swiss engineer. It was purchased through Intamin, A.G., Zurich, Switzerland. The coaster had two ends that were 139 and 111 feet high with a 72-foot vertical loop in between. The vertical loop had a 46-foot diameter. The train would climb the 139-foot end at a 70 degree angle. The ride's top speed was 54 mph and it had two dispatch buttons, which required two operators to press the button to activate the train. Foundation work was done by Curtis D. Summers, a professional engineer. Andy Vettel, Sr. supervised the construction of the new ride.
MIDWAY - A new midway was created behind Noah's Ark to connect the Enterprise with the new entrance under the Laser Loop.
MOON ROCKETS ride was removed from Kiddieland.
PONIES were moved slightly to walk under the new Laser Loop.
ROW BOATS had their final season on the Lagoon.
SPACE ODYSSEY had its final season. The Space Odyssey building was razed to allow room for the new Gold Rusher loading area.

1981

OPENING DATE: Saturday, April 18

32nd FALL FANTASY PARADE: Holidays on Parade
CHRISTMAS CARD: Lithograph of the Penny Arcade in 1928.

ARCADE was demolished after the season during the winter and replaced with a new Arcade.
CHRISTMAS TREE in lights was placed inside the Laser Loop for the first time during the Christmas season.
FIRE - A grease fire on the Jack Rabbit that caused little or no damage occurred on August 18.
GAMES DEPARTMENT took control of the sketch artist concession.
GOLD RUSHER dark ride opened. It was developed by Ayers Studios, Santa Cruz, CA. Maurice Ayers, a former Hollywood set designer, created nine frightening and comic scenes along the path of the 550-feet ride. The front of the ride featured a waterwheel, sluice, miner, and derrick to attract riders. The scenes included a charging locomotive, a dynamite explosion, a waterfall with a dousing surprise ending, and the Lone Stranger and Tonto (country coyotes). Cars and track were made by Bradley and Kaye, Long Beach, CA. The ride cost more than $550,000.
GRAN PRIX added three new cars purchased from French Rides Distributing Co., Inc., Pleasantville, NJ, for $1,250 each.
LANDSCAPING - 58 trees and four planters were added for $23,000.
LOG JAMMER was converted to a high tech ride with a printed circuit board.
NOAH'S ARK received two new scenes designed and built by Edward D. Hilbert of Unique Design, Inc. Finksburg, Maryland.
PADDLE BOATS painted bright yellow replaced the row boats on the park's Lagoon.
SKEE BALL - 15 new electronic alleys were purchased from the Philadelphia Toboggan Company, Lansdale, PA, for $2,100 each. Thirteen old alleys were sold for $5,250.
TORNADO MINIATURE RACE CARS, manufactured in England and radio-controlled, were added.
TURTLE CARS were rebuilt for $18,000, and a new $20,000 track was installed.

1982

OPENING DATE: Sunday, April 18

33rd FALL FANTASY PARADE: Magic Melodies on Parade
CHRISTMAS CARD: A small (10" by 15") poster of the Laser Loop with a Christmas tree.

ARCADE - A new steel building with a basement used for storage and a first floor Arcade was added. The structure was built by John F. Casey Company. The new Arcade was purposely kept in the same location as the old Arcade and was about the same size as the old structure. The new building was 90 feet wide by 100 feet deep. The wooden front had four roll-up aluminum doors, each 20 feet wide and 8 feet high.
BIG DIPPER ice cream parlor, formerly a vending stand, was built across from Noah's Ark. The stand featured marble counters.
CUDDLE UP moved to the former basketball location.
DIPPER roller coaster had 30 percent of its structure replaced, and the entire coaster was painted for 1982.
KENNYWOOD: ROLLER COASTER CAPITAL OF THE WORLD by Charles J. Jacques, Jr., was first published.
KIDDIE SPACESHIPS were sold.
LOOP-O-PLANE was sold to C & J Ride Exchange in Oxford, NJ.
MEXICAN FOOD STAND was opened near the Racer.
MINI ENTERPRISE kiddie ride with helicopters and spaceships was purchased from Zamperla Inc., East Brunswick, NJ. The ride was manufactured in Vicentina, Italy.
PIRATE, a 45-foot long swing boat, was purchased from Huss & Company, Bremen, West Germany. The boat swung with a pendulum motion, taking its riders higher on each swing. In full swing, the attraction rose 66 feet from ground level. It seated 54 adults divided into two groups that faced each other. The ride had an hourly capacity of 1,800 persons. It replaced the Cuddle Up next to the Laser Loop. The foundation plan was done by Curtis D. Summers, Professional Engineer.
RACER - Two new trains for the old coaster were purchased from the Philadelphia Toboggan Co., Lansdale, PA. The cars had electronic lap bars and seat dividers. The trains (two red trains and one blue) were 4-car, 3 seats per car with aluminum chassis coaster cars. One additional train was later purchased. Two old roller coaster cars were donated to the Pittsburgh History and Landmarks Foundation.

1983

OPENING DATE: Sunday, April 17

34th FALL FANTASY PARADE: Mother Goose on Parade
CHRISTMAS CARD: Drawing of a snowy Noah's Ark.

ARCADE - The wooden front was replaced with a new mirrored glass front by Golub Cales Corporation.
LE CACHOT dark ride's stunts were upgraded by Funni-Frite Inc., Pickerington, OH, for $4,671.
CATERPILLAR was removed from the park and put in storage.
CINEMA 180 and its dome were sold at the end of the season to Knobels Grove, Elysburg, PA, for $26,000. Carl Hughes liked to refer to Knobels Grove as "Kennywood East."
ENTRANCE - A new entryway was installed from the free parking lot. At the same time, the 88-foot-long tunnel that ran under Kennywood Boulevard was upgraded. More than $250,000 was spent on the landscaping, ticket booths, entrance gates, turnstiles, and tunnel. The new turnstiles were located in the park near the Turnpike ride. The entrance was designed by Thomas Borellis of Landscape Architects GWSM, Inc. The entrance plaza was raised 12 feet to make it level with the parking lot, thereby increasing its visibility. Over 250 white pines, 25 oaks, 600 Pfitzer junipers, and hundreds of ornamental azaleas, Bradford pears, and rhododendrons were planted.
FREE PARKING LOT was expanded.
GATE - A new wrought-iron gate was added to the free parking end of the tunnel. It was made by Duquesne Metal Products, Inc. The two-door gate carried a "K" and "P" as part of the design.
IDLEWILD PARK was purchased by Kennywood Park Corporation on January 26, 1983.
JUMPIN' JUNGLE planned for Kennywood's Kiddieland was transferred instead to Idlewild. The attraction cost approximately $325,000.
LOOP-O-PLANE was removed from the park.
NOAH'S ARK received new displays including a shark and a man in a boat from Edward D. Hilbert, Unique Design Inc., Finksburg, Maryland. The cost was $23,016.80.
RANGER, a swing ride that made a 360-degree loop, was manufactured by Huss & Company, Bremen, West Germany, and was leased through Huss Trading Corporation of America, Corfu, NY. The Ranger was placed on a site next to the '76 fountain by Kiddieland. In addition to the looping motion, the operator could hold the ride at the top of its arc in a stationary position and then swing the ride either forward or backward. Ranger was similar to Pirate, but had a boat-like cage that turned completely upside down in a huge circle. The attraction lasted only one season.

1984

OPENING DATE: Easter Sunday, April 22

35th FALL FANTASY PARADE: Circus on Parade
CHRISTMAS CARD: Drawing of Santa on the Raging Rapids.

BAYERN KURVE - A used model was purchased from a German showman.
CATERPILLAR TRAIN and JUNIOR WAVE SWINGER were added to Kiddieland.
DIPPER - It was the Dipper's final year of operation. The junior coaster was closed before the end of the season and demolition began so that work could start on the park's new white water ride.
GOLD RUSHER'S loading station was elevated off the midway with stairs to enter and exit the ride.
PONIES, which had been a Kennywood tradition since the turn of the century, were removed at the end of the season. Ridership had gone down, and there were too many small accidents with the ponies.
REFRESHMENT TICKETS were discontinued, and the refreshment stands went to all-cash sales.
STARVUE PLAZA demolition began in July to make way for the park's new white water rapids ride. Nationality events, which had formerly been held at the Plaza, were moved to Pavilion #7 behind the Turnpike ride.
SWING AROUND was leased from Huss & Company, Bremen, West Germany. It was placed on the Ranger site. The ride had 14 gondolas that spun its riders in a 360-degree position before each gondola began a separate back-and-forth motion, producing the feeling of a "swing within a swing." It remained in the park only one season.
TROLLEY VEHICLE was purchased from The Trolley Works and used in Fall Fantasy Parades and at other events both in and out of the park.
WAVE SWINGER was leased from manufacturer Josef Zierer of West Germany to replace Cinema 180 on a site across from Noah's Ark. The ride was particularly spectacular at night with computerized lighting. It was a newer version of the old chair plane ride. The ride telescoped into the air and then tilted after it was up to create a wave-like motion. Patrons rode in chairs that were suspended by two chains from the ride.

1985

OPENING DATE: Sunday, April 21

36th FALL FANTASY PARADE: Saturday Morning Live on Parade
CHRISTMAS CARD: Drawing of a trolley with Santa.

CARL E. HENNINGER, chairman of the board of Kennywood Park, died May 21, 1985. A graduate of Amherst College, Henninger devoted almost 50 years to Kennywood, serving first as general manager, later as president, and finally chairman of the board.

COMPUTERIZED ADMISSION was used by the park for the first time.
FROG LEAP game was purchased.
GOLD RUSHER improvements were made. A platform was added by Duquesne Metal Products, West Mifflin, PA.
PATIO CAFE was the new name for the Casino restaurant. Sit-down dining, which formerly had occupied half the restaurant, was discontinued in favor of total cafeteria-style dining.
PAY ONE PRICE - Every day in July and August became pay one-price days.
PICNIC PAVILION was added behind the Turnpike ride.   RAGING RAPIDS, a white water rapids ride by Intamin, A.G., Zurich, Switzerland, was built on the Starvue Plaza and Dipper coaster site. The ride opened in May. The course was approximately 1,300 feet long. Travel time was between 3 and 4 minutes with 30 seconds in the loading station. The ride had 20 six-passenger boats that gave the ride an hourly capacity of 1,400. Each boat had a diameter of 9 1/2 feet. The name was going to be "Raging Waters," but it was changed to Raging Rapids shortly before the ride open.
ROLL-O-PLANE was removed from the park.
SUPER ROUNDUP was removed and later sent to Idlewild.
TIN CAN ALLEY game was added.

1986

OPENING DATE: Sunday, April 20

37th FALL FANTASY PARADE: Cartoon Capers on Parade
CHRISTMAS CARD: The Flower of Kennywood (photos in ornament drawings).

FIRST AID STATION was moved from the Park Office to the Gran Prix Building.
GAMES BUILDING was constructed opposite Fascination along the midway that ran from Le Cachot to the restaurant.
GUEST RELATIONS AND GROUP SALES OFFICE BUILDING was constructed at the Laser Loop entrance.
KIDDIE SCOOTER ride was purchased from Roseland Park, Canandaigua, NY. The ride was manufactured by Zamperla, Inc.
KIDDIE WHIP, by W. F. Mangels, Coney Island, NY, was purchased from Paragon Park, Hull, Massachusetts. An earlier oval-style Kiddie Whip had been destroyed in the 1975 fire.
MINIATURE GOLF COURSE near the Gran Prix was removed at the end of the season and replaced with landscaping at a cost of $60,000.
PAY-ONE-PRICE ADMISSION - The park shifted from open gate and tickets to pay one price at the end of the school picnic season, June 26, 1986. This marked the end of a ticket system for Kennywood admissions.
OBSERVATION DECK, built by park employees, was added to the Raging Rapids. The deck was located between the rapids and the miniature railroad.
PICNIC PAVILION was added behind the Turnpike.
RAGING RAPIDS was made wetter with the addition of a triple waterfall that cascaded down a fountain 25 feet high. A huge pump projected 3,500 gallons of water a minute over the mountain. Two "pop up" geysers, controlled by a park employee were also added.
SKYRIDE was purchased from Roseland Park, Canandaigua, NY. It was intended for use at Idlewild but was not erected.
TOWER REFRESHMENT STAND (a.k.a. Voice of Kennywood Stand) was demolished at the end of the season.
WALK-IN GIFT SHOP, the park's first, was designed by GWSM, Inc. and was called Rue Orleans. It was located opposite Fascination.
WAVE SWINGER, manufactured by Zierer GmbH & Co. KG, Offenberg, Germany, was purchased by the park.
WONDER WHEEL, a giant Ferris wheel that was 85 feet high and had 24 gondolas each holding six passengers, was purchased in 1983 at a bankruptcy sale. The ride was manufactured by Soli, Reggio Emilia, Italy. It was installed on the site formerly occupied by the Super Roundup. The last time a Ferris wheel had operated in the park was 1980. Foundation plan was done by William L. Cobb.

1987

OPENING DATE: Saturday, April 18

38th FALL FANTASY PARADE: Music, Music, Music!
CHRISTMAS CARD: William Libby black and white lithograph of the Carousel with holly trim and ribbon.

CALYPSO was removed at the end of the season.
CAROUSEL DECORATIVE RAILING by Duquesne Metal Products, West Mifflin, PA, was placed around the park's Dentzel Carousel.
CENTENNIAL TIMEPIECE was added in a Victorian-themed park setting near the Merry-Go-Round. The centerpiece was an 1890 street clock manufactured by Canterbury International, Sherman Oaks, CA. It cost $22,700.
COMPUTERIZED LIGHTING was added to the Ferris wheel.
GOLD RUSHER'S trusses and exit stairway were added by Duquesne Metal Products, West Mifflin, PA.
KENNYWOOD PARK was designated a National Historic Landmark. A bronze plaque was unveiled by National Park Service historian James Charleton on August 28, 1987.
KIDDIE ELEPHANT RIDE was added in Kiddieland for $20,000.
LASER LOOP - Twenty-six people were rescued by ladder from the Loop when a car got stuck on a level section of the track on the far side of the ride about 10 feet above the ground.
MINIATURE GOLF COURSE - A new course was built near the Laser Loop entrance for $200,000. The site was prepared by Grove Industries. Originally there were 18 holes.
MUSIK EXPRESS, manufactured by Mack, GmbH & Co., Waldkirch, Germany, was added to the park. The ride traveled in a circle and bounced passengers at high speed in a roller coaster fashion to the beat of top 40 musical hits. The new ride cost approximately $250,000.
PAGODA REFRESHMENT STAND was built on the site of the old Tower or Voice of Kennywood Refreshment Stand. It was similar to the Kinesiske Tarn Restaurant in a pagoda at Tivoli Gardens, Copenhagen, Denmark, that Carl E. Henninger had always admired. The dragons used to decorate the structure had been on the front of the Old Mill boats. The building was designed by Maclachin, Cornelius & Filoni and cost more than $275,000.

1988

OPENING DATE: Sunday, April 17
(Saturday, April 16 was scheduled to be opening day, but because of bad weather the park did not open until the following day.)

39th FALL FANTASY PARADE: Fairy Tales on Parade
CHRISTMAS CARD: WQED Kennywood Memories poster.

BAYERN KURVE was removed at the end of the season.
BREAKING PLATES game was added.
FANTASTIC FOUNTAIN, a dancing 70-foot fountain made with imported tile, was installed at the site of the old miniature golf course. The fountain came alive with a "Magic Waters Show" featuring dozens of pulsating jets of water and colored lights that were synchronized to music with a computer. Twenty-foot high evergreens were planted behind the fountain. The area was designed by GWSM, Inc.
FLYING CARPET was a "boat-like" carpet ride that went back and forth as it advanced higher and higher until it went 360-degrees over the top. The ride could hold 40 passengers with half the riders facing the others. The ride was purchased from a New Jersey boardwalk amusement park, although it was manufactured by Zierer GmbH & Co. KG, West Germany. It was themed as an Arabian Nights carpet. The ride simulated a weightless, free-falling feeling similar to the Pirate. Flying Carpet was a high tech ride controlled by a circuit board. The ride cost $375,000. Foundation plans were designed by Milton Justh.
JACK RABBIT received a new retaining wall that cost $50,000.
KENNYWOOD MEMORIES, Rick Sebak's award winning documentary for WQED was shot at the park during the month of July. It was first televised on Wednesday, September 28, 1988.
LANDSCAPING - Over $15,000 was spent on new shade trees.
MINI SCOOTER RIDE, bumper cars for children, was moved at the end of the season to Idlewild.
PHOTO STUDIO, where pictures were taken and placed on a magazine cover, was placed in the Arcade.
PLUSH PITCH game was added where players threw quarters onto a plate to win.
POP GUN game, which required players to knock down three cups with a single shot, was added.
ROTOR (the park's third) was purchased from Chance Manufacturing Co., Wichita, Kansas. The rotor was located next to the Gran Prix. It held riders against the wall of a rotating cylinder with centrifugal force as the floor pulled away. The ride cost more than $135,000.
ANDY VETTEL, SR., designer of the Thunderbolt and Little Dipper coasters, died. As the park's master mechanic, he had lived in a house in the park for fifty years. The house was razed after his death.

1989

OPENING DATE: Sunday, April 23

40th FALL FANTASY PARADE: Americana on Parade
CHRISTMAS CARD: Marilyn Henry painting of "lead horse."

FIRE broke out in one of the park's concession booths on May 12.
MONONGAHELA MONSTER was moved from the Garden Stage to beside the Park Office. The ride was taken out of the park at the end of the season.
SAFETY CITY was added to Kiddieland. The park designed the attraction, which had replicas of buildings from downtown Pittsburgh along its route. The kids rode 4 x 4 jeeps, manufactured by Venture Ride Mfg., Inc., Greer, South Carolina.
SANDCASTLE, Kennywood's new water park in West Homestead, PA, opened on July 17.
SWING AROUND, manufactured by Huss & Co., Bremen, Germany, replaced the Monster on the platform above the Garden Stage. The swing ride had 14 gondolas that swung to a horizontal position where riders spun 360 degrees. Each gondola then began a back and forth motion creating a swing within a swing. It had made a one-season appearance in 1984.

1990

OPENING DATE: Saturday, April 14
(The park closed the following day, April 15, for Easter.)

41st FALL FANTASY PARADE: Golden Oldies on Parade
CHRISTMAS CARD: Christmas ornament with Santa on the Steel Phantom.

BALLOON RACE was purchased from Zamperla Inc., Parsippany, NJ, although the ride was manufactured in Italy. The ride held 32 passengers and could accommodate adults or children.
CATERPILLAR TRAIN was removed from Kiddieland and sent to Idlewild at the end of the season.
GAMES BUILDINGS AND FOOD STANDS (formerly Pastime Building and food stands) adjacent to the Racer and extending to the Jack Rabbit were completely rebuilt. Steel buildings were used and the fronts were designed to capture the look of the 20's. Layout for the new structures was by Milton Justh with the details by R & R Design. Games added included Wacky Wire and Sidewinder. String Game was removed from the Arcade.
GIFT SHOP (second) replaced the Frog Bog game located across from the Penny Arcade.
LADIES COTTAGE (#2 rest room) was renovated to 1990 standards.
LAGOON BRIDGE - Old wooden bridge was demolished by the park and a new steel and concrete bridge was built.
LASER LOOP was removed at the end of the season and sold to a park in Mexico City.
LOG JAMMER had a portion of its fiber glass flume trough replaced for $62,000.
PARACHUTE TOWER from Venture, Greer, South Carolina, was added to Kiddieland.
RACER'S 1927 front was restored. The previous front was removed and underneath workers discovered that much of the original 1927 front still existed; it required only minor rebuilding. Design work was done by R & R Creative Amusement Designs, Inc., Anaheim, CA, with the work performed by Kennywood's maintenance crew. Old photographs of the original front were used as guides.
RAGING RAPIDS sign and a new waiting area were added to the ride.
RING AROUND game replaced the Can Smash game. The new game challenged players to loop multi-colored rings on a revolving platform.

1991

OPENING DATE: Sunday, April 14

42nd FALL FANTASY PARADE: Storyland on Parade
CHRISTMAS CARD: E. "Spud" Pinkney color drawing of a snowy Noah's Ark & Steel Phantom.

BAND ORGAN on the Merry-Go-Round underwent extensive repairs. A worn out drum pad and air bellows were replaced by Gavin McDonough of B.A.B. Organ Company, Long Island, NY.
ICE CREAM PARLOR was converted from a walk-in food site to a midway walk-up operation.
JACK RABBIT had a tunnel again added between the first drop and the lift hill.
MINIATURE GOLF COURSE had a few holes removed to make way for the Steel Phantom.
PHYSICS DAY was held in the park for the first time.
STEEL PHANTOM coaster was erected. The roller coaster, manufactured by Arrow Dynamics, Inc., Clearview, Utah, was 163 feet high with one drop of 155 feet and a deeper drop of 225 feet into a ravine where it cut through the Thunderbolt's structure. The coaster was 3,000 feet long and had a loop, a boomerang, and a half corkscrew. Parts of the old Laser Loop loading station were used on the Steel Phantom. Engineering was done by Curtis D. Summers.
THUNDERBOLT TUNNEL was removed.

1992

OPENING DATE: Saturday, April 18
(The park closed the following day, April 19, for Easter.)

43rd FALL FANTASY PARADE: Kiddy Kapers on Parade
CHRISTMAS CARD: Marilyn Henry watercolor of the Thunderbolt.

CAROUSEL COURT was the name for the newly remodeled food court that was placed in the original Merry-Go-Round building. It was conceived by Hammer Designs.
FREE PARKING expanded by 1,000 additional spaces and a second tier was created. An escalator (called a People Mover) was installed.
GROUP SALES AND GUEST RELATIONS BUILDING was erected across the highway from the park and was designed by Maclachlan, Cornelius, & Filoni to look like an old inter-urban railway station. The building featured a clock tower, a shingle and brick exterior, glass block windows, and a roof with patterns made from different colored shingles. Since the building was located outside of the fenced in park, it was built with large steel doors that could be pulled over the windows in front and on the side that faced the park.
HISTORIC MARKER recognizing Kennywood was placed by the Pennsylvania Historical and Museum Commission outside the entrance to the park.
MINI ENTERPRISE returned to Kiddieland after an absence of several years.
PARKING - All parking was moved across the road for safety reasons. Pay parking on the park side of the highway was closed.
SINGLE ENTRANCE to the park via tunnel was inaugurated.
TRI-STAR was installed for one season in what would become the entrance to Lost Kennywood. The ride was manufactured by Huss Trading Company, Bremen, Germany.
WALK-IN GIFT SHOP was added. The shop was placed in the building near the Steel Phantom's exit when Group Sales was moved across the highway. It was the park's third walk-in gift shop, and it featured Steel Phantom merchandise.

1993

OPENING DATE: Sunday, April 18

44th FALL FANTASY PARADE: Mother Goose on Parade
CHRISTMAS CARD: E. Pinkney color drawing of the gazebo with a Christmas tree.

ENTERPRISE was removed for one season for refurbishing.
LOST KENNYWOOD construction started in 1993 and proceeded until the themed section was opened in April 1995. Construction was held up when part of the old swimming pool was discovered and had to be broken up and removed.
PITTSBURGH HISTORICAL SCENES replaced the hillbillies display on the miniature train ride. Mary Ann Spanagel, a freelance artist from Indiana, PA, who had made the floats for Kennywood's Fall Fantasy for 27 seasons, and her assistant David Schremp created the display. Passengers aboard the train experienced such historical scenes as Braddock's Crossing, The Whiskey Rebellion, and the Homestead Steel Strike (the latter complete with such figures as Henry Clay Frick and the Pinkerton men hired as strikebreakers). In addition, there was the imposing figure of Joe Magarac, the mythical, hulking steelworker, stretching more than 15 feet in the air. (It is fitting that Joe Magarac be placed along the bluff overlooking the Edgar Thomson Works of USX, the only remaining steel mill in the Monongahela Valley.) The display concludes with a wall bearing faces of several ethnic groups who have given the area its diversity and pride. The wall has six five-foot-tall facial sculptures. Spanagel used chicken wire to make the initial shapes, but more durable steel and concrete were used to make the final characters.
TOY SOLDIER entrance was added to Kiddieland.
GEORGE WASHINGTON - Mary Ann Spanagel with the help of her employees, David Schremp and Tracey Simmen, created a 9 1/2 foot statue of George Washington as a young colonel with the Virginia militia at the time of Braddock's Crossing. The bronze-coated statue weighed 1500 pounds and replaced the "1890" Street Clock in the small Victorian display near the merry-go-round.
WIPE OUT ride was purchased from Chance Manufacturing, Wichita, Kansas.

1994

OPENING DATE: Sunday, April 17

45th FALL FANTASY PARADE: Wild Wild West on Parade
CHRISTMAS CARD: card size copy of an old Luna Park poster announcing Lost Kennywood.

BAYERN KURVE bobsled ride returned after several years' absence.
ENTERPRISE returned after one year's absence.
ROTOR was removed from the park at the end of the season.
SKYCOASTER towers were constructed over the Lagoon with an entrance on the Lagoon Stage. The ride was designed by Sky Fun 1 Inc. of Boulder, Colorado, and cost over $200,000.
WAVE SWINGER was removed from the park for one season for refurbishing.

1995

OPENING DATE: Saturday, April 15
(The park is closed the following day, April 16, for Easter.)

46th FALL FANTASY PARADE: Holidays on Parade
(The parade was expanded to 18 nights.)
CHRISTMAS CARD: David Farmerie color photo of a cherub on Kennywood's Merry-Go-Round.

LOST KENNYWOOD, a five acre themed area, opened on April 15. The $7 million project was the largest single addition ever to the park in terms of acreage and cost. The area was designed by Bruce D. Robinson Architecture - Design, Inc., Cincinnati, OH.
PHANTASTIC LASER SHOW was designed by Techni-Flex and took place nightly in Lost Kennywood's reflecting basin.
PHANTOM PHLYER (generic name: Flying Scooter) was purchased when Idora Park, Youngstown, OH, closed in 1984. The ride was refurbished by Conklin Shows, Brantford, Ontario, Canada. Before going to Idora the ride had been located at West View Park, West View, PA.
PITTSBURG PLUNGE was a shoot the chute ride constructed by O. D. Hopkins Associates, Inc., Contoocook, NH, in Lost Kennywood.
ROLL-O-PLANE, built by ORI, Salem, OR, was placed in Lost Kennywood.
STREET CLOCK "1890" returned to the park and was placed in Lost Kennywood.
WAVE SWINGER returned to the park after a year's absence and was placed in Lost Kennywood.
WHIP returned to the park after a one year's absence and was placed in Lost Kennywood.
WHIP BUILDING was given a new concrete floor and converted into a picnic pavilion.

1996

OPENING DATE: Sunday, April 14

47th FALL FANTASY PARADE: Broadway on Parade
CHRISTMAS CARD: "Light the lights — hit the heights." Bob Pazuchak color photo of a Christmas tree in lights on the Steel Phantom.

CATERING BUSINESS - Stratigos Caterers, a White Oak-based company, was purchased by Kennywood Entertainment Company. Stratigos had done catering for Kennywood since 1979. The Stratigos family continued to manage the operation.
KENNY'S PARKWAY, a ski lift 1,550 feet long extending from the third-level parking lot to the park's front entrance, was built. It traveled at 3 mph and could carry as many as 396 passengers in its 99 seats. The ride was named by Sandy Evans of the Kennywood Games Department.
KENNYVILLE HIGH, a back-to-the-'50s entertainment area, replaced the Wipeout in the area between Noah's Ark, Potato Patch, and Le Cachot. A false front was built on the back of the Refreshment Company complex.
LAKE COMPOUNCE - Kennywood bought an interest in this amusement park located in Bristol, Connecticut.
LI'L PHANTOM, a junior steel coaster built in Florida, was added to Kiddieland. Adults who accompanied children could also ride it.
NOAK'S ARK was enlarged and practically rebuilt. David Moll, superintendent of the carpenters, was in charge of rebuilding the boat. Bruce D. Robinson Architecture - Design, Inc., Cincinnati, OH, designed the additions and modifications. Noah's Ark was not opened until August 12. Some of the high-tech devices were supplied by Techni-Flex, a California firm.
PHANTOM PHLYER was removed from the park and sent to Lake Compounce to make room for the Pitt Fall.
RAMBLER AUTOMOBILE from 1957 was acquired by the park and was used in the Fall Fantasy parade.
WIPEOUT was moved to the area between Lost Kennywood and the Musik Express.

1997

OPENING DATE: Sunday, April 20

48th FALL FANTASY PARADE: Incredible Journeys on Parade
CHRISTMAS CARD: Kennywood Centennial ceramic ornament with 100th anniversary logo.

KENNYWOOD RESORT was the new name for the Kennyville High entertainment area.
LAUGHING SAL, the mechanical lady originally manufactured by the Philadelphia Toboggan Company, returned after five years' absence to the entrance of the train ride.
PITT FALL, designed by Intamin A.G., Zurich, Switzerland, was at 251 feet the tallest free-fall ride in any amusement park in America. The ride carried 16 passengers in rows of four that formed a square around the cylindrical center tower. Braking for the ride was done using fail-safe magnetic brakes called LSMs, or linear synchronous motors. The ride was so high that FAA regulations required the park to install flashing lights.
VIRTUAL REALITY DISPLAY was put in the Arcade.
WHIP BUILDING that had been converted into a picnic pavilion had a small stage added.

1998

KENNYWOOD PARK CELEBRATED ITS 100TH ANNIVERSARY

OPENING DATE: Saturday, April 25
(The park was to open on Sunday April 19 but did not open that day because it rained all day.)

DISTORTION MIRRORS were resilvered and placed on the historic midway.
DRINK STATIONS added to the picnic groves.
LEVEL FOUR PARKING was developed.
MERRY-GO-ROUND HORSES were refurbished.
OLD MILL was painted and paddle wheel was rebuilt.
PARK FRIES were sold in Giant Eagle super markets.
SANITARY SEWERS – Some sewers were replaced.
STRING GAME returned after many years' absence along with FISH GAME, SCATTER BALL, and PAINT GAME.
THUNDERBOLT received new headlights
TURN-OF-THE-CENTURY MIDWAY was created with tents, flags and banners.

Pittsburgh artist Linda Barnicott's drawing of Kennywood's Turn-Of-The-Century Midway.
(COPYRIGHT BY LINDA BARNICOTT)

Kennywood Park's
Turn-Of-The Century Midway

...after all,
   Kennywood
      is just for fun!

(Kennywood's Turn-Of-The-Century Midway photographs by Charles J. Jacques, Jr.)

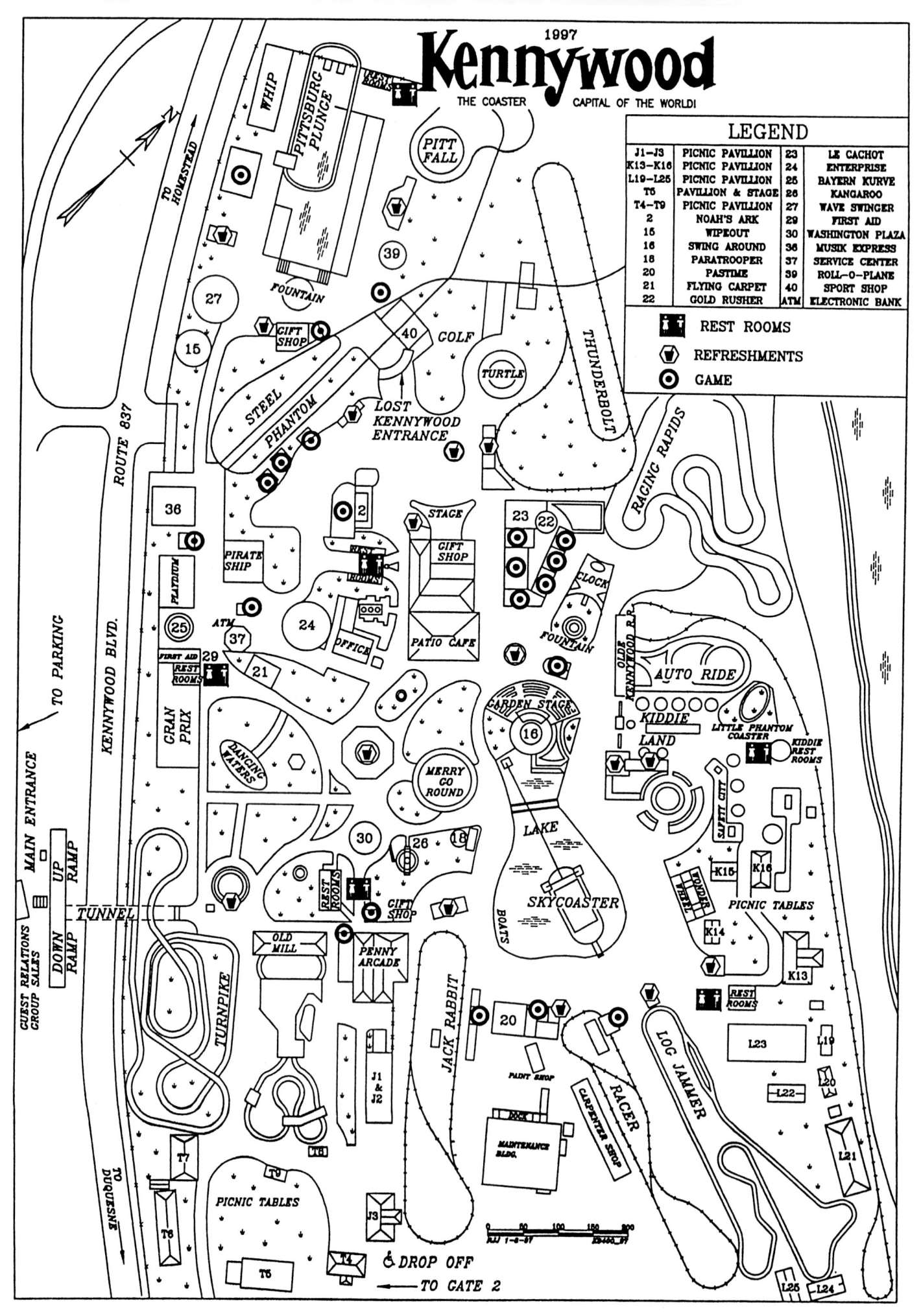

1997 Kennywood
THE COASTER CAPITAL OF THE WORLD!

LEGEND			
J1-J3	PICNIC PAVILLION	23	LE CACHOT
K13-K16	PICNIC PAVILLION	24	ENTERPRISE
L19-L25	PICNIC PAVILLION	25	BAYERN KURVE
T5	PAVILLION & STAGE	26	KANGAROO
T4-T9	PICNIC PAVILLION	27	WAVE SWINGER
2	NOAH'S ARK	29	FIRST AID
15	WIPEOUT	30	WASHINGTON PLAZA
16	SWING AROUND	36	MUSIK EXPRESS
18	PARATROOPER	37	SERVICE CENTER
20	PASTIME	39	ROLL-O-PLANE
21	FLYING CARPET	40	SPORT SHOP
22	GOLD RUSHER	ATM	ELECTRONIC BANK

- REST ROOMS
- REFRESHMENTS
- GAME

Acknowledgments

In addition to the persons that I acknowledged in *Kennywood: Roller Coaster Capital of the World*, this book would not have been possible without the further help of the following people:

Carl O. Hughes, chairman of the board of Kennywood Entertainment Company, who encouraged me and took an active interest in the book. He read the manuscript and helped with historical interpretations. His help was invaluable to answer many of the whys. He also wrote the preface to the book.

Harry W. Henninger, Jr., president and chief operating officer of Kennywood Entertainment Company, again shared his thoughts. He has a wonderful sense of humor and is a great story teller.

F. W. "Bill" Henninger, president of the Kennywood Refreshment Company, who like other members of his family, shared photographs, records, and his memories of the park. Bill, whose other love is landscaping and gardening, encouraged me to mention Kennywood's gardens.

Andy R. Quinn, grandson of A. S. McSwigan, shared his recollections of the park and his family's part in its development.

Ann Hughes, Kennywood's publicity director for many years and wife of Carl O. Hughes, was again very helpful. One of the reasons the park is so beloved and respected is Ann's work over the years. Mary Lou Rosemeyer, who followed in her mother's footsteps, is Kennywood's current publicity director. She was so patient with me and supplied me many things which I thought were lost or impossible to find. She made the park's newspaper clippings available as well as the photographic archives.

Significant information was gained from the personal recollection of the following people: Richard J. Henry, Susan Fontanese, Kenneth Garrett, Nancy Jane Jackson, William J. Rodgers, Keith Hood, Bob Henninger, and Norm Sweich.

Paul and Claudia Korol, longtime friends and collectors of amusement park memorabilia (among many other things), helped me with the research. Paul spent many hours at libraries and historical societies looking for articles on Kennywood and Idlewild.

Richard L. Bowker, who has one of the largest collections of amusement park postcards and Kennywood memorabilia, permitted me to use some of his postcards and photographs. Also providing photographs were Paul L. Ruben and Ken Simmons.

Rick Sebak, a WQED-TV producer, shared his photographs and memories of the park, which I used in the chapter on *Kennywood Memories*. Sebak shot most of the pictures in this chapter. I also wish to thank WQED for their help with the book.

Jim Futrell, the historian for the National Amusement Park Historical Association, permitted me to use pictures of Idlewild and Kennywood in the book. Jim also wrote an excellent article on Idlewild that appeared in Vol. 14, No. 3 of the *NAPHA News*.

Marilyn Holt and Gil Pietrzak of the Carnegie Library of Pittsburgh's Pennsylvania Department were very helpful to me as I researched this book. Many of the photographs that appear in my two Kennywood books have been given to the Carnegie Library of Pittsburgh and can be found in the Charles J. Jacques, Jr. Collection.

The Pittsburgh History & Landmarks Foundation and the Western Pennsylvania Historical Society provided material that was used in the book.

Karen Morrison, who designed the book's layout, did her usual fantastic job. Karen kidded about breaking my heart because there were many pictures that she could not use, but in the end, she was able to use so many that it did not break my heart but my budget. Karen did a superb job on the cover.

Rick Shale, Professor of English at Youngstown State University, edited the manuscript and brought a greater clarity to the text. He created the index and helped prepare the appendix.

Betty Jacques, my wife, took a number of photographs that appear in the book. Writing a book is a long, difficult process, and Betty has been incredibly supportive and willing to listen for months as ideas were developed, discarded, or revised until the final product emerged.

CHARLES J. JACQUES, JR.
March 1998

The material for this book comes from three primary sources: first, newspaper and magazines articles, many of which are cited in the text; second, correspondence, memos, and documents from the park and individuals; and third, personal interviews by the author.

For those interested in additional reading about Kennywood and other amusement parks:

Amusement Business
Box 24970
Nashville, TN 37203

Amusement Today
P.O. Box 5427
Arlington, TX 76005-5427

At The Park
P.O. Box 597783
Chicago, IL 60659-7783

The Carousel News & Trader
87 Park Ave. West, Suite 206
Mansfield, OH 44902-1657

Inside Track
P.O. Box 7956
Newark, Delaware 19714-7956

Merry-Go-Roundup
Publication of the
National Carousel Association
P.O. Box 4333
Evansville, IN 47724-0333

NAPHA NEWS
Publication of the
National Amusement Park
Historical Association
P.O. Box 83
Prospect, IL 60056

Park World
P.O. Box 54
Desborough, Northants
England
NN14 2UH

RollerCoaster!
Publication of the
American Coaster Enthusiasts
P.O. Box 8226
Chicago, IL 60680

Index

(**Bold**, *italicized* page numbers refer to photographic captions.)

Alameda Park, 156
Aliquippa Park, 11, 156
Allan Herschell Company, 29
Allez Oop, *36*
American Coaster Enthusiasts, 47, 126, 136
Arcade, *50*, *69*, *128*
Arrow Dynamics, Inc., 135-36
Astroworld, 46
Athletic Field, 8, *10*, 17
Auto Race, 15, *20*, *26*, 28, *31*, 89, *93*
Auto Ride, *20*, *31*
Auto Skooter, 18, *23*
Ayers, Maurice, 50

Ballroom, 32
Bandstand, 9
Bayern Kurve, 48, *51*, 109, 144
Beal, Frank S., *88*, 92
Bermuda Triangle, 116
Blackpool Pleasure Beach (United Kingdom), 167
Borellis, W. Thomas, 116
Bozo, the mechanical man, *31*
Braddock, General Edward, 85, 85-86, *94*, 94
Braddock's Crossing, 85, 86, 140
Brownie Coaster, 28
Bruce D. Robinson Architecture-Design, Inc., 153, 169
Bruwelheide, Jim, *100*, 102-3, 107, *109*
Bubble Bounce, *25*, *35*
Bug House, 17
Burke's Glen (Monroeville, PA), 16, 156

Cachot. *See* Le Cachot
Calhoun Park, 5, 10, 149
Calypso, *39*, 48, *48*, 79, 109
Camden Park, 63
Carousel, *4*, *38*, 38, 53, 85, *87*, 184. *See also* Dentzel Carousel; Merry-Go-Round
Carousel (Kiddieland), 28
Carousel Court, 137
Carousel Pavilion, *10*, 12, *86*, 87, 90
Carowinds, 46
Cartmell, Robert, 38
Cascade Park (New Castle, PA), 11
Casino, 2, 3, *3*, *5*, *7*, *10*, 37, 39, *46*, 81, 83, *87*, 87, 90, 140
Caterpillar, 15

Cedar Point, 36, 48, 55, 130
Celoron (Lake Chautauqua), 11
Charleton, James, *84*, 88, 90
Chatty, 26
Chester Park, 9
Chicago, IL, 30, 36
Cinema 180, *47*, 48
Circle Swing, *7*, 7, 9, *11*, 13-, 23
Cliffhangers, 116
Club Wet, 120, 123-24
Columbian Exposition of 1893, 151
Comet Ride, 28
Coney Island (Cincinnati, OH), 37
Coney Island (Neville Island), 10
Conneaut Lake Park, 11, 16
Cope, Myron, 78, *78-79*, 79-81
Cuddle Up, *38*, *45*
Custer Car Ride (Idlewild), 60
C. W. Parker Company, 15

Daffy Klub, 27, *34*
Danahey, Frank, 127
Dance Pavilion, 2, 8, *10*, *16*, 18, 25-26, 29, 32, *36*
Darlington, William, 57
Dayton Fun House and Riding Device Manufacturing Company, 15
Dayton Fun House Corporation, 60
Dentzel, Gustav A., 2, *4*, 15
Dentzel, Michael, 15
Dentzel, William H., 15, *15*, *87*, 87, 166
Dentzel Carousel, 12, *15-16*, 16, *26*, 53, *87*, 87, 126, 160. *See also* Carousel; Merry-Go-Round
Dipper (Little Dipper), 24, 28, 51, *69*, 71, 73
Dipsy Doodle, *22*, 22-23, 158
Disney, Walt, 36
Disneyland, 36
Dodgem, 15
Dollywood, 153
Doodlebug (Idlewild), *60*
Down-and-Out, 7
Dream City (Wilkinsburg, PA), 10
Dumbo the elephant ride, 95
Duquesne Gardens, 7
Duquesne, PA, 2, 85, 104

Edgar Thomson Works (Carnegie Steel Company), 4, 140
Electric Park (Kansas City), 151
Electric Theater, 8
Enchanted Castle, *36*
Enterprise, 38, 47-48, *81*, *139*, 144
Euclid Beach Park (Cleveland, OH), 36
Exposition Park (Conneaut Lake), 9
Eyerly, 18

Fairyland Floats, 8, 12
Fall Fantasy Parade, 30, 30-31, 64-65, 94, 139, *162-65*, 162-65
Ferris Wheel, 9, 15, *23*, 23, *32*, 35, *39*, 82
Ferris Wheel (Idlewild), 59, 60, *68*
Ferris Wheel (Kiddieland), 28
Figure Eight Toboggan Coaster, 6, 8, 12-13
Filoni, Al, 95
Fire Engine Ride, 28
floral calendar, *12*, *82*, 159
floral clock, *48*, *125*
Flyer, 36
Flying Cages, 29, *36*
Flying Carpet, 109
Flying Coaster, 37
Flying Saucers, *34*
Flying Scooters, *22*, 23, *36*, *159*
Fontanese, Sue, 152
Formula 1, *123*, 123
Frog Bog, 81
Frontierland (United Kingdom), 167
Frontier Zoo (Idlewild), 62

Garden Stage, 52, 70, 125, *126*
Garrett, Ken, 38, 83, *138*
Geauga Lake, 48
Ghost Ship, 82
Gold Rusher, *48-50*, 49-50
Graff, John R., *88*, 92
Grand Victorian Festival, *141*, *145*, 145
Gran Prix, *45*, 48, 109, 181
Great America, 46
Great Balloon Race, *128*, 128, *136*
Great Depression, 25, 35, 59
Great Pavilion (Idlewild), *56*, 58
"Great Western Train Hold-Up," 8, *8*

215

Grotto of Visions, 8
Guest Services Building, *138*

H2OhhhZone (Idlewild), 65, *65*, 113
Hardheaded Harold's Horrendously Humorous Haunted Hideaway, *40*, 48
Harton, T. M., 9, 12, *56*, 58
Henke, Ed, *145*, 145
Henninger, Carl E., 20, 24, 29-30, 35, 37-41, 47, 82, 95, 127
Henninger, Frederick W., 9-13, 16, 18, 20, 29, 35, 135, 150
Henninger, F. W. "Bill," 38-41, 55, 65, 70, 72-73, 87, 95, 113, 116, 137, 141, *167*
Henninger, Harry W., Jr., 38, 40-41, 43, 45-46, 55, 63-65, 67-68, 72-73, *74*, 74-75, 77, 81, 88, 95, 112-14, 116, 118-21, 125, 131-36, *136*, 142, 153-54, 168, 175
Henninger, Harry W., Sr., *29*, 29, 35, 37, 39-40
Henninger, Robert F., *29*, 29, 35, 39
Henry, Rich, 77, 109, 111, 126, 129, 136, 142, 155, *163*, 163-64, 172, 174
Hersheypark, 24, 48
Hilarity Hall, 8
Historic Village (Idlewild), 62
Homestead Steel Strike, *139*, 140
Homestead Steel Works, 114
Hood, Keith, *63*, 63, 172
Hootie & the Blowfish, 125
Hootin' Holler' (Idlewild), 64, *64-65*
Hot Tootsie, 121
House of Mystery, 9
House of Trouble, 7
Hughes, Ann, 51, *89*, 100, *101-102*, 102-104, 109, *130*, 146
Hughes, Carl O., *27*, 27, 35, 40, 49, 51, 55, 63-65, 68-69, 72-74, *74*, 76, 81, 83-84, 87-88, *89*, 90, 92, 94-95, 100, 105, 109, 112-16, 118, 120, 127-28, 142, 144, 146, 153-54, 159, 166-68, *173*
Hurricane, 29
Huss, 52, 70, 126, 137

Idlewild Express, 60
Idlewild Park, 11, 24, 54, *54-55*, 55-56, *57-58*, 57-58, *59*, 59-65, *65*, 66-68, 82, 109, 113, 128, 167, 172
Idora Park (Youngstown, OH), 10, 158-59
Ingersoll, Fred, 5, 6, 148, 151
Intamin, 74-75, 174-75
International Association of Amusement Parks and Attractions, 72, 88, 92, 128, 142
Island Stage, 29, 38, 51, 142
Italian Day, 96, 103, 146

Jack Rabbit, *4*, *13*, 13-14, *34*, 37, 43, 48, 51, 83, 89, *91*, 136, 141, 178
Jacques, Charles J., Jr., 53, 104
Jumping Frogs. *See Frog Bog*
Jumpin' Jungle (Idlewild), *64*, 64

Kangaroo (ride), 37
KDKA, 30
KDKA Orchestra, 26
Kenny, Anthony, 2, 37
Kenny, Thomas, 8687
Kenny Kangaroo, *71*, 71, *100*, *109*, 111, *125*
Kenny's Grove, 2, 21, 87

Kenny's Parkway, *171*, 171
Kennyville High School, *170*, 171
Kennywood Alumni Day, 160
Kennywood Boulevard, 42, *45*, 52, *85*, 86, 133, 138, 157
Kennywood Entertainment Corporation, 166, 168, 171
Kennywood Express, 21
Kennywood Memories, 70, *97*, 97-108, *108*, 111, 159
Kennywood Park Corporation, 37, 39
"Kennywood Park Waltz," 106
Kennywood Refreshment Company, 39
Kennywood Resort Hotel, 171
Kennywood: Roller Coaster Capital of the World, 52
Kentucky Kingdom (Louisville, KY), 175
Kiddie Auto Ride, 28
Kiddie Auto Ride (Idlewild), 60
Kiddie Boat Ride, *16*
Kiddie Cadillacs, *139*
Kiddie Caterpillar, 69, *103*
Kiddie Mill Ride, *34*
Kiddie Whip, 28, *139*
Kiddieland, 14, *20*, *26*, 27-28, *28*, *33-34*, 65, 69, 82, 95, 126, 128, *141*, 141, 162
Kiddieland (Idlewild), *58-60*, 61
Kiddie Swing, *146*
Kings Dominion, 74, 78, 130, 153
Kings Island, 37, 130, 153
Knobels Grove, 24
Knott's Berry Farm, 46

Laffing Sal, *105*
Laffing Sal (Idlewild), 61
Laff-in-the-Dark, 15, *24*, 53, 105
Lagoon, *3*, *6*, *10*, *16*, 23, 38, *41*, 47, 50, 82, 128, *147*, 184
Lake Bouquet, *54*, 56, 58
Lake Compounce (Bristol, CT), 171-72
Lake St. Clair, *54*, 57-58, *58*
Lambert, Jack, *68*, 68-69, *78*, 78-81
Laser Loop, 40, 42-43, *43-44*, 45-46, *47*, 47-48, 52, 76, *80*, 83, 95, *98-99*, 102, *106*, *129*, 129-35, 174
Laughing Gallery, 5-6, 9
Lavin, Nancy, *99*, 99-100, *101*
Lazy River, *116*, 116-17, *118*, 119, *119-20*
Le Cachot, 69-70, *126-27*, *154*, *176*, 179
Lightning Express, *114*, 116
Ligonier Valley Rail Road, 55, 56-57, 60-61
Lil' Phantom, 171, *172*
Little Choo Choo (ride), *26*
Little Dipper. *See Dipper*
Little Squirts (Idlewild), 65
Log Jammer, 38-41, 43, *46*, 47-48, *70*, 72-73, 76, *97*, 103, 128, 158, 176
Long, Radar, *97*, 100, *103*, 103-104, *105*
Looper, *25*, 29
Loop-O-Plane, 18, *47*
Lost Kennywood, 46, 144, *149-56*, 150, 153-60, *158-61*, 165-67, 170-73, 176, *177*, 182
Loyalhanna Creek, *54*, 57, 66
Loyalhanna Limited (Idlewild), 65
Luna Park (Cleveland), 151
Luna Park (Coney Island, NY), 152, 156
Luna Park (Pittsburgh), 10, 148-52, 155, 159
"Luna Phantastic," 159

Macdonald, C. C., 59-60
Macdonald, C. S., 62
Macdonald, Dick, 61
Macdonald, Grace, 59
Macdonald, Jack, 59, 61-62
Macdonald family, 61-63
Mach, Charlie, *16*, 20
Mackay, Scott, 123-24
Magarac, Joe, *140*, 140
Magic Carpet, 18, *110*
McAneny, Peter, 144, *175*
McSwigan, Andrew Brady, 13-14, 16, 18, 20, 22-23, 25, 27, 30, 32, *35*, 35, 41, 127, 151
McSwigan, Andrew S., 7-13, 35, 150
Megahan, A. F., 9-10
Mellon, Andrew, 2, 56-57, 59
Mellon, Judge Thomas, 56-58
Mellon, Richard, 56-57
Mellon, Thomas, 59
Mellon, Thomas A. "Tommy," 56-58
Mellon family, 61
Merry-Go-Round, 2, 8, 16, 53, 87, 89, 93, 166. *See also Carousel; Dentzel Carousel*
Merry-Go-Round (Idlewild), 58-59
Merry-Go-Round Pavilion, *3*, *4*, 27, 37, 137
Miller, John A., *11*, 13-14, 83, *91*
miniature railroad, *15*, 15, *50*, 82, *89*, 139
miniature railroad (Idlewild), 58
Mini-Caterpillar, 128
Mini Scooter, 109
Mister Rogers' Neighborhood (TV show), 67
Mister Rogers' Neighborhood of Make-Believe (Idlewild), 66, *67*
Modern Art Studios, Inc. of Chicago, 30
Moll, Dave, 128, *168*, 168
Monongahela River, 2, 4, 11, 25, 27, 85, 96, 111-12, 114-15, *117*, 118, *120*, *122*, 124, 130, 140, 143, 167, 174
Monongahela River Valley, *3*, *4*, 15, 136
Monongahela Street Railway Company, 2, 5, 90
Monster, 38, 48, 70, 125, 128
Moonlight Bay, 121
Moonshine Village, *50*
Mother Goose, 65, *65*
Mother Goose Tiny Tot Comfort Station, *33*
Mouse City, 18
Music Plaza, 26, 29, *33*, *35*, 35
Musik Express, *94-95*, 95

National Amusement Park Historical Association (NAPHA), 147, 156
National Association of Amusement Parks, Pools, and Beaches, 27, 151
National Carousel Association, 53, 109
National Historic Landmark, *84*, 84, 89-90
Nationality Days, 177
National Park (Aspinwall, PA), 16
National Park Service, 84, 87-88
National Trust for Historic Preservation, 146
New York World's Fair of 1939-40, 22, 27, *89*
Noah's Ark, 18, *31*, *36*, 37-38, *40*, 42, 46, *46- 47*, 52, 69-70, 89, *90*, *154*, *159*, *166-69*, 166-69, 175, 179

Oakford Park, 16
Oakwood Park, 5, 10
Oasis Miniature Golf (Sandcastle), *123*

Octopus, 29, *30*
Octopus (Idlewild), *68*
Old Country, 130
Olde Idlewild, 63, *68*
Old Mill, 4, 5, 8, 12, *24*, 37-38, *40*, 76, 89, *95*, 95, 164
Old Mill (Kiddieland), 28
Olympic Park, 16

Pagoda Refreshment Stand, *95*, 95
Palisades Park, 20, 36
Panama Canal (Old Mill), 12
Parachute Drop, *128*
Paragon Park, 82
Parkside Terrace, 140
Patio CafÈ, 81
Patio Restaurant, 140
Pennsylvania Amusement Park Association, 20
Pennsylvania Historical and Museum Commission, 86, *88*, 90, 92
Penny Arcade, *52*, 53, 175
Penny Arcade (Idlewild), 60
People Mover, *138*
Phantom Phlyer, 158, *159*, 172, 174
Philadelphia Toboggan Company, *17*, 18, 28, 34, 53, 59-60, *91*, 172
Physics Day, *145*, 145
Pippin, 13-14, *25*, 32, 35, 37-38, *38*, *93*
Pirate, *52*, 52, 70, 109, 171
Pitt Fall, *159*, *170*, 172, *173-74*, 174, *175*
Pittsburgh Exposition, 12
Pittsburgh History and Landmarks Foundation, 53, *86-87*, 87-88, 92
Pittsburgh Pirates, 23
Pittsburgh Railway Company, 3, 8-9, 149-50
Pittsburgh Steeplechase and Amusement Company, 6-7
Pittsburgh Street Railway Company, 5-7
Pittsburgh, PA, 3, 12, 25, 56, 69, 114
Pittsburg Kennywood Park Company, 9
Pittsburg Plunge, *151-52*, *156-57*, *156-59*, 181
Playland Park, 90
Pony Ride, 28, 47
Pony Track, *6-7*, 9, 25
Popcorn Wagon, *146*
Pop Over, *41*
Potato Patch, *65*, 108, *136*, 176
PTC #83 Carousel (Idlewild), 59, *66*, 66

Qualters, Robert, 99-100
Quinn, Andy, 100, 139, 146, 150, 163

Raccoon Lagoon (Idlewild), *66*, 66
Racer (1910-26), *6*, 11, *12-13*
Racer (1927-present), 14, *24-25*, 28, *33*, 37, *37*, 43, *46*, 48, 53, *81*, 89, *104*, 111, *128*, 128, 136-37, 143, *172*, 182
Rafters Run (Idlewild), *66*
Raging Rapids, *72-78*, 72-78, 80-83, 102, 112, 120, 136, 144, 174
Rainbow Gardens, 156
Ranger, 70, *71*
Revere Beach (Massachusetts), 159
Ricky the Raccoon (Idlewild), *67*
Ridee-O, 18, *20*
River City, *121*, 123

Riverplex, 124-25, *125*
Riverview Park (Chicago, IL), 30-31, 36, 156
Robinson, Bruce D., *150-51*, 153-55
Rockets, The, 22
Rock Springs Park (Chester, WV), 59
Rogers, Fred, 66-67
Rollo Coaster (Idlewild), *60*, 60
Roll-O-Plane, *47*, *158*, 158-59
Rosemeyer, Mary Lou, *146*, 146, 162-63, 167, 170
Rosen, Al, *97-98*, 98, *99-102*, 102, *104*, 107
Ross, Frank, 163-64
Rotor, 29, *32*, 109, 111
Roto Whip, 28
Roto Whip (Idlewild), 59
Rowswell, A. K. "Rosey," 17, 23
Rumpus (Idlewild), *60*, 60-61

Sacramento, Tony, 53, *86*, 109
Safety City, *126*, 126
Sandbar, 124
Sandcastle, *112-25*, 115-25, 142, 167
Satellite, 39
Scenic Railway, 5, 7-8, 11
Schmeck, Herbert P., *17*, 18, 28, 60
Schremp, David, 94, 140
Seaplane Swing, 28
Sebak, Rick, *97*, 97-99, *99*, 100-103, *103-104*, 104-105, 107
Senft, George, 57-58
Ship's Wharf, 53
Shockwave Coaster, 134
Shooting Gallery, 9, 13, 26
Shoot the Chutes, 148-51, 156
Shorty's Miniature Golf Course, *98*, 135
Simmen, Tracy, 94, *163*, 164-65
Six Flags Great America, 134
Skee Ball, *109*
Skooter Building, *40*
Skooter Building (Idlewild), *55*
Skooter Cars, *33*, *45*
Skycoaster, *142-44*, 142-44
Sky Diver, *41*, 48
Snapper, 22
Snodgrass, Beth, *105*, 106, *107*
Southern Park, 5, 10, 149
Spanagel, Mary Ann, *84*, *94*, 94, 139-40, *140*, *162-63*, 163-65
Speed-O-Plane, *7-8*, 11, 13, 42, 135
Splashdown, *112*, 115, *118*
Sportland Building, 49, 53
Starvue Plaza, 35, 71, 73
Steak-Out Restaurant (Idlewild), 54, 62
Steel Phantom, 46, 52, *129-35*, 129-37, *137*, 149, 153-54, 158, *170*, 171-73, 182
Steeplechase, 9
Story Book Forest (Idlewild), 54, *61-62*, 61-65, *65*
Stratoship, 18
Sunlite Pool, 35
Super Roundup, 38, *80*, 109
Swimming Pool, *14*, 14, *20-21*, 26, 32, 35, 47, 112-13, 125, 155
Swimming Pool (Idlewild), 56-57, 59, 65, 66
Swing Around, 70, *71*, 125-126, *126*

Tadpool, 116, 119
Teddy Bear Coaster, *17*, 18
13 Spook Street, *18*, 18, 27
Thunderbolt, 14, 37-38, *38*, 43, 47-48, 51, 68, 75, *75-76* 93, *102*, 103, 106, *127*, 129-31, 133-34, *134*, 136, *171*, 173
Thunder Run, *114*, 116, *118*
Tickler, 28
Tilt-A-Whirl, 15
Timberlink Golf Course (Idlewild), 54, 62
Tin Can Alley, 81
Tivoli Gardens, 95
Tomasic, Steve, *64*, 64
Toomer, Ron, 135
Tournament of Music Parade, *30*, 30
Tower Refreshment Stand, *14*, *17*, 35, 95
Tracy, Bill, 126
Traver, Harry G., 15, 18
Tri-Star, *137*, 137
Tuber's Tower, 116
Tumble Bug, *15*, 15, 51, 89, *93*
Turnpike, *37*, 37, 42, 45, 69, 83
Turtle, *15*, 51, 89, *93*, 179

United States Department of the Interior, *84*, 84, 88
USX (U. S. Steel), 114-15, 118, 140

Van Dusen, Dr. A. G., 88
Van Trump, James, *86*, 87
Vettel, Andy, 38
Vettel, Erwin, 20, 22
Voice of Kennywood (publication), 17, 27

Washington, George, 4, *84*, 85, *94*, 94
Wave Swinger, *70*, 70, *83*, *100*, *103*, *105*, 106, *107*, 144, *159*, 159
Weber, Fred, *128*, *137*, *164*
Wentzel, Franklin, 5
West Homestead, PA, 114, 119
Westinghouse, 32
West Mifflin, PA, 54-55, 88, 164
West View Park, 9-10, 37, *149*, 156, 158-59, 176
Wet Willie's Water Works, 124, *124-25*
Whip, 13, *92*, *151-52*, 157, 175
Whip (Idlewild), 60
Whirly-Whirl, 8
White City (Chicago), 152
White Swan Park, 156, 159
Wildcat (Lake Compounce), 172
Wild Horse Saloon (Idlewild), 64
Wild Mouse, *29*, 29
Wild Mouse (Idlewild), 66
William H. Dentzel Carrousells and Organs, 15
Windmill, *16*, *46*, 179
Wipeout, 139, 144, *154*, *170*, 170-71
Wonderland, 8
Wonderland (Revere Beach), 159
Wonderland Building, 5, *9*, *11*
Wonder Wheel, 71, *82*, 82, *144*
Woodland Beach (Ashtabula, OH), 10-11
World War II, 22, *23*, 26, 27, 37, 60, 114
WQED-TV, 70, 97-102, 104-105

Ziegler, Arthur P., Jr., *87*, 87, 92

Books From Amusement Park Journal

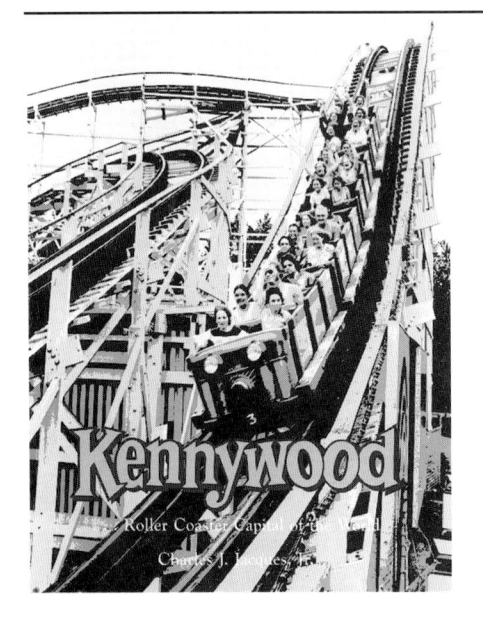

KENNYWOOD: ROLLER COASTER CAPITAL OF THE WORLD by Charles J. Jacques, Jr. This 212-page book was first published in 1982. The book has gone through six printings and has sold more than 23,000 copies. There are 450 photographs and other images that are not duplicated in Jacques' second Kennywood book *More Kennywood Memories*. Kennywood coasters from the 1902 Figure Eight to the Laser Loop are covered as are many other attractions such as Noah's Ark, Dentzel Carousel, circle swing, and funhouses. Size 8 1/2 x 11 inches.

This softcover book is available for $24.95, plus $2.50 for shipping and handling.

GOODBYE, WEST VIEW PARK, GOODBYE by Charles J. Jacques, Jr., a history of one of Pittsburgh's amusement parks from its founding by T. M. Harton in 1906 until it was closed after the 1977 season. Included in this 124-page book are many photographs of West View Park's terrific roller coasters, the Kiddie Dips, the Dips and Racing Whippet, designed by the Vettel family. Rare photographs of the carousel built by Harton with horses carved by the Muller brothers of Philadelphia, and West View Park's famous Danceland which played all of the major dance bands over the years. Size 8 1/2 x 11 inches.

This softcover book is available for $24.95, plus $2.50 for shipping and handling.

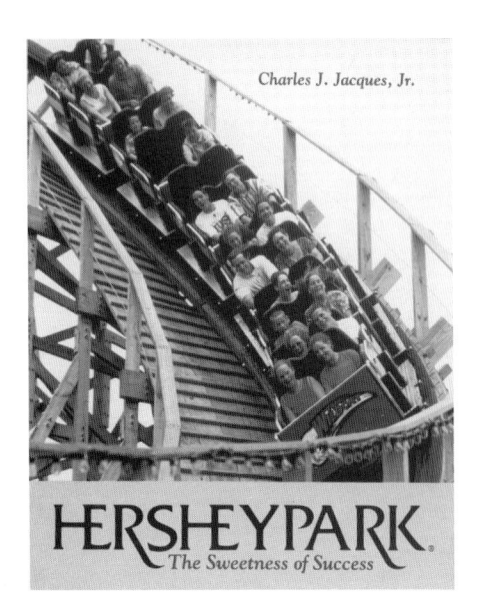

HERSHEYPARK: THE SWEETNESS OF SUCCESS by Charles J. Jacques, Jr. was published in 1997. The 224-page book tells the story of Hershey Park from its founding in 1907 by chocolate magnate Milton S. Hershey to the 1997 season. Hersheypark's roller coasters such as the Wildcat, Comet, and sooperdooper Looper and carousels along with the swimming pool, Kiddieland, the Whoops, TIDAL FORCE, and the Kissing Tower are included. The book has 483 photographs (36 in color). Size 8 1/2 x 11 inches.

This book is available at $29.95 for the softcover edition and $37.50 for the limited hardcover edition, plus $2.50 for shipping and handling.

AMUSEMENT PARK JOURNAL
P.O. Box 478 • Jefferson, OH 44047-0478
(440) 576-6531

Printed in U.S.A.
General Press Corporation, Natrona Heights, PA 15065